CULTURE AND COMMERCE

THE VALUE OF ENTREPRENEURSHIP IN CREATIVE INDUSTRIES

MUKTI KHAIRE

Stanford Business Books
An Imprint of Stanford University Press
Stanford, California

Stanford University Press
Stanford, California

Special discounts for bulk quantities of Stanford Business Books are available to corporations, professional associations, and other organizations. For details and discount information, contact the special sales department of Stanford University Press. Tel: (650) 725-0820, Fax: (650) 725-3457

Printed in the United States of America on acid-free, archival-quality paper

Library of Congress Cataloging-in-Publication Data

Names: Khaire, Mukti, 1973– author.
Title: Culture and commerce : the value of entrepreneurship in creative industries / Mukti Khaire.
Description: Stanford, California : Stanford Business Books, an imprint of Stanford University Press, 2017. | Includes bibliographical references and index.
Identifiers: LCCN 2016048652 (print) | LCCN 2016050258 (ebook) | ISBN 9780804792219 (cloth : alk. paper) | ISBN 9781503603080 (e-book)
Subjects: LCSH: Cultural industries. | Entrepreneurship. | Arts—Economic aspects. | Arts—Marketing.
Classification: LCC HD9999.C9472 K43 2017 (print) | LCC HD9999.C9472 (ebook) | DDC 658.4/21—dc23
LC record available at https://lccn.loc.gov/2016048652

Typeset by Thompson Type in 10/14 Minion

CULTURE AND COMMERCE

CONTENTS

PART IV

THE CREATIVE INDUSTRIES: PAST, PRESENT, AND FUTURE

PREFACE

I begin this preface by discussing two television shows—*UnReal* and *Project Runway*—a surprising choice given that I don't watch much reality television. However, the experiences I had with these shows nicely capture two main themes of the book, so, in the interests of introducing and motivating this book with some authenticity, I submit to the reader the following cases.

In the first example, my personal experience with the show *UnReal*, which premiered in June 2015, illustrates the importance of entities—critics, reviewers, and the like—that seem peripheral because they do not produce the works that are consumed but are actually part and parcel of the creative industries. I had seen promotions for the new show on Lifetime TV while flipping through my cable provider's on demand section. The font used in the advertisement; the way the title was presented; the title itself, which sounded like teen slang; and the fact that the show was aired on Lifetime TV, which I associated with cheesy, sentimental films, all put me off, and I paid no further attention to the advertisement. A few weeks after my initial dismissal, which was based on nothing other than gut instinct and evidence-free analysis (a classic situation of judging a book by its cover), I saw that Emily Nussbaum, the television critic for *The New Yorker* magazine had reviewed the show. I was surprised—the show had not struck me as typical *New Yorker* material. Moreover, Nussbaum had praised the show. The very next evening, I watched every episode of *UnReal* that was available on demand. I liked the show; it had feminist sensibilities, as Nussbaum had written, but was also hugely entertaining and brilliantly acted, and it opened my eyes to the true extent of the unseemliness and fakeness in the world of reality television shows (such as *The Bachelor*), while also shedding light on the complexities of human nature that make reality television possible. Even though I didn't like every episode of the first season, I nevertheless watched the second season, which aired earlier this year, brushing aside any reservations I had, secure in the knowledge that Nussbaum, the television critic at *The New Yorker*, had endorsed the show. I discovered and even appreciated the show entirely because of Nussbaum's review in *The New Yorker*.

The second example highlights the other main category of entities in the creative industries: the firms that actually engage in the production and sale of creative works such as books, films, music albums, television shows, and fashion apparel. These are the producers, and they are located at the intersection of art and business. Despite my research on the fashion industry and my particular interest in designers as founders of creative firms, I had never really watched the show *Project Runway* (on Bravo from 2004 to 2008 and then on Lifetime since 2009), which followed participants as they competed for the approval of a panel of judges comprising well-connected individuals in the fashion industry. It was never clear to me whether the judges on the show were looking for creativity (the next Alexander McQueen) or for commerciality (the next Ralph Lauren). It seemed to me that the show, and all other reality shows seeking the next talented individual, possessed a desire to be *both* arbiters of culture and promoters of commerce, a schizophrenic goal that was unlikely to be achieved to any substantial degree, let alone in full. I felt perversely vindicated then, on reading in *The New York Times*[1] that Christian Siriano, the high-profile winner of the fourth season of *Project Runway*, had apparently not truly gained acceptance into the inner sanctum of the high-fashion world, despite having parlayed his win into a viable fashion "line." The situation that Siriano found himself in was, I thought to myself, something I could have predicted, knowing that intangible, social assets do not always follow financial ones, although the reverse can and does happen. The so-called *nouveau riche* are familiar with this phenomenon, and anybody working in or observing the creative industries knows that greater status is accorded to the penurious artistic genius (writer, painter, sculptor, musician, filmmaker, and the like) than the creator of best sellers.

These two examples nicely preview the main themes of the book, which is about the nature, structure, and functioning of creative industries and how entrepreneurship in these industries can influence broader societal culture. As the examples above suggest, audiences are often suspicious or ignorant of new creative works until they are endorsed by critics/reviewers they trust. Thus producers in creative industries face the daunting task of having consumers discover and accept their product; in addition, producers constantly struggle to balance the cultural and commercial worlds that they must span to succeed as a commercial entity that sells cultural creations. These challenges raise some important questions: How and why does any entity (individual or organization) participate in these highly risky sectors of the economy, let alone introduce new products? How and why do consumers purchase cultural goods? What do critics stand to gain from introducing audiences to new works? This book attempts to address these and other relevant questions.

The Key Factors: The Art World, the Market World, and Entrepreneurship

Although my interest in the creative industries was originally spurred by a desire to understand the paradox of growth and scaling in commercial firms that are dependent on selling the work of a single founder (for example, high-fashion firms are founded to sell the creations of the founding designer), who presumably cannot create at the scale or speed of an automated process, I gradually became more interested in how the worlds of art and business co-exist, interact, and even flourish in the context of creative industries. When I began to explore the topic in more detail, I found research that described an entire ecosystem of entities that needed to function together in a particular pattern of interactions, a situation that engendered stability. Because entrepreneurship is another area of my interest, I became intrigued by the entrepreneurial activity and artistic innovations that were occurring throughout the creative industries, stability notwithstanding, and how these activities affected both the creative industries and society more generally. This book is the result of my inquiries into the entities that populate the creative industries—artists, critics and reviewers, and producers—and is informed by decades of prior academic work that addressed many of these questions from various angles. I integrate my empirical observations with prior scholarly work to derive conceptual frameworks and models that describe the system of entities, which I call the value chain, that constitutes the creative industries and facilitates the market exchange of cultural goods (the baseline case). In addition, I explore the implications of the nature and structure of the baseline case for entrepreneurship and new market creation. Underlying my interest in entrepreneurship is the belief that entrepreneurship that overcomes the stability of the creative industries and creates markets for radically innovative artistic goods, an act I label pioneer entrepreneurship, can have a profound impact on society and culture. I am aware that this last statement—that commerce can change culture—is likely to be controversial and therefore is worth interrogating at multiple levels.

THE ROLE OF THE MARKET IN THE ART WORLD

First, I would like to address the pro–market orientation of the statement that commerce can change culture, which is a prerequisite for claiming such importance and power for entrepreneurship. Given that the market world and the art world are considered not just different but antagonistic, the extensive focus on the market in this book may seem out of place. In particular, my stance that markets play a central role in promoting cultural change may raise some eyebrows. I want to emphasize here that not only do I not believe that the market has a uniformly positive influence on art and culture, but I also do not believe that the market is integral to either artistic creation or cultural production. The market, in my opinion, is but one way to support artistic creation and consumption—state and nongovernmental not-for-profit institutions can also support these endeavors. For good or ill, however, the market is currently the primary mechanism that enables the dissemination and enjoyment (and therefore the creation) of artworks. Although this situation should be cause for concern, there is no question that state control of artistic creation and dissemination is not an optimal situation either, given the potential for abuse inherent in that arrangement, as observed at various times and places in history. Further, nonprofit organizations can become financially unsustainable, especially when they depend primarily on philanthropic sources of money. Additionally, in nonprofit organizations, the need to remain financially viable has negative operational implications, namely that fund raising takes an inordinate amount of effort. Finally, readers should keep in mind that not all artists need or desire to engage solely with the market; some decide to stay out of the market, and other public and state institutions serve to provide that choice to artists. Notably, then, an ecosystem of complementary means and mechanisms is necessary to maximize society's access to art works.

THE POWER OF ART TO CHANGE MINDS

Second, although the claim that art is transformative and inspiring is a cliché, it is worthwhile to question this claim, especially because it is central to the book's premise that (creating markets for) radically new works of art can change society. Although I myself can attest that several books and works of art have influenced me deeply, I certainly would not say that any single work has changed my worldview completely. Rather, individual works have influenced different aspects of my thinking, and jointly they have shaped the person I am. I am not alone in having a sense that various forms of artistic

expression have influenced my beliefs about not only society and appropriate social behavior but also the kind of society in which I would like to live.
For several years, I have asked students to name three creative works that
have had an impact on their lives; invariably, students don't produce simple
lists but rather detailed and moving descriptions of exactly how the works
have changed their perspective in some way. In addition to this anecdotal
evidence, recent experiments[2] have shown that exposure to works of art increases children's capacity to engage in critical thinking. At least for existing works, therefore, it appears that the ideas the works represent do indeed
percolate through and become embedded in our psyches. Given this result,
radical artistic innovations, which manifest new ideas and do not align with
any existing conventions or criteria of worth, should have an even more profound influence on people's thinking. Confronted with a radical work of art,
individuals struggle to make sense of the underlying idea and do not consume
the work until they understand the idea. If consumers purchase such work,
therefore, the market mechanism must have changed their minds about the
value of the work, which is to say that the new idea represented by the work
must have seeped into the collective psyche and been accepted, that is, the
work must have changed the way they think. This process, I suggest, is how
commercial interest in creating a market for radically innovative art works
leads to cultural change and thus motivates the book's focus on pioneer entrepreneurship, which is the act of creating a new market.

THE IMPORTANCE OF ENTREPRENEURSHIP IN THE ART WORLD

Third, I would like to address the significance I attach to entrepreneurship within creative industries. Certainly, such a strong focus on entrepreneurship—a phenomenon much more closely associated with technological
or financial innovations than with cultural goods—is suspect in a book
about cultural and artistic production. Moreover, entrepreneurship is directly and closely linked to the "market," which has negative connotations
in the context of culture. In broadening the definition of entrepreneurship
and applying it to the creative industries and markets for cultural goods,
I am only extending a recent trend both in the academy and in practice,
which is evident in the frequent use of terms such as "institutional entrepreneurship" and "social entrepreneurship." I am proposing a parallel category,
cultural entrepreneurship. Additionally, if one thinks of markets as "audiences," the process of creating an audience for new a cultural product is not
so different from creating markets, and indeed I treat the two (audiences

and markets) as equivalent in the book. For these reasons, I believe that the liberal use of the terminology and conceptualizations of entrepreneurship should not seem out of place.

With regard to the terminology surrounding entrepreneurship in this book, the distinction between a pioneer entrepreneur and an entrepreneur is worth clarifying here. Whereas the term *entrepreneur* used by itself is applied in the usual sense to describe an individual who starts a new venture, *a pioneer entrepreneur is one who creates a new market for a radically innovative good, which is either not understood and thus not valued by consumers or was previously undervalued and thus did not have a market*. A pioneer entrepreneur, therefore, does not have to found a new venture to be classified as such and in fact does not have to be associated with a firm at all; any entity (individual or organization) whose efforts contribute significantly to the creation of a new market is a pioneer entrepreneur. The definition, therefore, resides in the object—a new market—rather than the subject—a venture—of entrepreneurship. Using this definition, the book explores pioneer entrepreneurs and entrepreneurs in both the producer position and the intermediary position within the value chain. Pioneer producers and pioneer intermediaries create new markets, whereas entrepreneurial producers and intermediaries are new producer ventures and new intermediary ventures in well-established, smoothly functioning market categories.

A Few Caveats and Clarifications

Having attempted to clarify several of the choices I have made in structuring the book, I turn to a few disclaimers that provide greater context for the ideas about creative industries and entrepreneurship expressed here, in the hope that readers will keep them in mind as they read the book. Specifically, I attend to four issues here: the properties of intermediaries, the purpose of art, the role of recent technological and socioeconomic changes, and the absence of social class and race in the forthcoming pages.

THE INDEPENDENCE AND EXPERTISE OF INTERMEDIARIES

The descriptions of the "baseline case" that I provide in this book are necessarily ideal normative. Thus, while the creative industries operate in more or less the manner described in the book most of the time, there are certainly exceptions. As one example, readers' experience may suggest that two features that I describe as prerequisites for intermediaries—independence and expertise—are actually not that common. As a result, readers may believe that these properties represent an overly idealistic view of the world, that a complete absence of bias is impossible, that incorruptibility is a pipe dream, and that expertise is restrictive, snobbish, and unnecessary, especially in the case of cultural goods, which are governed by subjective evaluations. I agree that my description of these properties represents an ideal situation, but I do not believe that these features are either impossible or unnecessary. Certainly digitalization (addressed in Chapter 9) has made it quite difficult to maintain financial independence while making it easy to substitute the "wisdom of the crowds" for singular expertise. However, as I argue in the final chapter, discarding economic independence is certainly not beneficial for civil society in the long run and, perhaps more pertinently, is not good a business move, either. The same is true of expertise, although arguably to a lesser extent. Aside from these pragmatic arguments, I want to stress the importance of optimism. Although I understand the appeal and logic of skepticism, even to the level of cynicism, I would like to advocate for the belief that society will self-correct (in the long run, at the very least) to the correct ethical position. Until that correction occurs, however, it is up to us, as consumers of the discourse produced by intermediaries, to remain vigilant and insist that intermediaries establish and maintain visible independence from the influence of producers. The notion that consumers can, through their purchase decisions, motivate businesses to change their practices is widely accepted, and I suggest that consumers should utilize this process to maintain the value of independent and expert evaluation of cultural goods by intermediaries.

ART FOR INTELLECTUAL STIMULATION; ART FOR ENTERTAINMENT

Although art can be enlightening and inspiring, individuals do not want or need to be enlightened every time; entertainment is important, too. Thus, I want to be clear that although cultural prestige and financial success are often at odds, neither should be considered superior to or consistently more desirable than the other. Firms focused on gaining cultural prestige are needed to stimulate intellectual growth and challenge societal norms and assumptions, whereas firms focused on achieving financial success fulfill the significant need we have for entertainment and amusement, even to the point of mindless silliness.

DIGITALIZATION AND GLOBALIZATION

Despite all the focus on entrepreneurship and innovation in the book, with a final chapter (which examines the effects of digitalization and globalization on the creative industries) titled "New World, Old Rules," I run the risk of coming across as a Luddite, or, at the very least, a denier of technological change because it may initially seem that I am making the claim that these changes are not significant. Nothing could be further from the truth—I agree entirely that digitalization, especially, has had a substantial impact on the nature of creation, production, and consumption. Once again, however, I must emphasize that the book focuses primarily on the ideal-normative scenario and takes a descriptive stance; in other words, the goal of the book is to describe how the creative industries ought to be (and are) structured, given the unique characteristics of cultural goods and the nature of their consumption. As I emphasize in that last chapter, digitalization has not significantly changed these fundamental aspects of cultural goods, which in turn means that the baseline case described throughout the book has not changed in any pervasive way—intermediaries continue to be integral to the creative industries and therefore must continue to be both independent and expert, and producers must still contend with the tension between the art and business worlds.

The reader may ask: Even if the nature and functioning of the system *need* not change, *should* it change, given the vast difference between the digital and the analog worlds? My answer is a firm "no." I believe that the way in which the system functions and the requirement for intermediaries to be independent and expertise are good for society. I would argue that not everyone can or should be a creator or producer or intermediary, and that quality is not an elitist concept. Although I think the digital medium is indeed a democratizing force, I contend that the focus of democratization should be maximizing access to the discourse of expert intermediaries, as well as exposure to excellent art works, rather than maximizing participation in the creation of art and/or commentary. Because this is an unpopular assertion to make these days, I want to clarify that I am making this claim in the narrow context of valuation, pioneer entrepreneurship, and markets. In contrast, it is certainly desirable to allow everyone to create for their own pleasure or self-actualization, and it is even desirable to have as many individuals as possible weigh in on the quality of cultural goods. However, I make a distinction between these activities and the processes that occur once goods enter the market and consumers are making monetary and psychological decisions about these goods—I would much rather place my trust in an independent expert intermediary than in the "crowd," let alone individual idiosyncratic consumer reviewers. This is especially true for cultural goods, which manifest ideas; I would like to offer a plea for us to treat our minds with the same respect that we treat our bodies— just as we would not seek medical advice from a random individual whom we do not know or buy drugs manufactured by an unknown firm, I suggest that we should not blindly celebrate the growth in artistic creation wrought by the digital medium. Although there is room for technological change in the old system, I would suggest the new world should not entirely replace the old. I neither disparage nor deny the impact of digitalization. Instead, I merely recommend that we remain circumspect about this transformation so that it elevates our existence, rather than reducing our artistic experience to an echo chamber devoid of discovery and challenge and filled with anodyne mediocrities.

THE ROLE OF SOCIAL CLASS

Finally, readers will notice that social class and race, both of which are significant aspects of cultural production and especially consumption, are included in this book in only a marginal sense. The notion of "highbrow" and "lowbrow" cultural products (discussed in Chapter 7) is, in effect, a reflection of class. Highbrow cultural goods—those perceived as artistic, intellectual, and culturally prestigious—are considered the domain of upper-class individuals, and lowbrow cultural goods—those perceived as simple and entertaining— are considered to cater to the lower classes. Although the topic of social class is obviously relevant in the context of cultural goods, I nevertheless ignore this issue for two chief reasons. First, there is an entire literature on the relationship between social class and cultural consumption, and any proper treatment of the topic would fill at least an entire book if not several. Moreover, given that there is an assumed correlation between cultural value and social class (highbrow goods = higher social class, and lowbrow goods = lower social class) but no clear understanding of whether this correlation is due to the quality of the goods or exists solely for historical social reasons, many scholars deplore both the terminology (which originated from the racist and later discredited theory of phrenology) and the concept. The second and main reason I choose not to address the topics of social class and race, however, is a simple one: the core focus of the book is business and entrepreneurship in the creative industries, rather than class-based and race-based distinctions among consumers.

These are the choices, inclusionary as well as exclusionary, I made in writing this book. Accordingly, the reader will note an emphasis on describing markets—their structure and functioning and their constitutive entities—for cultural goods, with a view to shedding light on their role in society and offering models from the past and prescriptions for future entrepreneurs whose value is the ability and desire to harness the power of commerce to change culture.

ACKNOWLEDGMENTS

This book would not have been even possible were it not for the support of a collective of kind, generous, and intelligent individuals whom I have been privileged to know. Without the guidance and insights I received from the writings of Patrick Aspers, Jens Beckert, Luc Boltansky, Pierre Bourdieu, Richard Caves, Clement Greenberg, Lewis Hyde, Wesley Shrum, Laurent Thevenot, and several other scholars who have written about specific industries, I would not have known the first thing about creative industries. Further, were it not for a number of individuals and entrepreneurs in the cultural sector who graciously and generously responded to my cold calls and offered me their time, access to their archives, and answers to my questions, I would never have been able to build a repertoire of cases, examples, and evidentiary support for the conceptual frameworks I propose here. Although this group of individuals is large, I would like to acknowledge the following individuals specifically: John Galantic, Aditya Julka and Osman Khan, Karl Lagerfeld, Ruby Lerner, Tom Pritzker, Keri Putnam, Evan Ratliff, Robert Redford, René Redzepi, Dinesh and Minal Vazirani, and Claire Zion.

I owe a large debt of gratitude to my friend and colleague Dan Wadhwani, who has been an intellectual sparring partner and coauthor on one of the two large research projects that laid the foundation for this book. Always sharply analytical and also funny, a perfectionist, and an inveterate reviser and refiner of written material, Dan makes work easy, fun, and satisfying. Also crucial to this book and the various research projects underlying it were three research associates—Erika Richardson, Eleanor (Elsie) Kenyon, and Hannah Catzen—whose age belied their wisdom and whose contributions to my work have gone well beyond their formal job descriptions.

All the case studies that inform the book as well as two large-scale research projects (on the creation of the Indian art market and the emergence and evolution of the high-end fashion industry in India) were conducted during my time at Harvard Business School. This book would therefore not have been possible without the unsurpassed resources and access provided by that institution. More intangibly, but no less importantly, several senior colleagues at Harvard Business School provided moral support throughout the process. Nitin Nohria was the first to plant the idea of a book in my head, and I am grateful to him for believing I could do it. Teresa Amabile, Tom Eisenmann, Joe Lassiter, Bill Sahlman, and Noam Wasserman—all fellow dwellers of the Rock Center, home of the Entrepreneurial Management Unit at HBS—provided guidance, encouragement, and ideas as well as much-needed relief from the tedium of writing a book. Outside the unit, I could always count on Rohit Deshpande, Geoff Jones, Dutch Leonard, and Henry McGee to take a genuine interest in my work, offer me advice and insights, talk me up to everyone they knew, and take me to lunch or accompany me on a walk.

Within the larger academic community, one tends to find one's own tribe, a small world that provides intellectual and social sustenance. Because of my cross-disciplinary interests, my tribe is eclectic, but they have in common kindness and generosity of spirit and, of course, intellectual chops. Howard Aldrich, Paul DiMaggio, Walter (Woody) Powell, Hayagreeva (Huggy) Rao, Mark Suchman, and Viviana Zelizer have not only influenced my work and thinking but have also shown me, by example, how to be a good citizen within the academic community. Candace Jones, Roger Friedland, Mike Lounsbury, Ashley Mears, Jesper Strandgaard Pedersen, Roy Suddaby, and Silviya Svejenova have spent many hours reading and discussing my work; sharing their expertise on creative industries, markets, and institutions; and pushing me to sharpen my thinking about the issues covered in this book. I cannot thank my tribe enough for all these years of enthusiastic engagement with my work and with me. But I would not have even been in this academic community if it weren't for Heather Haveman and Peter Roberts, who have been founts of energy and education since my graduate school days; it gives me great joy to offer my thanks to them in one more manuscript.

One of the biggest joys of teaching is learning from the students. I have been fortunate to have several students I have learned from over the years, and I am grateful to them for having challenged me to draw the more subtle insights from any situation or experience. Thanks are also due to those students whose thoughtful ideas made their way into my thinking about the creative industries and entrepreneurship. Three peers who reviewed earlier versions of the manuscript will also, I hope, see the influence of their ideas and suggestions in this final version of the book. I am grateful for the time they took to patiently and painstakingly read the manuscript and help improve it—at least this reviewing task will not go down as having been a thankless one. I have benefited tremendously, and so has the book, from the work of Jennifer Eggerling-Boeck and Angela Palm, both of whom went well beyond the call of duty as copyeditors to provide meaningful substantive comments that significantly improved the clarity and readability of the book.

Starting a book project is very difficult but not as difficult as completing it, and neither would have been possible in this case were it not for my wonderful editor at Stanford University Press, Margo Beth Fleming. With her incisive clarity and forthrightness combined with a disarming charm and persuasiveness, Margo has shaped this book more than anyone else, and I feel very lucky to have worked with her. I know I have tried her patience and severely prolonged the process of completion—I will always appreciate how human she was in understanding and forgiving my tardiness. Also important at the point of completion of this book are my colleagues in my new professional home, Cornell Tech in New York City: Dan Huttenlocher, Vrinda Kadiyali, Chris Marquis, and Doug Stayman. I am grateful for the opportunity they have given me by bringing me closer to the geographical center of the creative industries in the United States, to a campus focused on fostering entrepreneurial thinking—perhaps another book will come out as a result of the next few years.

Friends have lent their hand to this writing project in many ways. Elisabeth Köll and Mary Tripsas made me look forward to coming to the office. They have promised to read the book, and for that I am almost as thankful as I am for the many walks and talks we've shared. There is much talk of mentorship in the workplace these days, especially by women for women, but Elisabeth and Mary went beyond mentorship, offering me true friendship. I could not have done any of this without them. A sisterhood outside of work kept me connected to the rest of the world and heard me out no matter what I had to say; Rasika Krishnamurthy, Swati Kulshreshth, Avanti Paranjpye, Anita Patil-Deshmukh, and Jahnavi Phalkey are due much more than thanks for their love over the years.

Much as I otherwise love breaking with tradition, I will follow the custom of thanking family members and use this opportunity to attempt to express how I feel about them. My parents Vishvanath and Umadevi Khaire have given me unconditional love, and words cannot adequately express my gratitude to them. They are my role models. My amazing father, author of several books, made writing seem deceptively easy (I have found out that it is not easy at all). My mother's passion for all things beautiful, from pottery and textiles to the written word, has, I am convinced, influenced my choice of research subjects. Both always had a sympathetic ear and encouraging words at the ready and seemed to know exactly when I needed them. To my mother and father, I owe everything. But they live far away in India, and in their physical absence my sister, Pradnya Patil, stepped in as their surrogate. She loved me and fed me, and more importantly she kept me grounded. Ever proud of me, she nevertheless reminded me that work was not everything, and for several years she has helped take my mind off the trials and tribulations of writing a book. She, as well as my brother-in-law, nephew, and niece, made me an honorary member of their family with all the benefits of membership and none of the responsibilities. Finally, there is one person who is present in every word in this book and every moment spent on it: my smart, warm, funny, exceedingly hardworking, and entrepreneurial husband, Samir Patil. He challenges me, teaches me, loves me, encourages me, pushes me to my limits and beyond to bring out the best version of me, and inspires me. Samir, this is for you—thank you.

CULTURE AND COMMERCE

Part I

MARKETS, ENTREPRENEURS, AND CULTURE

THE BUSINESS OF CULTURE

The work of an artist is . . . to change the value of things.

—Yoko Ono[1]

Paul Durand-Ruel was a successful and astute businessman in mid-nineteenth-century Paris. He also changed the course of art history. As an art dealer who was willing to take risks and defy the authoritative diktats of art academics and the sensibilities they reinforced about what constituted "good art," Durand-Ruel cultivated a group of high-status collectors and convinced them of the aesthetic, social, and economic value in the unusual paintings of a group of radical French artists who were ridiculed as "Impressionists" by many art critics and commentators of the era. Labeled as such because their works comprised landscapes and real-life scenes in bright colors and fluid brushstrokes that rendered a general "impression" of the scene rather than a detailed representation, these artists' paintings looked nothing like "good art" as defined by the rigid academic conventions of that time, which called for historical or religious subjects and portraits, depicted realistically and precisely in muted tones and dark colors. Art critics and other commentators deemed the new style of painting an outrage—strange, bewildering, even subversive—and the Impressionists were banned from the official shows that were, at the time, the primary means for artists to garner critical attention and cultivate customers. Although the new art and the artists were marginalized for a time, Durand-Ruel and a few other brave and visionary art dealers and critics defied prevailing conventions to promote the genre among collectors and thus create a market for it.

The story of Impressionism (as the style came to be legitimately known) is the story of many innovations. When first presented, radical ideas that defy or deviate from accepted conventions, standards of quality, and prevailing norms about appropriateness face an indifferent reception, if not outright hostility,[2] and yet a few of these ideas overcome this initial resistance and gain attention, acceptance, and respectability, as well as (high) value in a market. Though initially banned, Impressionism as a genre was soon accepted, and eventually desired and coveted, as it is today.

A similar story unfolded in early twentieth-century France in a different creative field—fashion—where cultural norms were arguably more rigid, influential, and powerful than in art, and social pressure to conform to these norms was more extreme. At the time, society women were expected to wear elaborately restrictive dresses that were considered appropriate because they signaled wealth and status (of the women's husbands and/or fathers). Coco Chanel's radically minimal, modern aesthetic in clothes, introduced in 1913, changed this notion of acceptable fashion over a decade that also witnessed social upheaval and changes in other cultural norms. Chanel's influence can still be seen in the wardrobes of today's women, which typically contain several staple pieces—the little black dress, a handbag with a shoulder strap that leaves the wearer's hands free, and costume jewelry that is boldly attractive but not ostentatious, for example—that derive from Coco Chanel's original ideas about what women should wear.

These examples from the art and fashion worlds are similar in two key respects. For one, the trajectory of both innovations—from marginal to mainstream—required a transformation in the established cultural norms regarding what was appropriate, accepted, and valuable. Second, in both cases this cultural change was facilitated by entities operating in the market (dealers of Impressionist art and Coco Chanel's eponymous firm, respectively). The role of business ventures in the cultural arena is, at first glance, puzzling: growing revenues by selling more seems to be at odds with pushing artistic and cultural boundaries, which typically occurs through the introduction of radical, innovative works that consumers do not usually want to buy (at least initially). Even though the production of cultural goods in a market economy by private firms is now the most common mode of cultural production, such firms presumably and understandably wish to grow revenues (by selling goods that consumers want to buy). Under these circumstances, introducing radical innovations that defy conventions of acceptability and appropriateness and are unlikely to be desirable to consumers would seem not to be the best business strategy.

Many individuals and firms nevertheless succeed in juxtaposing these two seemingly conflicting goals to build cultural acceptance, as well as new markets, as the preceding examples indicate. These two episodes are not isolated instances: record companies Sugar Hill Records and Def Jam were central to popularizing rap in an era when disco and classical rock were de rigueur; Sylvia Beach published *Ulysses*, a modernist novel that not only broke all traditional narrative conventions but also gravely offended the social sensibilities of its time and yet is today considered an exemplar of modern literary fiction, and the Sundance Festival is widely acknowledged as being primarily responsible for changing the public's tastes in movies by promoting an alternative to big-budget blockbusters—independently made films that shine a spotlight on new and diverse stories and viewpoints.

How and why does this interaction of business and culture occur? Who are the entities generating this type of economic and cultural change? This book addresses these questions, taking as its starting point the (somewhat counterintuitive) premise that, as in the preceding examples, the creation by commercial ventures of a market for a new, radically different category of cultural goods is an entrepreneurial act that occurs in conjunction with changes in cultural norms, despite the seeming contradictions between the commercial and cultural worlds. The specific process by which commercial ventures in the creative industries create a market for novel cultural goods is related to the nature of value in markets, as well as to the particular characteristics of cultural goods, all topics on which this book will shed some light.

Understanding markets and consumption requires comprehending how and why people develop affinities for particular objects or goods, a process that is particularly complex and slow in the case of novel items that are unintelligible to most consumers and are even considered controversial or unacceptable by many. How consumers begin to covet once unfamiliar goods—sometimes to the point of becoming willing to pay exorbitant prices for these goods—is a complex puzzle. Further, the acceptance of radical novelty is particularly challenging to understand in the case of cultural goods, which don't always offer the consumer value in the form of objective utility or measurable improvements relative to prior iterations or alternatives in the way that, say, a faster and more powerful car, computer, or smartphone does. Cultural goods (such as music, literature, films) have greater symbolic than material or utilitarian worth,[3] and the value they provide to consumers falls primarily in the realm of art or entertainment; these factors slow down the pace at which consumers' tastes in these goods change.

Indeed, cultural goods are not much more than physical manifestations of ideas. Chanel's little black dress, for example, was not merely a garment but also a comment on modernity and the changing roles of women in society. Sergei Diaghilev and the Ballets Russes provide another helpful example. Diaghilev's choreographies fundamentally departed from the conceptualization of proper ballet (and, at an extreme, dancing as a whole) at the time— they were a manifestation of Diaghilev's ideas about movement, music, and performance in an increasingly social and globalized world. In the cases of both Chanel and Diaghilev, the resulting product is something the consumer does "use" in a certain capacity—even products that have less utility than clothing or food, such as fine art or classical music, still have a use, oftentimes as entertainment—but the product is far more than a purely utilitarian object. It is the idea of the artist manifested in a physical form. Another way of understanding cultural goods (and the artistic endeavors that typically result in the creation of such goods) is to view them as products of actions that use concrete resources to convey intangible ideas that have intellectual and symbolic value: paintings made from paint and canvas, clothing made from textiles, and theater created via performers, sets, and costumes.

In both understandings—cultural goods as physical manifestations of ideas and cultural goods as the symbolic output of material inputs—there is a juxtaposition of the symbolic value of the object, related to its underlying meaning, and its material value, which is the result of the physical properties of the object. What is manufactured, bought, and sold is an amalgam of both kinds of value. In this way, cultural goods are quite different from most other objects that are bought and sold in markets;[4] consequently, the artistic or cultural paradigm and the market paradigm are generally regarded as different and often contradictory.[5]

Of course, these two paradigms do intersect and interact in the putative creative industries: art, music, fashion, theater, film, publishing, and haute cuisine. Since the end of the system of royal patronage of the arts, firms in these industries have brought cultural goods to consumers via the market mechanism. In this process, multiple entities translate and convert the symbolic value of artistic creations into economic value through discourse that renders the goods intelligible, acceptable, and valuable.[6] However, when new artistic goods embody radically innovative ideas, they may be slow to gain acceptance in the market. Therefore, entrepreneurial firms in the creative industries must work to render new categories of cultural goods acceptable and desirable in order to create a new market; in so doing, they may engender cultural change.

Understanding the nature of artistic endeavors and the resulting cultural goods, the structure and functioning of markets for these goods, and the process of market creation by entrepreneurs will shed light on the relationship among business, entrepreneurship, and cultural change. These mechanisms and processes and their social and cultural implications are the central topics in this chapter. As a first step in investigating the creation of markets for novel cultural goods, this chapter addresses two questions: what events, entities, actions, and processes engender transformations in the perception and reception of novel categories of cultural goods? And how can the creation of such new markets inform the scholarly understanding of the relationship between business and cultural norms?

A Conceptual Understanding of Value and Markets

Markets are physical (or metaphorical) venues in which certain entities supply goods and/or services in exchange for money (in most cases) from other entities that demand these goods and/or services.[7] The price at which an exchange occurs reflects the value placed on the good by the customer who buys it. In this understanding of markets, two sets of players—sellers and buyers—exchange goods for a strictly objective and commensurable value. Sellers are part of a larger group of entities—*producers*—that broadly comprises firms and individuals that have a direct economic interest in the good exchanged in the market because they are involved in its procurement, production, distribution, or sale (or some combination of these).[8] *Consumers* are the individuals and/or groups that acquire the good in exchange for a commensurate amount of money, time, effort, or other tangible or intangible resource (or some combination of these). Thus, markets are perceived as objective realms in which goods must be rendered perfectly comparable and commensurable in quantitative, economic terms. The value assigned to goods, however, is never purely objective, a fact that has significant consequences for the conception and conceptualization of markets. In fact, scholars have suggested that "every determination of value is subject to forces that are part of the dominant context" and that "no evaluation is purely rational."[9]

The perceived value of a good is determined by a complex amalgam of individual preferences and collective (at a societal or communal level) interpretations of its appropriateness and worth in the context of certain social norms, customs, and practices.[10] Conceptualized in this way, value depends on a shared understanding of the good and of the attributes that shape its desirability or importance, all of which depend on *values*,[11] that is, the collective norms and principles held by a social group. To value a good, therefore, consumers must first *understand* it and then assess its appropriateness and desirability based on its congruence with prevailing personal and shared *norms* regarding what is acceptable and suitable.[12] In this sense, value can be understood as a social construction rather than an inherent, predetermined property of the good.[13] Value is thus relative, deeply subjective, and fundamentally dynamic.

Because social norms play a central role in determining value, conceptions of value must be generally shared and accepted (that is, intersubjectively agreed on) to ensure smooth exchange among the entities that make up markets. As a result, value construction is predicated on broadly disseminated discourse, composed of texts and/or narratives that contextualize an object or concept/idea with the goal of explicating it and communicating its meaning.[14] This discourse can take a variety of forms, ranging from publications and texts such as magazines, books, and advertisements to events such as conferences, conventions, and award ceremonies.[15] The need for intersubjective agreement on value mandates that the process of value construction must be distributed across multiple actors. The social construction of value therefore occurs along a nonlinear and iterative path that involves repeated interactions among various entities, each of whom performs a different, sometimes redundant, role in contributing to a shared understanding of a good and its value. These entities constitute a value-construction chain, which is conceptually and materially very different from a supply chain, primarily in that it is nonlinear and the interactions and engagements that occur along the chain are symbolic.

THE VALUE CHAIN: ACTORS AND PROCESSES

Although consumers are the primary and intended audience for the discourse generated in the value chain, the iterative nature of the process of value construction suggests that the discourse provides information and evaluation to all entities involved, directly or indirectly. In addition to consumers, the value chain comprises two types of actors—*producers*, who have a *direct* financial stake in the sale of a good; and *intermediaries*, who do *not* have a direct financial stake but still produce discourse that contributes to the understanding of the value of a good. Producers are often responsible for contributing material/physical attributes of value (for example, raw materials, workmanship) to the good and for conferring intangible markers of value on it via their discourse, which consists of promotional materials such as advertisements and brochures. Although it may seem that producers inhabit a position of power within the value chain, their acknowledged incentive for increasing the perceived value of the good in the marketplace works against them, lowering their credibility among audiences and weakening the influence of their discourse in the value-construction process (a topic discussed at greater length later in the book). Notably, in the creative industries, producers are often distinct from *creators* (that is, the individuals who create works of art and cultural goods). However, creators also have a vested interest in the symbolic and economic value of their creations. Therefore, for the purposes of understanding markets in the manner described here, creators and producers are equivalent, as are their respective discourses.

Two aspects of the value chain, (1) the conflict between the interests of producers/creators and the interests of consumers in the valuation process (the fact that producers/creators have an incentive to elevate the value of a good, and to manipulate consumers into buying it) and (2) the need for narrative and discourse in the process of value construction that underlies market exchange, necessitate the existence of a third party (in addition to producers and consumers) in markets. These third-party actors are *intermediaries*, which are entities—individuals or firms—that do not have a direct economic stake in the valuation of a good, that is, neither a higher perceived value of the good nor a corresponding increase in sales revenues directly affect the revenues of intermediaries. Organizations such as schools, museums, trade associations, and specialized trade or consumer publications, as well as the individual critics and reviewers who write in these publications, are all examples of intermediaries. Given their lack of direct involvement in economic transactions (buying and selling of the goods) and the resultant absence of conflicting incentives and economic interests, intermediaries tend to have greater influence than producers in the process of constructing value and thus shaping consumers' preferences.[16]

The combined discourse of producers, which is more promotional in nature, and that of intermediaries, which tends to be more objective, shapes consumers' beliefs and preferences, which, in turn, determine the value they perceive in goods and govern their consumption patterns. In this manner, market mechanisms and markets, for all their reification as definitive and transactional means to an end, are, in fact, socioculturally constituted and circumscribed.

VALUE IN CREATIVE INDUSTRIES

In the case of cultural goods, a particularly complicated equation determines value. The socially constructed nature of the valuation process in markets is most clearly visible in the creative and cultural industries because creative works such as art, books, music, and fashion have *greater* symbolic than material value. For example, readers value books not because of the physical materials (such as paper and ink) that go into the writing and publishing of a book but because of the ideas that the book symbolizes. Special knowledge is required to interpret, understand, and convey this symbolic value and to evaluate cultural goods; individuals need to understand something about art, the history of aesthetic movements in the art world, and the evaluation criteria for art (for example, originality, rarity, technique) to know not only why works by Raoul Dufy are valued but also why they are less valued (and therefore, also less expensive) than those by his contemporary, the abstract artist Pablo Picasso. Thus, the symbolism inherent to cultural goods—which distinguishes them from strictly utilitarian goods, such as, for example, paintbrushes[17]—creates a barrier to their understanding and valuation.

This barrier means that intermediaries such as critics, reviewers, and awards play an especially significant role in the interpretation and evaluation of cultural goods. Consumers rely on intermediaries and their discourse to understand the symbolic value of these goods. In addition, social norms, cultural beliefs, and preferences influence the value-construction process by providing virtually the entire contextual scaffolding within which consumers understand cultural products. Through the value-construction process, these goods are assigned an economic value and market price commensurable with their symbolic worth,[18] which allows them to be bought and sold in the market.

Notably, the high-end luxury segments of some other sectors, such as automobiles, real estate, and consumer technology products, also derive their monetary value largely from the symbolic and signaling value, beyond their utility, that they signify. However, this valuation is distinct from the value-construction process for cultural goods, which have limited, if any, utilitarian or functional aspects. In theory, any car is a means of transport, and, with some differences in comfort and perhaps durability, an inexpensive automobile will perform the function just as well as one that is priced orders of magnitude more. Some consumers nevertheless pay these high prices because they derive considerable status from luxury automobiles or other luxury items. However, the value of expensive cars, homes, and computers as status signals is the result of the carefully crafted promotional discourse and branding activities of the firms that produce these goods; third parties or formal intermediaries, which do not have a direct economic stake in the sale of the good, are rarely involved in this process beyond a basic verification of the functional claims made by the producer. Compared to intermediaries in the creative industries, intermediaries in such luxury sectors are not as essential to valuation and do not perform the same functions. *Consumer Reports*, for example, is an important intermediary but focuses primarily on evaluations, verifications, and rankings and less on interpretation and explanation; in contrast, one rarely sees a formal film review that does not include analysis and interpretation of the film.

The boundaries and distinctions between the creative industries and other sectors, however, are not always sharp and clear. First, some segments of creative industries also lack this need for extensive explanation and interpretation. For example, mass-market films, pop music, and the clothes sold in chain stores such as Old Navy and Target do not require decoding of their meaning or symbolic value. Yet each of these products has a highly symbolic counterpart (independent film, classical music, haute couture) that bears the distinct mark of cultural goods. Second, and at the other end of the spectrum, even haute cuisine and haute couture, while suffused with symbolism and complexity, do have utility as nourishment and cover, respectively, and thus have some similarities with the luxury segments in other industries in the manner in which value is constructed, conveyed, and established. Third, the commodification of many utilitarian goods has led producers to attempt to differentiate these goods (to increase their perceived value) by incorporating aesthetic elements and design (refrigerators with a "retro" look are an example).[19] Much like the consumption of cultural products (such as music, books, or films), individuals' consumption of such aesthetically differentiated and expensive counterparts to commoditized products is often driven by a desire to express personal identity and uniqueness. However, as in the case of luxury goods, these markers of aesthetic value, which translate into economic value, are incorporated by producers, and intermediaries play a limited role.

The socially constructed nature of value and the value-construction process have implications for understanding markets and the relationship among markets, entrepreneurship (defined in this book as the process of bringing new goods to market[20]), and culture, especially in the context of cultural goods and the creative industries. Importantly, these characteristics of value and valuation imply that markets are socioeconomic, rather than purely economic, arenas and must be analyzed as such. The following section presents a conceptualization of markets that, while applicable to all goods and sectors to a certain extent, is especially pertinent for cultural goods due to the nature of value in creative industries as described in the preceding pages.

A Framework for Understanding Markets in Creative Industries

Markets are created when two conditions are met: supplying entities and buying entities agree on value, and stable conditions enable smooth exchange.[21] Because markets require intersubjective agreement on value, they emerge at the intersection of *commerce, commentary, culture,* and *consumption,* which interact in recursive and mutually reinforcing ways (see Figure 1.1). Commerce and consumption (selling and buying, respectively) are the traditional constituents of a market, and the framework used here adds a consideration of the ways in which culture and commentary influence the market creation process to more comprehensively and accurately reflect the social processes that influence economic exchange. The next section describes the relationship and interaction among these four elements.

COMMERCE, COMMENTARY, CULTURE, AND CONSUMPTION

Commerce, perhaps the most straightforward of the four elements of a market, requires the least explication. Commerce is the process of selling things—the phenomenon of producers introducing a good for exchange, that is, placing a good in a venue where consumers may pay a sum of money equivalent to its

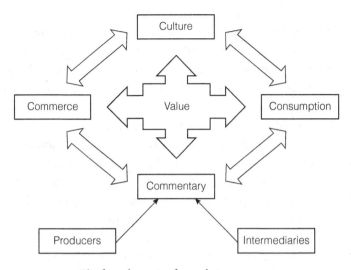

FIGURE 1.1. The four elements of a market.

perceived value to acquire it. In the case of creative industries, commerce is performed by producers, including galleries and auction houses (in the art market); fashion firms, distributors, and retailers; publishers and bookstores; and record labels and music stores. These firms source works from creators and provide them at a particular price that is acceptable to consumers based on how much they value the works.

Commentary consists of the discourse generated by producers and intermediaries, which helps determine both the value of the specific item as well as more general guidelines regarding what types of items are considered valuable. In theater, for example, both the discourse of theater critics (intermediaries) and the director's notes provided in programs qualify as commentary. Commentary may also shape and influence the creation and production of goods because creators and producers who seek to meet consumers' needs will pay heed to the criteria of value espoused in the prevailing commentary. In the example of theater, commentary circulates among not only consumers and theater patrons but also theater producers and owners, directors, critics, other actors and actresses, festival organizers, and other producers.

Producers contribute to the commentary via advertisements, catalogues, and other promotional materials. This type of discourse is meant to encourage sales of the item and is therefore focused solely on positive and attractive features that render the item desirable to consumers, or sometimes on negative attributes of competitors' goods.[22] Intermediaries, in contrast, are expected to generate materials that are more evaluative, objective, and circumspect. Their discourse not only provides a more evenhanded assessment of the item but also places the item in context so that consumers understand why the item is desirable (or not).

Fundamentally, the importance of commentary to the market lies in the ability of language and discourse to "signify" goods[23] with meaning and value beyond their intrinsic properties or qualities and well beyond their functionality and utility.[24] Thus, commentary does not merely describe the good but also contextualizes it with respect to other goods in its own and other similar categories, provides a decoded explication of the underlying idea and symbolism, and enables consumers to engage with the good in a meaningful manner. This process constructs the value of goods and enables market exchange. At the same time, however, commentary helps establish general conventions of value and criteria of quality, which are disseminated among all sectors of society and intersubjectively agreed on. Thus, commentary contributes to the development of norms of appropriateness and value.

The meaning and value conferred by commentary goes beyond the intrinsic elements of the good and produces a socially constructed, shared understanding of the good across broad sections of consumers. Barthes, writing about the process by which clothing is signified as fashion, suggests, for example, that people would wear two blouses at the same time if the prevailing discourse defined one of the blouses differently and described the wearing of two blouses in language that effectively endorsed the practice by infusing it with a particular social value.[25,26] Although Barthes's imagined scenario may seem to imply that consumers are mere pawns at the hands of commentators (both producers and intermediaries), believing what they are told to believe and doing as they are told to do, such a conclusion is excessively cynical and privileges institutional structure too much. A more realistic understanding is that individual consumers engage in consumption as a social process,[27] deriving psychic benefits from being part of a community with an intersubjectively shared reality.[28] Further, although the structural stability engendered by this shared institutional process of meaning and value construction may seem immutable, it is not. Entrepreneurial activity intermittently brings about changes in the shared beliefs in a society, thus changing the perceived meanings and value of goods, which, in turn, reinforces and consolidates the changes in beliefs in a recursive manner.

Commentary, through its discursive representations, is the scaffolding for the social structures that build, and are built of, *culture*. Culture is the set of shared norms (that is, rewards and sanctions) that govern behavior by defining what is appropriate and desirable.[29] The discourse of producers and intermediaries contributes to culture by generating a shared understanding among consumers about what is appropriate and valuable through the repetitive and recursive process of value construction; this understanding then becomes codified as a set of cultural norms. In the context of market exchange, these norms have a direct and substantial influence on what consumers believe is worth doing and what goods are worth owning.

In addition to referring to shared norms, the term *culture* also refers to an item (that is, a cultural good). Although these two ideas are distinct, they are clearly linked, and it is useful to understand the precise nature of their relationship. The sociologist Simmel[30] contended that the term *culture* (as in a cultural good) denoted material objects that would not have come about through a natural course of action without human intervention. Cultural goods are thus embodiments of the ideas and desires of individuals, who changed and shaped the physical and material qualities of the raw materials to create something that connotes a unique significance that is the result of actions that went well beyond the natural. The ideas, beliefs, and desires of human beings can be thought of as cultural values—the state of mind shared by members of a society in a particular time and place. These values, in turn, shape the production of a cultural good. Culture and cultural goods are thus closely intertwined—culture determines both means and ends; it provides a worldview and a way of understanding one's surroundings and also normalizes and valorizes elements of one's existence and interactions, so that people strive to achieve and/or maintain these elements. This linkage is crucial to understanding how markets for cultural goods influence culture, which is described later.

Consumption of a good produced for commerce is the fourth component of the framework. In sum, patterns of demand are a function of the shared conceptions of value (culture) in a society, which are determined by commentary, whereas the good itself is supplied (for consumption) by firms engaged in commerce. In this manner, markets are created at the confluence of these four elements, rather than simply at the intersection of supply and demand. Especially in cultural industries, cultural norms and commentary play significant roles in this process of market creation.

As an example, consider the market for high-fashion clothing, which is created by creators (designers) and sold by firms in stores (*commerce*). Each season's style is rendered desirable (*culturally* normative) by the discourse (*commentary*) in fashion magazines' coverage of fashion shows and endorsement of specific styles (intermediaries' discourse) and the ads of design firms and stores (producers' discourse), as well as in the more diffuse and informal commentary prevalent in a society. This process induces sales of the clothes (*consumption*). In a steady state, the four elements of a market exist in a mutually reinforcing balance: consumers buy items that they believe are congruent with shared norms of appropriateness, which are driven in large part by the broader discourse generated by various entities in society; firms, seeking to generate revenues and profits, provide those items to consumers. This steady state, however, is disturbed and thrown into disequilibrium when a new type of good is created and introduced in commerce or described in the commentary. The novel good and resulting disequilibrium requires the creation of a new market, in which all four elements are once again in alignment.

CREATING NEW MARKETS

New and unfamiliar cultural goods sometimes face hostility because any new, unconventional product or product category that does not conform to prevailing cultural norms is unlikely to be understood, let alone perceived as desirable. In this scenario, the attributes of the product being sold (commerce) are misaligned with the criteria consumers use to understand and evaluate it (commentary) as appropriate and valuable (culture); as a result, the consumption of new product categories is unlikely, if not downright impossible because the prevailing balance among the four elements of the market cannot assimilate new goods. A market for such goods, therefore, must be *created*; its emergence is not teleological. A new market emerges when value conceptions (cultural norms) change in a way that renders the new good valuable. New value conceptions can be generated and established through the commentary of market creators, who are referred to as pioneer entrepreneurs in this book. Such pioneer entrepreneurs may be producers (pioneer producers) or intermediaries (pioneer intermediaries). In this process of market creation, cultural change can be wrought when discourse valorizes and endorses the attributes of the new product, thus producing new criteria for assessing the worth of a product and changing consumers' value systems. The seeds of cultural change, therefore, are embedded within the very system that maintains cultural values and beliefs; however, these changes are set in motion only in response to the ingenuity, drive, and perseverance of pioneer entrepreneurs.

Importantly, the novelty discussed here is of the *radical* kind—the type of idea that is not an incremental or horizontal change relative to what existed before but rather a near upheaval of the prevailing order. This is a significant point because the *creative* industries, by definition, are associated with change and novelty borne of individual creativity. However, the focus here is not on mere changes to hemlines or the release of new songs or albums. Rather, think of the radical change wrought by the introduction of an entirely new category or genre, which cannot be evaluated or understood using existing criteria and conventions; colloquially, such a change would be perceived as "rule-breaking" and "unconventional."[31]

The modern Indian art category is one example of a cultural good that required the creation of a new market.[32] Prior to 1995, art created in the twentieth century in India was consumed only in a small, disorganized market—both in India and abroad—and was characterized as provincial or parochial and derivative (of Western modern art).[33] The basis of this characterization was a widely accepted belief about which attributes rendered art aesthetically and economically valuable. In the Western world, where art markets were well developed and established, a clear set of evaluative criteria for art prevailed. These criteria had evolved throughout the history of Western art via the discourse of academics, historians, curators, critics, and gallery owners. For example, originality—defined in a very particular way, in juxtaposition with the artistic traditions of Western painters—was a sine qua non of good modern art and was valued more highly than many other attributes. In that context, modern Indian art, with its heavy emphasis on iconography, was perceived as folk art and was consequently not aligned with the prevailing norms of value. The art existed and was for sale but had limited, if any, value in the Western (or, for that matter, Indian) market. The supply existed (commerce), but, in the absence of commentary that would cast it as appropriate and valuable in the minds of consumers (culture), sufficient demand did not exist to motivate a set of transactions (consumption) extensive enough to create an equilibrated market.

However, the commentary pertaining to modern Indian art began to undergo a substantive change in the 1990s.[34] Academics and art historians began to characterize this art as modernist, with a particular original aesthetic that they asserted was just as valuable as the aesthetic of Western modern artists, albeit different. These academics began to shift the evaluative criteria and frameworks for describing, characterizing, and understanding modernism itself, making these criteria more inclusive and thus allowing twentieth-century art from India to be newly categorized and positioned as "modern" art. Once this discourse was broadly disseminated and intersubjectively accepted, the art was perceived as complying with prevailing norms of appropriateness and value. Because of this commentary, auction houses dealing with twentieth-century Indian art found consumers willing to invest in the works. In sum, a new market was created when commentary changed the value conceptions of consumers, thus generating demand for an item that had previously existed (as had some commerce in the category) but had not been valued highly by consumers because of the earlier prevailing norms.

Naturally, the same model can be applied to a de novo good, an item that is materially new and did not exist prior to a creator's having created it or a producer's having attempted to sell it.[35] There are many examples of such goods including the novel as a literary form, Impressionism as an art genre, and the *le smoking* (trouser suit) for women introduced in 1966. Take, for example, the market for organic foods, which was created as a result of the changing commentary around food, health, the environment, and the interrelationships among the three.[36] Although organic foods are not a creative or artistic product per se, the introduction of this category provides a straightforward and universally relatable exemplar of the interactions among the four elements that lead to the creation of markets. Prior to the introduction of organic food, the U.S. population had grown accustomed to thinking of the use of chemical fertilizers and pesticides to grow produce as a sign of progress and the primary factor behind much-desired increases in productivity that had made food more affordable. In contrast, the term *organic* did not have much meaning for most people and probably carried negative connotations associated with an atypical lifestyle—among the majority of consumers, organic food was considered neither desirable nor valuable. However, when the scientific and (subsequently) popular press published discourse denouncing the chemicals in pesticides and fertilizers for their negative impact on the health of humans and animals, consumers gradually began to accept organic food and consider it both appropriate and desirable. Coupled with increased access to organic foods and produce (commerce) as well as certification procedures that allowed people to trust the quality of produce being offered, this widespread discourse changed value conventions (that is, societal beliefs regarding what was appropriate and desirable food) and rendered organic food valuable. This value shift then led to the increased consumption of organic foods by consumers.

A proximate but more creative instance of a new category of products is "New Nordic" cuisine, which was introduced by chef René Redzepi in Copenhagen in 2003. Previously associated with "gray, drab food,"[37] primarily meat and potatoes, Nordic cuisine received a complete image makeover due to Redzepi's innovative and creative menus and (important in this context) his other efforts to legitimize the new culinary category through events such as symposia to discuss creative foods and cooking techniques. As a result, Copenhagen is now considered a top gastronomic destination.[38]

As shown by these examples, the introduction of a new good disturbs the mutually reinforcing balance between the four interlinked elements, creating a need for adjustments on all sides before a market for the new good can be created. This process of adjustment and rebalancing to create markets, as well as the characteristics of the pioneer entrepreneurs who are responsible for the process, is described in detail in Chapter 2. The following section examines the cultural impact of the process of market creation as initiated by pioneer entrepreneurs.

Linkages among Pioneer Entrepreneurs, Markets, and Cultural Change

The chief proposition of this chapter, and indeed the premise of this book, is that creating a market for creative works—books, paintings, music, performances, design in the fields of architecture and fashion, films—has the potential to initiate broader cultural changes (that is, changes in social norms, beliefs, and ways of thinking) due to the nature of creative works and their creation as well as the functioning of markets (for these goods).

THE UNIQUE NATURE OF THE CREATIVE INDUSTRIES

The importance of the alignment of culture, commerce, and consumption to the smooth functioning of markets stands in stark contrast to the popular perception of artists as free-willed iconoclasts. In fact, this oppositional re-lationship between the need for conformity and the iconoclasm of creativity is what makes the creative industries and artistic works the setting for the initiation of cultural change through market creation for unfamiliar and sometimes threatening new goods. Since the rise of modernism—a movement that emphasizes novelty and promotes departures from tradition following an examination and critique of prevailing social practices[39]—original ideas have been the currency of the art realm, lowering the importance of traditions handed down over generations. As a consequence, works of art in the modern era are embodiments of the ideas of their respective individual creators, who create without deference to the status quo and prevailing practices and be-liefs.[40] Such works of art, essentially manifestations of new and original ideas, may not be easily accepted by society initially; significant changes in norms of acceptability may be required before such works acquire market value, thus linking culture and commerce through market creation for radical, original artworks, as described next.

Raw, ineffable creativity, materialized as an original idea or a new good, has quite often been deemed dangerous (such as rock 'n' roll, the novel *Ulysses*). Even if new goods are not exactly dangerous, an unbounded creative process operating in the context of markets that are influenced by the prevail-ing commentary and culture gives rise to the potential for conflict. This con-flict arises because the nature of the creative process is such that the creators of cultural goods and/or artistic works do not reliably create "for the market" and instead tend to push the boundaries of creativity and novelty as far as they can.[41] Maverick artists, with their disregard for rules and norms, would not be able to sell their subversive works, which flout these rules, in markets that, as previously described, require goods to meet the prevailing criteria for the appropriateness and value of products. Because artists seek to push boundaries, new categories of cultural goods are quite often radically differ-ent from existing categories, rather than being incremental improvements on the goods already available. Moreover, art serves to make the unimagined and unknown seem possible, plausible, and known. When artists employ their creativity to achieve this goal in a work, the resulting product often pushes against prevailing beliefs and cultural values, inciting suspicion and hostil-ity. Such radically new works cannot be assessed and valued using existing conceptions and norms of value; rather, new criteria and conventions of value are needed. The dissemination and acceptance of new evaluation criteria for such products leads to a change in conventions of appropriateness and value, rendering the new category valuable in the minds of consumers. This allows audiences to discern, understand, and accept the idea underlying the work and consume it. The consumption of new categories of cultural goods thus implies the occurrence of a change in value norms, that is, a cultural change.

Radical artistic works, by their very nature, present an invitation to pause, assess, and reflect—a challenging proposition. Acceptance and consumption of these works (and therefore the idea within the works) is an implicit agreement to question what came before to the degree that the work itself questions and challenges the status quo. Further, the assessment and reflection motivated by artistic works, when properly contextualized and explained, can lead consumers to question beliefs that were previously accepted without question, thus causing a change in the way the audiences of these works *think*. In contrast, objects that afford a utility of some sort—objects that make life better, more comfortable, less strenuous, or improved in some other way—change the way consumers *behave* but not necessarily how consumers *think*. Thus, even though all objects brought to the market must be contextualized and their value must be constructed, acceptance of most novel utilitarian objects does not change the very fabric of people's identity and way of thinking (although this type of acceptance may facilitate that process, as will be clear later) in the way that acceptance of new categories of cultural goods and works of art does.

This unique role of novel cultural goods is related to the nature of these goods,[42] their role in our lives, and their close association with our sense of self and identity—we are defined by, and attempt to define ourselves by, our tastes and preferences in music, literature, clothes, films, and other artistic works, but we are also eager to fit in with others in society. Due to the intense nature of consumers' relationships with specific cultural goods, they are particularly resistant to accepting new goods without a broader, more intersubjective agreement on new conceptions of appropriateness and value. The introduction of new goods in a market, therefore, necessitates commentary that presents new conceptions of meaning and value, which, if accepted, change our preferences and beliefs.

HOW BUSINESS CHANGES CULTURE

The contention that business is closely intertwined with culture should not be controversial at any level. It has become commonplace to talk about consumer products, services, or infrastructure elements (such as electricity and the Internet) as having "changed culture." Examples of items that are routinely put forward as culture changers include the automobile, the personal computer, cell phones, the iPad, the U.S. highway system, Facebook, Google, and many others. Although these items have certainly had an enormous impact on people's lives and led to behavioral change on a very large scale, they have not brought about changes in *beliefs*. Because changing culture entails changing minds (beliefs), not just lives (behavior), the acceptance of new *ideas* can influence the broader culture, but the acceptance of new products by itself cannot have the same effect. Rather, products such as the automobile and the personal computer (or Facebook's online social network that eases communication and dissemination) have facilitated cultural change because they have undoubtedly greatly expanded access to new ideas, whereas cultural goods, being material manifestations of new ideas, are more directly able to influence and change minds. It follows, then, that the firms that bring cultural goods to market are capable of changing culture.

In summary, the successful creation of a market for a radically new cultural good is indicative of the occurrence of a cultural change. The fact that cultural goods are often symbolically and conceptually, rather than materially, differentiated means that the consumption of new categories of cultural goods (that is, new ideas) is the result of a virtuous cycle that brings about and reinforces a change in cultural norms by changing how people think about what is valuable. Thus, creative industries have a particularly emphatic impact on culture in society at the intersection of commerce, commentary, culture, and consumption, through the creation of markets for new goods.

The market for rap music provides an instructive illustration of the way in which a radical artistic work can change culture. Rap music originated in inner-city neighborhoods with predominantly African American populations and was heavily influenced by reggae and Jamaican culture. Consisting of spoken verse, rhythmically rendered live over existing music, rap (literally meaning "conversation") was unlike any music that was popular in the late 1970s in the United States. Some listeners questioned its very categorization as music. The *Billboard* Top 10 list for 1979 (the year Sugar Hill Records first released a rap album by The Sugar Hill Gang), which includes songs such as Gloria Gaynor's "I Will Survive" and The Village People's "YMCA," offers a sense of the type of music that was popular in the marketplace when rap was introduced.[43] The first rap single by The Sugar Hill Gang ("Rapper's Delight") not only differed dramatically from the type of music that was broadly accepted at the time but also originated in a context very different from the one in which most music buyers lived, which made the music seem even more unfamiliar and suspicious. Perceived as "ghetto music," rap struck a discordant note and was alien to most buyers' worlds and sense of self. As a consequence, rap did not become a cultural tour de force until several commentators and firms engaged in value-constructing commentary to change consumers' understanding of the new music. Firms such as Def Jam (a producer), magazines such as *The Source*, and music schools such as Berklee College of Music (both intermediaries) all contributed[44] to the generation of a new set of criteria and values that allowed consumers to understand and evaluate rap music on its own terms, rather than those of pop or disco music.[45] Once consumers recognized the value in rap music, they also understood the social context in which it originated, which further reinforced the appropriateness of the new value frameworks. In turn, perceptions of black culture changed in a significant way—critics and social commentators have asserted that hip-hop "transformed America's racial vocabulary and cultural landscape, [making] 'urban' refer to 'vital, hip, and desirable,' rather than 'poor, marginal, untouchable.'"[46] Once hip-hop was accepted and consumed, therefore, the music wrought broader changes in cultural norms of appropriateness.

CULTURAL CHANGES: GOOD AND BAD, PROFOUND AND PLAYFUL

Not all pervasive cultural changes ensuing from the introduction of novel cultural goods will be seen as "good." For example, hip-hop itself has been criticized for legitimizing sexist and racist stereotyping by glamorizing hypersexuality and disseminating a certain image of African American youth.[47] This book contains no judgments about whether cultural changes are for the better or for the worse but rather focuses only on how the actions of firms and entrepreneurs can engender cultural change. This withholding of judgment is in keeping with the fundamental modernist notion that the creation of art is in the service of nobody but the artist and the work itself, the "art for art's sake" principle.[48] Advocated by the nineteenth-century writer Theophile Gautier, this agenda of the modernist movement held that works of art could not be held responsible for upholding and/or ushering in moral values among society and that works of art were nothing but the purest articulations and manifestations of the artist's imagination and drive to expression through creation.[49] Thus, although arguments abound about whether good art can either uplift the soul and instill desirable values among its audiences or arouse the baser instincts of humans, it is not the intent of this book to take sides in this argument. Rather, the position taken in these pages is that novel creative works have the potential to change the way people think.

The resulting change may be desirable from the point of view of the greater good or some abstract and absolute moral standard, as is generally believed to be true of Harper Lee's book *To Kill a Mockingbird*. Conversely, the change may be offensive to modern sensibilities, as illustrated by the extensive hand-wringing over the way in which films have normalized and glamorized violence.[50,51] A category of cultural goods may even have both effects, as the ongoing debate over the impact of hip-hop demonstrates: some see the genre as denigrating women, fetishizing violence and criminal activity, and further deepening the negative image of the African American community, whereas supporters argue that hip-hop has rendered U.S. inner cities less threatening and more appealing and engendered a greater appreciation of urban and/or black culture and conditions. Regardless of which verdict one subscribes to, however, it is difficult to ignore the impact that exposure to the hip-hop genre has had on people's thinking. This phenomenon—novel artistic works changing people's beliefs—is the focus of this book.

Just as subsequent cultural changes can be either "good" or "bad," they can also pertain to either significant and even profound issues (for example, race, gender, class) or more playful and entertaining factors; whatever the importance of the target, each form of creative expression has the potential to change how consumers think. When society comes to accept new and different attributes and criteria as indicators of the appropriateness and perceived value of an object, thus recasting as valuable objects previously viewed as valueless, cultural change has occurred, even when the focus is something that would be generally considered frivolous, such as the attributes of delicious food or the criteria for physical beauty. The key is that cultural change involves change in beliefs and not merely behaviors.

Summing Up and Looking Ahead

This book describes the social, cultural, and business implications of the nature and structure of markets for cultural goods, building on the conceptual foundations explicated in this chapter. Key aspects discussed in more detail include the constituents of the value chain—producers, intermediaries, and consumers—and the four elements that constitute markets—commerce, commentary, culture, and consumption. Chapter 2 shines a spotlight on pioneer entrepreneurs—entities who create markets for new categories of cultural goods—by describing the types of entities that can undertake the task, the challenges they face, and the paths they follow. Crucially, both the interplay between commentary and consumption and the resulting importance of discourse to the creation of markets reinforce the central role of intermediaries. Chapters 3, 4, and 5 closely examine intermediaries, describing their raison d'être, their functions, and their characteristics, and explaining the implications of these dimensions of intermediaries for business and entrepreneurship (pioneering and otherwise).

Chapters 6, 7, and 8 examine the other category of actors in the value chain, producers. All producers face the challenge of bridging the market and cultural realms (which, as previously mentioned, are seen as standing in opposition to one another). The mutually reinforcing nature of the relationship between the four elements that constitute a market creates a tension— between the decision to reflect prevailing norms and the more risky strategy of changing norms—common to creators and producers. The former strategy is more commercially viable, because the product will find a market easily. That said, radical change does at times occur in markets and societies because producers have ways of alleviating, if not resolving, this tension to balance their financial/market and cultural imperatives. The nature and implications of these challenges and the strategies producers use to deal with them, as well as other aspects of producers and pioneer entrepreneurs among them, are the topic of Part III.

The final chapter, in keeping with the focus on entrepreneurship, turns to contemporary developments in the business and cultural worlds—specifically, globalization and digitalization—that have significant (positive and negative) implications for pioneer entrepreneurs and resulting cultural change. The twin forces of globalization and digitalization have been responsible for the introduction of new categories of cultural goods (through commerce and commentary) in unprecedented volume and at unprecedented speed and will likely continue to spur the introduction of novel goods that collide with the prevailing culture and face challenges to consumption. The final chapter addresses the most prominent questions for people who follow these two developments: what has changed, and what has stayed the same? Who are the winners and losers? What has been lost, and what has been gained? Although admittedly not providing definitive answers to these questions, the last chapter integrates the conceptual underpinnings of the entire book into a thesis that provides a way to analyze and understand these developments and their consequences for business, culture, and society.

However, before delving into analyses of these large-scale changes that have the potential to affect not only commerce but also culture, it is necessary to understand the nature and functioning of pioneer entrepreneurs, who predominantly feature in the interaction among radical innovations, creative industries, and cultural norms. These influential entities are the topic of the next chapter.

PIONEER ENTREPRENEURS

Creating Markets and Changing Minds

He who molds the public sentiment . . . makes statutes
and decisions possible or impossible to make.

—Abraham Lincoln[1]

The Man Booker Prize, awarded annually since 1969 to "the best novel published in Britain during the year, by any novelist from Britain, the Common-
wealth or the Republics of Ireland and South Africa,"[2] was in the news twice
in the span of two years, and not just for the announcement of the prize. First,
in 2011, the short list for the prize included a popular "thriller" in addition to
the typical literary fiction usually found on the list.[3] This led to celebration or
hand-wringing, depending on whether one perceived this breach in tradition
as dilution or inclusion. Then, in 2013, the Man Booker Foundation removed
the qualifying restriction on novelists' origins or residence.[4] In so doing, the
foundation exposed itself to a barrage of both criticism and praise from writers and commentators reacting to what was perceived as another step in the
dissolution of a constructed literary category, sometimes called "postcolonial
fiction [in English]."[5] The Booker Prize had always been controversial for having created—for better or for worse—a new literary category in a move that
also made publishers more money by increasing the visibility and therefore
the sales of both the winning book and the books selected as finalists for the
award. Whatever the literary or business antecedents and merits of the prize,
it certainly brought more consumers' attention to a type of fiction and a group
of writers that they may not have otherwise noticed, appreciated, or valued.
Because the prize—or, more accurately, the foundation that established the
prize—created a market category with which it is now indelibly associated,
the decisions to expand the category by relaxing the eligibility criteria were

the topic of much debate. Although these decisions created a market for a wider variety of books by including them in the category and the prize, some believed that the decisions, by diluting the category that the prize had helped create, lowered the literary value and therefore the economic value of the books in the category.

Such tight associations between specific entities and entire market categories— "Whole Foods Market" and "organic food"; "Penguin" and "paperbacks" and "classics"; "Sundance Festival" and "independent cinema"—abound in consumers' minds. Even though these firms were not necessarily the first in the market (Whole Foods was preceded by several local organic stores in various parts of the United States), or the only player in the category (Penguin is not the only publisher of paperbacks), or even a creator or producer of the goods in the market category (Sundance is an intermediary), they are closely and inextricably linked to the creation of markets for these categories of goods— they are pioneer entrepreneurs. This chapter focuses on these market-creating pioneer entrepreneurs.[6]

Pioneer entrepreneurs foster the creation of new markets for either de novo categories of goods, whose value must be constructed from scratch, or for existing but recategorized goods, whose perceived value must be altered (that is, increased) in the minds of consumers.[7] Pioneer entrepreneurship of the first type entails introducing new categories within existing fields, as the Robinsons of Sugar Hill Records did in 1979 with the then-new genre of rap. In the second type, pioneer entrepreneurs recast an existing category as valuable, as the Sundance Institute did for independent cinema, which, in the post-*Jaws* era of big-budget films, existed but was languishing on the sidelines of the industry.[8] Pioneer entrepreneurship of both types involves bringing goods to the attention of consumers in one of two ways—either by physically placing goods in the marketplace or by explicating goods via discourse that constructs their value for consumers so they are perceived as desirable and subsequently consumed.

Pioneer Entrepreneurs:
Who They Are and What They Do

What types of entities can be pioneer entrepreneurs? Perhaps somewhat counterintuitively, given popular conceptions of entrepreneurs as founders of new ventures, a pioneer entrepreneur does not necessarily have to found a firm or enterprise and does not even have to be associated with a firm or an enterprise (although most are because such an association has distinct advantages). Indeed, a pioneer entrepreneur does not even need to be a producer of goods for sale but can be an intermediary; the Sundance Institute and the Man Booker Foundation are examples of such pioneer intermediaries. To create a market, pioneer entrepreneurs must help consumers understand the value of new and original—even potentially subversive—ideas and goods so that consumers buy them—literally and figuratively. Pioneer entrepreneurs accomplish this by generating an understanding of the attributes, quality, and therefore the value of the good, thus making the works intelligible, meaningful, and desirable. Consequently, the discourse that educates consumers about the good is as essential to the market as the good itself, which is why intermediaries, who make no contribution to the production of the good, may still be pioneer entrepreneurs—they are involved in the "production of belief"[9] in the value of the product.

In addition to firms, individuals can also act as pioneer entrepreneurs.[10] Consider two examples: first, a hypothetical college professor who (in a defiant move, at least for the time) assigned Joyce's *Ulysses* in the 1940s or early 1950s when it was still considered profane and was not viewed, as it is today, as the canonical modernist novel; second, Robert Hughes, the art critic, who made modern art intelligible to the layperson. Individuals such as the hypothetical college professor (who operated outside the market) and Robert Hughes acted as intermediaries and most certainly contributed to an outcome that parallels the accomplishments of the Sundance Institute. Although the two types of pioneer entrepreneurs (individuals and firms) move toward this goal in slightly different ways, both types generate an understanding of new and unfamiliar work, making it possible for consumers to value the work and thereby creating a market for it.

The entity (perhaps surprisingly) least likely to be considered a pioneer entrepreneur in this framework is the creator, whose innovative and original idea is the basis of the new product category being brought to market. The notion that a creator is likely not a pioneer entrepreneur is less surprising than it sounds—artists often create without regard to prevailing consumer preferences or existing cultural norms, driven by the desire to materialize a creative idea or vision. A creator who forges a work that does not fit into existing market categories, and therefore cannot be understood and/or evaluated, is certainly a *pioneer*. However, the work of the pioneer *entrepreneur* goes beyond being a visionary: a pioneer entrepreneur bridges the visionary world of the artist and the more mundane and pragmatic sensibilities and institutions of the market, which includes consumers who tend to seek comfort in the familiar. The work of the pioneer entrepreneur begins after the pioneer artist has completed her task, when a market for the work must be created. The task of *market* creation, not merely *creation*, is the core of pioneer entrepreneurship.

Even though markets are composed of institutions that evolve to be resistant to change because stability is beneficial for all participants, change and evolution in the form of new market creation is not an infrequent occurrence. Institutions comprise individuals, at least some of whom are nonconformists with a vision that deviates from the institutional script they are expected to follow. These mavericks are willing to risk their reputations—and sometimes, by founding firms, even their fortunes—to go against the grain. These nonconforming individuals may not be artists themselves, but they have the ability to see the spark of artistic greatness that others may overlook. By identifying the value of something new—even if the novel good does not fit into prevailing norms of appropriateness (and therefore value)—pioneer entrepreneurs expose consumers to new ideas and objects. However, change is never easy. When such an opportunity is spotted and seized by a pioneer entrepreneur, appropriate discourse that changes the commentary is essential to neutralizing the challenges inherent in the creation of a new market.

The Importance of Discourse in Pioneer Entrepreneurship

A pioneer entrepreneur must disrupt the equilibrium that exists among commerce, commentary, culture, and consumption to create a market for a new good. Because its attributes likely do not align with prevailing cultural norms, a new category elicits confusion, or worse, hostility among consumers.[11] A pioneer entrepreneur, therefore, faces the difficult task of changing the cultural status quo to prompt consumption. This change primarily requires commentary, but any product new to the market naturally lacks the commentary that would render it understandable. Thus, one of the primary tasks of pioneer entrepreneurship is the creation of new commentary. Pioneer entrepreneurs face several challenges as they work to create this new commentary to create a new market.

The resistance to novelty is particularly intense when it comes to radically novel cultural goods. Because such goods don't possess much direct utilitarian value,[12] innovations in cultural goods tend to be parallel to extant categories rather than a new and improved iteration of existing goods. For example, rock 'n' roll is not an objectively better version of previous music (such as opera) but rather a novel category of music. The unfamiliarity and unacceptability of a radically new category of cultural good, then, cannot be easily mitigated by demonstrations of improvements in utility or clear advancement in benefit to consumers.

Furthermore, consumers' tastes in art, music, books, films, and the like are all heavily influenced by when and where they grew up, as well as by the particular experiences to which they were exposed.[13] These tastes become an integral part and expression of consumers' personal identity—who they are, who they want to be, and how they want to be seen by others. This makes society rather more resistant to new categories of cultural goods and art works than to novelty in other kinds of goods because such new goods often challenge the self-perceptions and worth of the majority of its members, as was the case with rock 'n' roll.

Even if we were to believe that every innovation would not encounter the kind of extreme and blatant hostility that rock 'n' roll faced, new cultural categories, however seemingly innocuous, raise a problem for their promoters and supporters. The subjective attributes and high symbolic content of cultural goods entail the need for high levels of explication before consumers can understand the meaning and value of these goods.

Pioneer entrepreneurship in the creative industries is therefore difficult, and market creation—encouraging and driving consumption of new categories—requires copious amounts of discourse so that commentary and culture are in alignment and drive consumers to value the good. The crucial importance of discourse to the creation of a market has two chief implications for the study as well as the practice of pioneer entrepreneurship. First, the centrality of discourse means that intermediaries (not just producers) can be pioneer entrepreneurs and market creators. The inclusion of intermediaries has additional nuanced implications in that the relationship between pioneer producers and pioneer intermediaries tends to be symbiotic. Given that explication is such a central part of value construction and market creation, and due to producers' known vested interests in creating a market for the good,[14] pioneer producers on their own cannot achieve a complete transformation in the perceived value of a good. Instead, intermediaries play a major role in market creation because, to be market generative, producers' reorientations or constructions of value must be broadly accepted and endorsed by an independent and objective intermediary.[15] At the other end, the value-constructing dialogue of a pioneer intermediary will not result in the creation of a market without (pioneer) producers that steadily provide those goods to consumers.

The first important challenge of pioneer entrepreneurship, therefore, is that intermediaries and pioneer producers must work together in the process of market creation. Indeed, because pioneer producers have a known vested interest in creating a market for the good, and, because pioneer intermediaries cannot provide a steady supply of goods to consumers, neither type of pioneer entrepreneur is sufficient on its own—both entities are necessary, and they are connected in a symbiotic relationship. The crucial importance of intermediaries' discourse and the economic commitment required of producers mean that the pioneer producer must take on an unenviable economic risk. The work of a pioneer intermediary, although not entailing the same potential for economic loss, is not risk free. The economic risk of putting one's weight behind an unproven, unfamiliar radical innovation is limited for pioneer intermediaries by the very definition of an intermediary; however, the reputational risks these entities face are not insignificant.

The need for pioneer intermediaries and pioneer producers to work in concert is strengthened in the creative industries due to the manner in which consumers' preferences evolve and stabilize. Although commentary can introduce new ideas into a sociocultural context and cause a shift in general beliefs among the population, the potential for commentary to effectively bring about such change is neither unbounded nor simple, due to the nature of consumers' interactions with cultural norms. An important feature of cultural norms and the process of developing preferences based on those norms is that consumers accept and follow them from a desire to align and identify with some collective, which may be of varying size, legitimacy, and direct connection.[16] This collective may be convenient (family and physically colocated friends), chosen (because of affinity and similarity, which is admittedly endogenous but nevertheless important because it reinforces preferences), or aspirational (role models, celebrities). The chief implication of this need to belong to and identify with some social group is that a single voice within the overall commentary, attempting to change beliefs and criteria of validity, will not suffice; rather, consumers have to see the particular discourse take root and gain ground among the relevant social group. Even in being different, individuals like company and rarely venture into totally uncharted (or even undercharted) territory. A single source of commentary that proposes and supports a new idea, definition, or set of evaluation criteria or standards of quality will likely not be impactful unless that discourse is disseminated widely and reinforced in the general commentary.[17] Without intersubjective agreement over the value of the new idea, most consumers, unsure of the social validity of adopting it, will not change their beliefs and preferences. It is important, then, that the new conventions be generally circulated and accepted and bolstered by multiple relevant stakeholders—intermediaries as well as producers—for the commentary to become pervasive enough to have an impact on the norms in society. When exposed to similar discourse from multiple sources they can trust or identify with, consumers are much less likely to be suspicious of the new norms or to worry that this might be a fringe movement, participating in which would lower their social credibility. They thus would grow more accepting of the new conventions. This, in turn, would increase the likelihood that the newly introduced good would be seen as valuable and a market would be created for it.

The second implication of the importance of discourse is that pioneer entrepreneurship can take the form of recasting a particular existing category of goods as valuable through commentary, to create a stable market for it. Pioneer entrepreneurs accomplish this recasting in one of two ways: first, by highlighting particular attributes of the good that seem more familiar, and therefore more valuable, to consumers; or, second, by intersubjectively altering the relevant criteria of evaluation so that the good is perceived as valuable. Both processes change how the good is perceived by consumers—the first by changing (the perception of the) good so that it meets existing criteria of value and the second by changing the evaluation criteria. Notably, however, the boundary between these two modes of recategorization/revaluing is blurred, both because the attributes that define a good and the criteria used to evaluate a good are inherently and recursively linked and because parsing out discourse in this manner is incredibly difficult, as illustrated in the following examples.

Discourse that recasts value is apparent in the example of the market for modern twentieth-century artworks from India.[18] As a category, this art lacked a robust global market until the mid-1990s. Having been largely dismissed as parochial and derivative, it was therefore perceived as having little or no value in the fine art context. In the 1990s, however, academics and some critics began to recast these works as exhibiting a distinct type of modernism and originality. As this reframing gained traction, it was difficult for the market to dismiss the entire category, and thus the value of the works began to increase. The academic discussion around these works, which described them as having a particular sensibility and originality (that is, the attributes) that Western modern art possessed, also simultaneously questioned and cast as problematic the prevailing notions and criteria of modernism in art more broadly. In effect, two linked discourses—one specific to Indian artwork (focused on attributes) and one encompassing modernism in general (focused on evaluation criteria)—emerged. As a whole, however, the reorientation of the value of modern Indian art was predominantly a process of demonstrating and highlighting attributes of the genre that had previously been overlooked and less about changing the definition of modernism itself.

A contrasting example is the case of American chef James Beard, who promulgated a new vision and definition of haute cuisine as being a culinary category characterized by attributes such as freshness, simplicity, and regional (American) flavors.[19] This shift was a clear case of changing the evaluation criteria for an existing category, haute cuisine. The acceptance of Beard's conceptualization lent credence to the notion that haute cuisine need not be limited to European cooking traditions and repertoires and thus generated an appreciation among consumers for modern American cuisine, concocted by chefs such as Beard and Alice Waters (of Chez Panisse, a modern French-inspired locavore American restaurant near San Francisco) and effectively dissipated the perceived inferiority of this cuisine.

Although both means of recategorizing/revaluing cultural goods can originate from either producers or intermediaries, the broad intersubjective agreement on value criteria and standards required for market creation is more likely to emerge when there is a certain amount of independent objective discourse (such as that of intermediaries). In the case of Beard and new American cuisine, for example, the commentary of Craig Claiborne, food critic at *The New York Times*, played a significant role in establishing the validity of the reimagined conventions of haute cuisine in the United States, the same as art historians in the case of the market for modern Indian art.[20]

Characteristics of Pioneer Entrepreneurs

Although the roles that producers and intermediaries play in market creation are somewhat differentiated, as shown by the previous examples, pioneer entrepreneurs of both types nonetheless share certain characteristics that are a sine qua non for undertaking the risky task of creating a market for a new category.

First, all pioneer entrepreneurs must have the foresight and vision to understand the significance and importance of new—potentially incomprehensible or even offensive (to the sensibilities of the majority)—cultural goods, and they must want to create a world in which these goods find a market. Without a compelling vision to drive them, pioneer entrepreneurs would likely succumb to the despair and frustration that is part and parcel of the long, uncertain, and arduous process of market creation. The ability to envision the end goal—a state in which the new category of goods is widely understood and accepted and therefore consumed—enables pioneer entrepreneurs to plot their path toward this goal and strategize effectively to accomplish it.

Their second typical feature is that like the pioneering artists whose works they attempt to bring to market, pioneer entrepreneurs must also be driven substantially by nonpecuniary motivations.[21] Although the goal of a pioneer entrepreneur is to create a market for a cultural good, because the task is extremely challenging and the desired outcome is uncertain at best, the accrual of sales revenues cannot be the chief driving force behind the undertaking, even in the case of pioneer producers, who stand to gain direct economic returns from success in creating a market for the goods they sell. Sometimes pioneer entrepreneurs are motivated by the potential for impact; as described in the previous chapter, pioneer entrepreneurship has implications for cultural change. Specifically, most pioneer producers are driven primarily by a dual desire to obtain visibility and acceptance for creative and visionary artistic work and to financially support such visionary artists. The publisher of *Ulysses*, Sylvia Beach, for example, supported Joyce throughout the long process of his writing the book, which was much delayed.[22] Moreover, having read parts of the manuscript while Joyce labored on the tome, she must have anticipated the trouble the book could cause and the difficulty she would have selling it, let alone garnering any profits. Publishing *Ulysses*, then, was by no means a guaranteed way to make a profit, and therefore Beach's motives were arguably nonpecuniary.

Pioneer intermediaries—who by definition do not stand to make money as a result of their efforts—are motivated solely by the promise of intangible gains. Certainly pioneer intermediaries may enhance their reputations (for being visionaries or trend spotters and market creators) and status, which may be parlayed into future gains, tangible and/or intangible. Yet the prospect of even these potential future benefits cannot be the sole drivers of their work because their efforts could end disastrously, with their name in disrepute, being derided for having discovered and supported an unworthy artist and/or category of work. Thus, for both producers and intermediaries who act as pioneer entrepreneurs, working toward a goal beyond pecuniary gain is a necessity.

Finally, because pioneer entrepreneurs cannot work in isolation and must build intersubjective alignment and agreement, they need to create momentum among all the players necessary to the market. Unless the discourse is broadly disseminated, generally accepted, and reinforced by multiple entities, the new evaluation criteria and value construction are not likely to find their way into the general culture—that is, into the minds of a sizeable population of consumers—and therefore are not likely to lead to the construction of a sustainable and substantial market. Consequently, pioneer entrepreneurs must be collaborative consensus builders, nearly evangelical in their relentless pursuit of broad acceptance of their perception of the new good and its value.

Paths Taken by Pioneer Entrepreneurs

Pioneer entrepreneurs can adopt several strategies as they seek to create a market for a new category of goods. One of the most common strategies is to render the new good less unfamiliar to consumers.[23] Strategies that facilitate effective market creation address both the cause and effect of the unfamiliarity of the goods introduced by pioneer entrepreneurs. Thus, pioneer entrepreneurs attempt to assuage consumers' fears of standing out among their social group, which makes them less receptive to new goods and also makes those goods seem more familiar and attractive so consumers are less unwilling to consider and consume them. Several different actions fall under this broad rubric (the specific relevant action varies slightly depending on whether the pioneer entrepreneur occupies the structural position of a producer or an intermediary).

DEVELOPING A DISCOURSE FOR NEW CATEGORIES

Pioneer entrepreneurs generate discourse about the new product to promote an understanding of the product and construct its value. The discourse can take different forms, such as printed texts or high-profile events. For example, Saffronart, the auction house (and thus pioneer producer) that played a decisive role in creating a market for twentieth-century Indian art, engaged in market-creating discourse by producing detailed catalogues describing the artwork, the artists, and the overall context of modern Indian art.[24] Although the auctions were all conducted online, the firm still produced physical catalogues, which are a common discursive genre in the art world and especially for art auctions. In another example, the annual Sundance Festival for independent cinema constituted the chief discursive implement of the Sundance Institute, the pioneer intermediary widely regarded as having created a stable market for independent cinema in the United States.[25]

Regardless of the form it takes, the discourse generated by pioneer entrepreneurs fulfills two goals: explicating the product so that it is broadly understood by consumers as well as other producers and intermediaries and delineating the criteria that guide the evaluation of the product and the establishment of quality standards. Discourse can achieve these goals directly and explicitly, as in Saffronart's catalogues, or indirectly and implicitly, as in the Sundance Institute's choices of which films to feature at the Sundance Festival. Although the festival's programming staff had received some broad and diffuse directions ("What I sought in the Festival was variety," said Robert Redford, the festival's founder)[26] regarding the types of films they hoped to promote at the institute and festival, these directions, which were essentially evaluation criteria, were not put forth in a public forum. Yet repeated exposure to a certain type of film at successive festivals—small-budget, plot-driven films with somewhat subversive themes—led to festival goers, as well as society at large (through press coverage of the films and the festival) to understand a certain set of attributes as defining characteristics of a prototypical "indie" film.

Because pioneer producers stand to directly benefit from greater revenues and thus have a limited influence on how the product is valued, they benefit from co-opting discursive elements from pioneer intermediaries that are independent and therefore more credible and objective authorities, as Saffronart did when it included academics' writings in its catalogues. Without the incorporation of this type of independent explication and evaluation, a pioneer producer's own discourse may be viewed as purely promotional and self-serving, lowering its impact.

PIQUING INTEREST AND REDUCING ANXIETY

To successfully create a market for an innovative cultural good, pioneer entrepreneurs frame the new category in a certain fashion. Specifically, pioneer entrepreneurs attempt to pique consumers' interest in the novel category while reducing worries about social rejection. Consider Coco Chanel's simple modern dresses, made from inexpensive jersey cloth, which were, in many respects, quite inappropriate for women in the sartorial context of Paris in the first quarter of the twentieth century, and certainly would have drawn criticism for their subversive aesthetic.[27] Chanel's designs challenged the prevailing belief and custom that clothing served to indicate social class and standing rather than personal tastes and preferences. Previous fashions signified a woman's status as a privileged damsel who was able to lead a life of leisure because her husband or father earned enough to ensure that she did not need to perform any worklike activities. In contrast, Chanel's practical clothing, in which a woman could move easily, would not (initially) convey a high-status image.[28] Purchasing and wearing these dresses, then, signaled the wearer as a deviant and rebel, and only a brave individual would be willing to take on that kind of social vulnerability. Embracing a new cultural good, then, requires a willingness to shed an existing identity as well as question one's beliefs and thus stand out among one's peer group; pioneer entrepreneurs have to address the anxiety that often accompanies this process.

As the example of Chanel's designs illustrates, although consumers may find novel stimuli attractive and interesting, their fear of ridicule is one of the main obstacles to acceptance of new cultural categories. When faced with a new product, then, consumers are likely to be wary but also intrigued. To induce consumption of their innovative product, pioneer entrepreneurs must take advantage of the intrigue while quelling the wariness. These dual objectives are best achieved by framing the product as novel enough to be perceived with interest by consumers willing to take a chance on something new (the classic experimenters or "early adopters"[29]) but also similar enough to existing, accepted, and well-understood products that it is not perceived as threateningly unfamiliar—a strategy of "optimal framing."[30]

Pioneer entrepreneurs can achieve this delicate balance in several ways, but most involve some discursive repositioning and framing, given that the actual product likely cannot be altered to make its features seem more familiar. The task of pioneer entrepreneurs, then, is to shape the narrative about the new product in such a way that it highlights the familiar and comforting aspects of the product, emphasizes those aspects that are more closely aligned with prevailing criteria of propriety and value, and either downplays or casts in a positive light those features that are most threatening or unappealing to a majority of consumers. In some cases, it might even be possible to alter or design the product in ways that conform to the narrative and the framing chosen by the pioneer entrepreneur. Piquing consumer interest while reducing consumer anxiety, via both discursive and material changes, rather than just one of these, will increase the chances of successful market creation as the product will appear to be in alignment with its narrative framing.

An excellent example of optimal framing that achieved the dual objectives of piquing interest and reducing anxiety, through discursive as well as material means, occurred among the earliest fashion designers in India, where, until the mid-1980s, clothing culture followed the "tracht" model rather than the "mode" system.[31] In other words, women dressed according to traditional customs—choosing, either due to personal preference or pressure to conform to social norms, to wear saris[32] or the *salwar-kameez*[33]—rather than trendy styles dictated by a fashion system.[34] Traditional clothing styles used handwoven and/or hand-block printed textiles, often featuring additional decorations such as beadwork, embroidery, or surface layering with precious and semiprecious metals and stones. Because organized retail was relatively absent in the country at the time, Indian women were dependent on local tailors to make their garments. As a result, the first local high-fashion designers faced skepticism regarding the value of their products—they were viewed as glorified tailors with vastly overpriced products. Early fashion designers in India, therefore, primarily created and sold traditional Indian garments such as *lehengas*,[35] *salwar-kameez*es, and saris. Arguably, these garments did not involve much design innovation per se, but focusing on these styles was an economic necessity for early designers because, as one explained, "In India nobody is going to pay a high price for innovative patterns—only for embroidery."[36]

In this case the pioneer entrepreneurs (designers) were able to attract consumers (Indian women) by focusing on familiar garments but adding novel design elements to arouse the interest of more daring consumers. Designing within the parameters of traditional Indian garments allowed designers to add novelty and value via the use of heavy surface embellishments and luxurious fabrics while still maintaining the visual integrity of the traditional clothing. Further, the use of these textiles and heavy decorations served three purposes. First, these ostentatious decorations and fabric choices fulfilled the requisites of a natural product segment: wedding attire. Notorious for their extravagance, Indian weddings are important social occasions; because clothing serves as a status symbol during the festivities, expensive clothing is a sine qua non for the event, especially for the bride and close members of the wedding party. Second, the grand embellishments and luxurious fabrics justified the higher prices charged by designers: consumers could see and feel (and, most important, recognize) the value of the garment they were purchasing, even if they were uneducated in the importance of style or cut. Third, perhaps the most important element of the designers' framing strategy was that it provided a means to overcome resistance to the seemingly elitist nature of high fashion in a country rife with poverty, especially in rural communities. By creating traditional garments from handwoven fabrics and embellishing them with handcrafted decorations—all sourced from rural artisans who were part of a long and varied tradition of textile excellence in India—designers could assert that such clothing was relevant and important on nationalist and preservationist grounds. Even if the clothes seemed ostentatious and outrageously priced, designers argued, their purchase helped support the ancient, but dying, primarily village-based practice of textile craftsmanship. According to the designers' framing, the preference for handwoven fabrics and heavy embellishments served a higher purpose: preserving national identity and promoting superior Indian crafts and skilled craftspeople.

In the case of Indian fashion, pioneer entrepreneurs used both discursive and material means to pique consumer interest while reducing anxiety. However, changing the material aspects of the product was possible only because this case involved pioneer producers—design firms—that were founded by the creators themselves. Other types of pioneer entrepreneurs, both pioneer producers and pioneer intermediaries, have much less ability to influence the material properties of the product because they are limited by either the creator's individuality and artistic integrity or other aspects of the product or its presentation to consumers. However, even when pioneer entrepreneurs have little ability to change the material properties of the product, they can alter the narrative, as well as engage in other material actions that, without altering the product itself, still make it seem more familiar to consumers.

Whole Foods Market, for example, knowing that at the time of the firm's founding consumers associated organic food with unsavory images of hippies as well as perceptions of deprivation and a lack of taste, designed their stores to be bright, clean, inviting, and unlike any "crunchy-granola health food" store that existed at the time.[37] Moreover, the early stores exuberantly projected an image of decadence with chocolate fountains, luxurious bath and body products, and eye-catching merchandising, so that consumers would no longer associate organic foods with deprivation and drudgery. Finally, to this day, the stores stock a mix of organic and "conventional" produce and products because the management knows full well that a store that sells only organic foods will fail to attract a broad swath of the mainstream consumer market. Also worth noting is the subtle messaging implicit in the use of the word *organic* against the word *conventional*. In reality, organic farming was the norm until chemical fertilizers and pesticides were introduced in the late nineteenth century,[38] so "organic" is, in fact, "conventional" in historic terms. Moreover, "organic" is not the parallel counterpart to "conventional"; rather, "unconventional" would be the right descriptor. However, not only would the label "unconventional" for organic foods have, on the one hand, sounded too radical and novel, but, on the other hand, calling organic food "conventional" would have removed the novelty and the associated positive feelings around the new category. The framing, both discursive and material, thus was optimal, also because the term *organic* was already more broadly in use beyond Whole Foods at the time of the firm's founding. This is an important advantage because broad acceptance of the new conventions of value and criteria of quality and propriety promulgated by pioneer entrepreneurs is crucial to the creation of a market for a new category of cultural goods, as discussed earlier, and the basis of the next strategy of pioneer entrepreneurs.

DEVELOPING BROAD AND GENERAL ACCEPTANCE OF NEW CATEGORIES

The importance of broad intersubjective agreement on the appropriate way to view, understand, and evaluate a good is crucial to both existing markets and new markets for novel categories of goods, especially in the creative industries. Due to the acutely social nature of the consumption of cultural goods, the hasty adoption of a new category—prior to its general acceptance—could have a negative impact on the social standing of a consumer (in addition to an economic impact). Therefore, the discourse generated by pioneer entrepreneurs must be adopted by other entities in the value chain that will then disseminate and reinforce the discourse.

The dissemination and adoption of pioneer entrepreneurs' discourse, however, is neither inevitable nor easy to achieve; it cannot be strategically orchestrated because the impact of the discourse is contingent on other entities adopting it of their own volition. The commentary of pioneer entrepreneurs, therefore, must stand and gain ground on its own merits, rather than through persuasion and/or coercion.

If a pioneer entrepreneur cannot be instrumental in increasing the adoption of new value conventions, it might seem that there is little else, if anything, to do other than wait and hope. However, the reality is not this dire. Some individuals and firms have preexisting reputations and prestige, which grants them credibility and thus increases the likelihood that their value-constructing discourse (rather than another entity's discourse) is disseminated and accepted. Reputed producers, known for discovering worthy artists with innovative ideas and works, thus stand a greater chance of having their discourse believed and accepted. Similarly, some pioneer entrepreneurs are likely in the dually advantageous position of both possessing the right reputation and occupying a structural role in the value chain, which allows them to disseminate their opinions broadly. A well-established critic or reviewer who works at a reputed media organization (such as a magazine, newspaper, or television network), for example, likely has a significant ability to disseminate new value conventions for novel categories of goods.

As in successful social movements[39] (and related to the framing strategies already described), dissemination and adoption are most likely when the new value conventions and the related discourse resonate with relevant stakeholders for a variety of reasons. Of course, pioneer entrepreneurs cannot accurately predict what constitutes a resonant discourse (and therefore cannot plan or design such a discourse); however, these entities tend to have "an ear to the ground" and possess what is informally known as an intuitive or innate sense of what will resonate. In this regard, pioneer entrepreneurs are not that different from the artists whose works they promote; just as it is difficult to pinpoint with even a modicum of confidence what exactly it is about a painting by Picasso or a song by the Beatles that makes these works wildly appreciated and successful among critics and consumers alike, there is, to a certain extent, an art of pioneer entrepreneurship that may be difficult to describe systematically via a checklist of actions and discourse characteristics. Further, both artists and pioneer entrepreneurs are strongly motivated by nonpecuniary goals, and both groups believe it is imperative to make the most authentic attempt at expressing their vision of value.[40] As a result, both artists and pioneer entrepreneurs can hope for the best but must, in the end, leave the reception and acceptance of that vision to the stakeholders.

Garnering intersubjective agreement is less problematic for pioneer intermediaries than for pioneer producers because intermediaries have no direct economic interest in the market. Relative to pioneer producers, then, pioneer intermediaries such as academic institutions and individual academics, critics and reviewers, and award-granting bodies likely find it easier to achieve the broad dissemination and acceptance of their new value conventions.[41] That said, intermediaries are useful and relevant only when consumers perceive them to be beyond the influence and control of producers, that is, as being independent entities. Therefore, pioneer producers cannot actively court intermediaries to promote the adoption of their discourse. However, pioneer producers can borrow credibility from other entities that have already constructed a new discourse (as Saffronart did with academics' writings). In this case, the discourse of producers and the discourse of intermediaries are mutually reinforcing and jointly engender change in the beliefs and norms of consumers.

Summing Up and Looking Ahead

The rest of the book is about firms and entrepreneurs—pioneering and not—in the creative industries (see Table 2.1). Pioneer entrepreneurship is clearly challenging, and yet it occurs repeatedly if not frequently, in the creative industries. It is possible that the potential for cultural change—changing minds, not just lives—that can be wrought (as described in the previous chapter) through pioneer entrepreneurship and market creation for new categories of cultural goods is what continues to drive entities to engage in this difficult task. Their impact on cultural change makes pioneer entrepreneurs relevant to society, and it is therefore important to understand them. This can be achieved only by understanding the structure and functioning of creative industries. Conversely, the framework of pioneer entrepreneurship and market creation is useful for understanding the creative industries, the firms

TABLE 2.1. Types of firms and entrepreneurship.

		New	Existing
		Market category	
Firm (producer or intermediary)	*Existing*	Entrepreneurship: Pioneer (A)	Baseline (C)
	New	Entrepreneurship: Pioneer (B)	Entrepreneurship: New venture (D)

operating in these industries, and the markets for cultural goods because the creation of a market by pioneer entrepreneurs for radical new categories represents an extreme case of the market creation that has to occur every time a new cultural good (radical or not) is brought to market (as detailed in the following discussion). Finally, entrepreneurship, even when it is merely the founding of a new venture and not of the pioneering kind, is important in the creative industries because of the ferment of new ideas that new ventures generate. The rest of the book, therefore, builds on the concepts and frameworks elucidated in these first two chapters to shed light on the interrelationships among the various entities in the value chain of creative industries, with the aim of understanding the functioning of these industries and their implications for entrepreneurs and pioneer entrepreneurs operating in the intermediary and producer roles.

This chapter has emphasized the importance to pioneer entrepreneurs engaged in market creation of commentary comprising the discourse of producers and intermediaries, intersubjective agreement over the conventions of value elaborated in the discourse, and the discursive framing of the new category in optimally balanced ways that render it simultaneously exciting and comforting. These three aspects of market creation are central to markets for all cultural goods, new or not. Although new categories of creative works face high levels of uncertainty in the market, the nature of the creation, production, and consumption of cultural goods is such that every new iteration of a cultural good (even if the product is not the first in a new category) requires a certain amount of market creation. Continual market creation is required primarily because creative works are singularities,[42] meaning that each one is unique, so that even works that fit into a well-known category must be explicated *each time* a new one is brought to market. Every film, book, song/album, dress, or painting is new and distinctive relative to its predecessors on multiple fronts, so when it is brought to the market for exchange, its meaning and value must be decoded, constructed, and conveyed by the value chain in creative industries. Once a category has been established as valuable in the marketplace, subsequent units do not undergo the same rigorous evaluation and description; they must, however, be evaluated (with regard to the extent of their conformity to existing accepted criteria of value) and explicated.

As a consequence, the entrepreneurial act of market creation has to occur across the value chain each time a new cultural product is placed in the market, albeit in a less challenging or thorough manner than for an entirely new, radically innovative category of cultural goods. The subsequent chapters examine intermediaries and producers in the value chain in creative industries in more detail—what they do, how they do it, why they exist, and what their characteristics and functions imply for entrepreneurs in these sectors. Each of the following chapters first explicates how (existing) intermediaries and producers operate in existing categories or markets of cultural goods—the "baseline" case (cell C in Table 2.1). Building on this foundation, each chapter then explores what these fundamental concepts mean for new ventures in new (cell B—pioneer entrepreneurship) as well as existing (cell D) categories while also shedding light on the role of incumbents (cell A) in the creation of new categories (pioneer entrepreneurship). Above all, the book underscores the importance of systematically examining two processes, the production and consumption of culture and how change and innovation occur in the notoriously institutionalized stable creative industries. At the same time, building on the proposed model of the structure and creation of markets and the concept of pioneer entrepreneurs and their impact (through discourse) on norms, the book makes a case for understanding the creative industries, not merely as producers and sellers of culture but rather as entities that engage meaningfully and successfully with society and shape its culture.

Part II

INTERPRETING CULTURE

Intermediaries in Creative Industries

INTERMEDIARIES

Constructing Meaning and Value for Markets

A review should make you want to run out to a play, flip on
the TV, wake up to new possibilities. A negative review should
be exciting too; why shouldn't bad art make you angry?
—Jonathan Landman, culture editor, *The New York Times*[1]

In 1981, John Lack, executive vice president of programming and marketing
at cable operator Warner Amex Cable Communications (WACC), envisioned
a new television channel, "Music Television" (MTV). He imagined the channel as a "visual" radio station that would be "both promotional, and entertainment for its own sake."[2] Lack planned to show music videos all day, in
stereo sound, thus introducing audiences to new music and giving advertisers
a way to reach twelve- to thirty-four-year-olds, a very desirable demographic
that would be likely to gravitate toward such programming. The idea worked;
MTV showed that music videos could both attract viewers (and therefore, advertisers) and sell albums. A survey conducted by *Billboard* magazine in October 1981, soon after the channel launched, indicated that regions carrying
MTV cable signals experienced an increase in sales of tapes and records.[3] A
separate Nielsen survey in 1982 reported that 85 percent of participants were
MTV viewers and 63 percent of those stated that viewing a music video had
prompted their purchase of the album.[4]

Although MTV had a considerable impact on the music industry, this effect was impossible to know ex ante, particularly for record labels, which, after
an initial period of resistance, spent large sums of money to create attractive
music videos and give them gratis to MTV. Record companies chose to provide videos to MTV rather than trying to reach customers through their own
music video channels, which would have given them greater control. In the
marketplace, consumers began to rely on MTV to discover new music, which

influenced their purchase of new albums. It seems everybody did, indeed, need MTV, just as the channel's promotional campaign—"I need my MTV"—proclaimed. The importance of MTV, which acted as an intermediary in the market for music albums, and its impact on both producers and consumers are functions of the nature and structure of markets in general and of cultural goods in particular. This chapter, the first of three chapters on intermediaries, introduces intermediaries in creative industries, explaining their role in markets, their particular importance in creative industries, and their modus operandi, as well as the implications for entrepreneurship of these aspects of intermediaries.

Markets: Structure, Actors, and Information

Markets do not comprise only buyers (consumers) and sellers (creators[5] and/or producers).[6] They also require third parties—intermediaries such as MTV—that do not have a *direct* economic stake in the revenues generated from the sales of those goods but that provide crucial objective information about goods that enables and facilitates transactions between buyers and sellers.

Markets are not merely transactional exchanges but rather complex interactions that involve production, exchange, and consumption of goods and services, influenced by cultural and social factors,[7] and are therefore rife with uncertainty. Information that alleviates this uncertainty (and consequently eases market interactions) plays a crucial role in enabling valuation and exchange; indeed, a functioning market is predicated on the existence of discourse that provides such information.[8] As a consequence, markets abound with informational commentary, which comprises the discourse of both producers and intermediaries, in the form of advertisements, brochures, and catalogues (producers' commentary) as well as reviews, articles, books, message boards, event lists, conferences, and awards (intermediaries' commentary).

Markets for cultural goods are even more dependent on information (because of the unique properties of these goods; see the following pages for a detailed discussion) and thus are replete with commentary, generated by several entities, each with different and potentially competing objectives. With large amounts of information available in the market, to arrive at a good decision, consumers must consider the source and the intended purpose of the commentary. Not all commentary is created equal, and consumers are aware of the variation introduced by differences in the market roles, objectives, and incentives of the sources. Understanding the differences between sources of market information is crucial to understanding the role of intermediaries.

The chief distinction between the sources of commentary lies in the goals and incentives of the commentary-generating entities. Of the two primary sources—producers and intermediaries—of commentary that influence consumers' perceptions of value and desirability of the goods in a market, only producers stand to gain direct financial benefit from generating beliefs among consumers that the good is highly desirable and valuable; intermediaries, in contrast, have no such direct (economic) stake in increasing the value of the good. This distinction has material implications for the functioning of markets. Firms that earn revenues from selling goods (producers) must attempt to persuade consumers in various ways to buy more goods, to pay higher prices, or both.[9] Therefore, producers have ample incentive to circulate information—via advertisements, promotional and publicity materials, and other media—with a strong positive bias toward their own products, and/or a negative bias toward competitors and their products.[10] Producers also often engage the services of publicists, who are responsible for generating and circulating positive news and information about the firm and its products that will enter the public consciousness. The awareness of producers' goals and the intent behind their promotional materials is elemental to consumers' metacognition of markets[11] (their set of beliefs about the marketplace). Consumers know that the discourse generated by producers and their paid agents is intended to persuade them to buy goods. This discourse, therefore, triggers "coping mechanisms"[12] that help consumers make sense of these communications from producers. One primary coping mechanism is to discount the validity and veridicality of communications generated by producers and, therefore, turn to other unbiased sources of information and evaluation—intermediaries—for knowledge about goods. This knowledge influences consumers' preferences and consumption. Thus, intermediaries are essential to the functioning of the market because their discourse exerts a greater influence than that of producers (or of their paid agents) on the preferences and value perceptions of consumers.[13]

Clearly, consumers benefit significantly from intermediaries and their discourse, but it is not immediately evident whether and how producers benefit. If anything, it would appear that the objective information provided by intermediaries—because it cannot be controlled and molded by producers to their own advantage—would be problematic and therefore unwelcome to producers. Yet, not only are intermediaries tolerated, but producers also actively engage with them, as shown by the willingness of record companies to incur great costs to create music videos for MTV. Why do producers engage with intermediaries? One reason is that, in the case of MTV, if record labels had simply created their own music video channels, one for each firm, the endeavor would have been futile because such channels would have been understood as more promotional messaging from producers, albeit in a different and unusual format. Producer-created channels, therefore, would not have had the same impact on consumer behavior and preferences. Moreover, when MTV was founded, the music industry was in decline. Consequently, record companies, desperate to generate sales, were willing, albeit grudgingly, to try something that would give them greater visibility among consumers. That said, even—and arguably, especially—in a thriving industry, producers benefit from the existence of intermediaries, whom they incorporate into their production processes.

In creative industries, intermediaries are especially important to producers because they enable consumers to understand the symbolic value inherent in cultural goods and translate that symbolic value into commensurate economic value. The discourse of intermediaries affects either the aggregate value (total sales) of the product or the specific value (price) of an individual item, depending on the nature of the good itself.[14] In the case of goods such as films or books, which tend to be uniformly priced or priced before they appear in the marketplace, intermediaries such as film critics and book reviewers influence the number of consumers who recognize, understand, and pay for the value of the good (that is, they influence the total sales of the good). In the case of artworks or other sui generis items, intermediaries influence the perceived value and price of each individual work in the marketplace. The obverse is also true—strongly negative evaluations can undoubtedly destroy the market for a good, as any producer of a poorly received Broadway show knows well. For example, the all-around disastrous reviews of *Spider-Man: Turn off the Dark* (the musical incarnation of the original film) led the production to shut down within a few weeks of its New York preview and not open again until nearly a year later when sufficient changes had been made to the lyrics and music, cast, and direction.[15]

The manner in which intermediaries exert their influence on market transactions is why the use of the term *intermediary* is appropriate for these entities, although it has a somewhat different meaning in this book than in common usage. The term usually indicates an entity that is "in between" two actors, through which goods must pass as they make their way from sellers to buyers. In the context of creative industries, intermediaries are similarly integral to the passage of cultural goods from producers to consumers, their most important task being to convey the meaning of the cultural good and thus establish its value. In the art market, for example, galleries and auction houses are producers (although, in the usual sense of the term, they would be seen as intermediaries between artists and collectors), and art critics and museums are intermediaries. Just as wholesalers, distributors, and retailers (which are commonly referred to as intermediaries that connect manufacturers to consumers, although in this book they act as producers) are essential in other industries, the entities described in this section are essential for producers wishing to reach consumers. However, although in the usual sense of the term intermediaries connect products and consumers through the physical transfer of goods, the nature of creative industries is such that these intermediaries connect artworks and consumers through their discourse; without intermediaries' discourse, consumers would find it difficult, if not impossible, to discover, understand, and evaluate cultural goods such as artworks. Specifically, the term *intermediary* emphasizes that, although cultural goods in the market do not physically pass through these entities, intermediaries are crucial to the smooth functioning of markets, from the perspective of both producers and consumers.[16] Every producer—publishers, record companies, studios, restaurants—knows that being noticed by intermediaries is crucial to its business and financial performance and thus enacts specific rituals and procedures—providing review copies of books or tickets to press showings of films prior to theatrical release—that attest to the importance of the coexistence of intermediaries and producers in creative industries.

The Importance of Intermediaries in Creative Industries

Assigning such importance to an entity that is engaged primarily in the production of discourse aligns with the socially embedded view of markets,[17] which is especially applicable to the creative industries, due to the nature of cultural goods. The unique and specific properties of cultural goods are also the reason intermediaries are particularly important for the smooth functioning of markets for these goods, as described next.

CULTURAL GOODS HAVE HIGH SYMBOLIC VALUE

The fundamental feature of the products of creative/cultural industries is that their symbolic value is greater than their material value.[18] The symbolism inherent in cultural goods makes it difficult for consumers to understand and assess their value. Who, then, validates these works and establishes their value? Multiple entities—a "field of cultural production"[19]—contribute to the explication of the meaning of works of artistic production and the construction of their symbolic worth for consumers. Because works of art possess symbolic (and therefore economic) value only if they are recognized as such by all relevant entities/stakeholders, the "production" of artworks is more than a straightforward physical or material process of creating the work. Production, in the case of works of art, also includes the symbolic process of constructing the meaning and value of the work.[20] Thus, the entities in the field of cultural production that construct the "meaning and value of the [art]work"[21] for consumers include producers, intermediaries (for example, critics and reviewers), and educational institutions. The efforts of these entities produce— among society at large but more specifically among consumers or potential consumers—a "belief in the value of the [art]work."[22] However, for the reasons already mentioned, intermediaries have a stronger influence on consumers' perceptions of the value of the goods than producers. Intermediaries help consumers understand creative/cultural products through interpretation, explication, and judgment; the symbolism inherent in cultural products and their socially contextualized consumption make such interpretation a necessary step in the smooth functioning of markets for cultural goods. For example, consumers may not understand (the value of) highly symbolic, conceptual works such as modern art, free verse, magical realist novels, molecular gastronomy, rap music, or auteur films that subvert traditional storytelling formats; intermediaries, such as critics and reviewers, can address this problem by explaining the codes and symbolism in these works and delineating criteria for their assessment. The writings of noted art critic Robert Hughes are a good example of such explanatory and evaluative discourse. His BBC show, "The Shock of the New," has been called the "best synoptic introduction to modern art."[23] Hughes's commentary provided succinct descriptions of the important features of various works of art, which implicitly conveyed the criteria used in assessing those works and also modern art more generally, thus rendering the genre more accessible and comprehensible to lay consumers.

CULTURAL GOODS ARE EXPERIENTIAL AND SUBJECTIVE

Most, if not all, cultural goods are so-called experience goods,[24] whose quality is difficult to judge ex ante, although sampling may occasionally be possible, such as by browsing a book before buying it. Moreover, the quality of cultural goods is highly variable and difficult to discern.[25] Consumers, therefore, find it difficult to arrive at purchase decisions. Intermediaries experience and evaluate the goods in the market, and in turn their assessments of the quality of the goods help consumers make decisions. Restaurants are an excellent example of producers that sell an experiential good that would be prohibitively costly, literally and figuratively, to sample. As a result, restaurant reviews are invaluable to diners and, by extension, to restaurants, because reviews provide visibility and evaluation, both of which are prerequisites to consumption.

The variable quality of cultural goods and their experiential nature also means that their assessment entails subjectivity—individual consumers can use any criterion they wish to evaluate a product. Because individual tastes vary widely, this subjectivity leads to significant uncertainty about the potential demand for goods. Intermediaries address this uncertainty through discourse that influences tastes by systematizing the relevant criteria to be used for evaluation.[26] Individuals' tastes (their "predisposition to like and seek exposure to certain types of things")[27] are a central aspect of their decision to consume goods, especially creative works.[28] These tastes are influenced by prevailing cultural norms, which are beliefs about what is appropriate and desirable. In effect, tastes are shaped by intermediaries' commentary, which is responsible for generating and disseminating criteria and standards of quality. These criteria and standards, when shared and accepted more broadly, establish what is desirable and appropriate, shaping consumers' tastes and preferences and therefore determining what is valuable in the market. Although such discourse is particularly influential in the so-called high culture[29] segment (art, literature, classical music, and dance), which comprises highly symbolic works, the so-called low culture segment (film, pop music, genre fiction) is not entirely immune to these standards either, because consumers enjoy the emotional security that comes from knowing that a credible source has validated the quality of the work according to some widely accepted criteria.

CULTURAL GOODS HAVE SOCIAL MEANING

Cultural goods are consumed in a social context: the value of cultural goods lies not only in what they symbolize or mean for the consumer[30] but also in what they convey about the consumer to others. An art collector, an opera aficionado, or a fashionable individual uses an artwork, references to the opera, and cutting-edge clothes to signal a certain persona not only to friends and acquaintances but also (especially in the case of fashion apparel) to strangers. The desired and/or intended projection may be of refined taste or an avant-garde outlook. Alternatively, the individual may simply be trying to fit in with her or his peers by signaling conformity with prevailing norms that define what is desirable and valuable—hence the preponderance of "picture postcard" photographs from vacations.[31] The discourse of intermediaries facilitates the interpretation and understanding of a creative work, knowledge consumers need to make decisions that will be seen as socially appropriate.

A critic's favorable opinion of a cultural work, avant-garde or otherwise, can not only give comfort to a buyer but also generate consensus among the broader public—of which the buyer is a part—about its quality and importance. Such discourse can therefore generate a collective and shared understanding of cultural goods among consumers, which is a precursor to establishing their value and consequently enabling their consumption. Because the understanding of the goods and their meaning is shared and collectively agreed on, the consumption of particular goods then conveys impressions about the consumer, contributing to his or her social and cultural capital.[32]

CULTURAL GOODS ARE PRODUCED IN PROLIFERATION

There are vast numbers of creative artists in the world, and, as a result, a large number of cultural goods are produced every year in every country. As evidence, consider that more than 100,000 (book) titles are published every year in the United States. [33,34,35] This proliferation increases the importance of intermediaries because consumers find it difficult, if not impossible, to be aware of all these artists, let alone all of their works. And yet, having access to and information about the entire range of products available for consumption is a critical facilitator of consumption—a product will have meaning and value only if it is visible to potential consumers. Professional intermediaries can keep track of producers and products in ways that time- and attention-constrained consumers cannot, which allows intermediaries to provide important information to consumers.

Understanding Intermediaries and Influence

These social, symbolic, and subjective dimensions of cultural goods and their consumption all render interpretation and evaluation essential to the creation, existence, and operation of markets for cultural goods. Although such interpretation and evaluation is formally performed by intermediaries, other informal factors also influence consumers' perceptions of value and their buying decisions.

FORMAL INTERMEDIARIES

Formal intermediaries are explicitly engaged with the tasks that influence beliefs and perceptions about specific categories of goods. In contrast to informal forces of influence, the influence of formal intermediaries is not incidental, nor is it diffuse and unrelated to the market or particular good. Formal intermediaries fall into one of two main categories: entities that are integrated into the commercial realm of the market, operating as an essential part of the production and distribution of cultural goods; and entities that are, to a certain extent, outside the direct purview of the market. Entities in the former category—*market intermediaries*—are directly involved with the market and incorporated into production and distribution systems and decisions. Entities in the latter category—*nonmarket intermediaries*—are responsible for reproducing stable tastes and preferences among consumers.

Market intermediaries are entities whose presence and activities are acknowledged and supported by creators and producers selling cultural goods to the public. They are usually integrated into the production and distribution cycle of cultural goods. For example, record labels create music videos for MTV, publishers set aside complimentary review copies of books, movie studios conduct exclusive screenings of films for film critics, and artists and authors submit prints and/or manuscripts to juries, award committees, and festival committees. Producers and creators, knowing that these intermediaries play a large role in constructing the value of goods in the market, engage directly with these intermediaries and readily submit to their evaluation and discourse.

The case of nonmarket intermediaries such as museums and schools is somewhat different. These entities engage in discourse that shapes the general dispositions and norms in society, rather than the perceived value of specific cultural goods in the market. For example, a reputed and respected museum that decides to showcase pre-Raphaelite artworks may create a general predisposition toward paintings of this particular style. The museum's decision and its selection of works acts as a statement that leads members of the public to presume the aesthetic superiority of that style because the museum (or, more precisely, the curator) is viewed as an authority on the subject of quality in art. That said, museums do also have a more direct influence on value (and prices) in the case of secondary markets for art. In these markets, the fact that a particular artwork was acquired by a prestigious museum functions as an indicator of its quality and contributes to a higher asking price than would be applied in the absence of the museum's validation/endorsement.[36] In comparison, schools and the general dispositions that their curricula generate tend to be even further and more consistently removed from commercial processes in the market.

Formal intermediaries that produce interpretations and valuations to enable and enact a market for cultural goods come in a multitude of forms. Both firms and individuals may perform the tasks of an intermediary. Entire organizations dedicated to providing discourse about a particular cultural category, such as the Sundance Institute or the Pritzker Foundation, are crucial elements of the value-construction process and are therefore intermediaries. Individuals acting as intermediaries within bigger, more generalist organizations include book reviewers, such as Michiko Kakutani and James Wood at *The New York Times* and *The New Yorker*, respectively, which publish more than just book reviews. Slightly different from both of these examples is the fashion magazine *Vogue*, a publication that is clearly devoted almost entirely to covering fashion, even though it sometimes provides commentary on other related topics as well. The magazine has certain writers and editors who have the stature of Kakutani within the fashion industry (Grace Coddington, for example). However, *Vogue* itself is widely perceived as a key player in the fashion value chain, whereas *The New York Times*, its fashion coverage notwithstanding, is not considered a fashion publication per se. Therefore, *Vogue* and other similar entities would be considered intermediary firms, and the individuals employed by them—like Coddington—would be considered individual intermediaries.

The distinction between individuals and organizations is relevant because it influences the functioning of intermediaries as well as the organizational structures and business models that are put in place to maintain the impact of intermediaries on valuation and markets. In addition, this distinction is relevant to the issue of entrepreneurship, especially as it relates to the process of creating a market for a new product category by constructing and conveying its value (that is, pioneer entrepreneurship).

Although formal intermediaries are the chief topic of this section of the book and the most relevant to the other topics covered in the book, it is nevertheless useful to briefly explore the essential elements of informal sources of commentary, which also influence consumers' decisions by permeating culture and being manifest as cultural norms and beliefs regarding appropriateness.

INFORMAL INFLUENCES

When consumers are asked why they bought a particular record or book or watched a particular film, a frequent and likely response is, "Because [somebody they know] recommended it." This social process of discovery and evaluation is one of the informal ways in which preferences/tastes and consequent acts of consumption are shaped and influenced; individuals, embedded in a web of social connections and opinions, are susceptible to the influence of other individuals whom they respect, admire, or like.[37] The influence of one's social network is not only potentially stronger, more proximate, and more direct than the influence of advertisements and brochures but also more likely to "seal the deal" after professional opinions and recommendations have been considered.[38]

Aside from being influenced by their social networks, individuals' preferences are also informally influenced by diffuse and indirect commentary generated by entities beyond individuals' direct social connections. Especially in the world of fashion, celebrities' choices have significant influence on lay consumers' preferences and purchase decisions; for example, lace, which was once considered old-fashioned for the twenty-first century, suddenly became a popular embellishment in various garments (not only gowns) after Catherine Middleton married the UK's Prince William in a wedding gown adorned with intricate lace in 2011.[39] Other influential entities include writers, presenters, and social and cultural commentators who shed light on phenomena, events, objects, people, and other issues and, in so doing, affect individuals' opinions and beliefs about goods.

Consider the case of organic foods. Although many formal and social processes undoubtedly influenced perceptions of organic foods, making them more desirable and valuable in the eyes of consumers, the role of other texts, which were not originally meant to be directly related to organic food, also pulled weight. For example, Rachel Carson's *Silent Spring* has been credited with forcing society to acknowledge the unforeseen negative consequences of scientific and technological advances and causing people to rethink and reevaluate their beliefs about, say, chemical fertilizers and pesticides in agriculture. These new societal beliefs regarding the (in)appropriateness and (lack of) value of certain practices that were, until that point, broadly accepted as good were an important component of the beliefs about food production practices that eventually influenced individuals' preferences for, and consumption of, organically grown foodstuffs. Nevertheless, Carson did not set out to write about the desirability of organic food per se and was therefore not formally or explicitly involved in shaping consumers' beliefs about the value of the market category. Indeed, Carson and commentators like her (Michael Pollan, who writes about ethics and health in the food industry, is a good present-day example) are not engaged in consciously influencing perspectives about a particular category of goods in the market but rather seek to shape broader frameworks for norms that, in turn, shape overall consumer tastes and preferences.

Informal intermediaries affect consumer beliefs through vastly different processes. The distinction between schools that act as nonmarket intermediaries, for example, and informal commentators like Rachel Carson can be described along two different dimensions, intent and scale. Schools and their curricula (which are usually uniform within a socially, geographically, and/or temporally circumscribed unit) are able to influence beliefs on a much larger societal scale and at a more fundamental level than the types of informal entities previously described. In addition to scale, intentions differ across these two types of informal intermediaries. There is a systematic intentionality behind the design of school curricula, in terms of both the frameworks and ideas that are endorsed and the subjects of study. Thus, a literature curriculum intends to establish (and succeeds in doing so) ways of understanding, analyzing, and evaluating literature, which is a cultural good. Such a curriculum is required to cover this subject in a particular way that not only reinforces the canon but also reinforces the broadly accepted ways of understanding and evaluating these works. The intention of a school's commentary is thus quite different from the intention of a commentary that, in a general, diffuse way, influences individuals' thinking about an idea, concept, or event, which then becomes the preferred lens used to examine and assess cultural goods (just as *Silent Spring* indirectly engendered a belief in the value of dining at a restaurant that sources only local ingredients).

Doing Business as an Intermediary

This section returns to the main topic of this chapter—formal intermediaries, especially market intermediaries—after the preceding pages highlighted the variation among intermediaries. The extent of this variation means that it is difficult to develop a single generalized understanding of the nature, structure, and operations of intermediaries. That said, all intermediaries face three common challenges: creating a revenue stream, avoiding conflicts of interest, and managing a dual identity.

GENERATING REVENUES

The business models of intermediaries are uniformly complicated by the very definition of an intermediary; despite being integral to the market for a good, their raison d'être mandates an inability to benefit from high values of the goods about which they engage in discourse. Intermediaries' lack of vested interest in the value of the goods they construct is what gives them their position of credibility and authority in the market. As a result, intermediaries cannot sell cultural goods and must instead "sell" their value-constructing discourse to remain financially viable. However, there is no obvious market for this discourse; consumers don't necessarily recognize the need for or value of the discourse of intermediaries even though they do, in fact, benefit from the discourse.

Given the constraints generated by this situation, one of the most common business models among intermediaries is a two-sided platform[40] in which users on "one side" of the platform subsidize the users on the "other side." The best-known example of such a business model is a magazine, which has two sources of revenues that reinforce each other. Magazine subscribers are subsidized by the advertisers that buy ad space in the magazine in the hopes of reaching subscribers and other readers; without regular subscribers, the magazine would not be able to attract the right advertisers at the right price, and, without advertising revenues, subscription rates would likely be prohibitively high. Only rarely do magazines or other publications have content of such high quality and broad appeal that consumers are willing to pay the full cost of production, although, of course, books are commonly sold in this way. Further, despite using a two-sided revenue model, few intermediaries earn subscriptions solely on the strength of a value-constructing discourse that is directly pertinent to the focal market. For this reason, *Vogue* and *Rolling Stone* publish articles on topics other than fashion and music, respectively, and *The New York Times*'s restaurant and film reviews reach a wide audience of readers who read the newspaper for news rather than the reviews.

Intermediaries also employ other means of generating revenues. Some intermediaries earn revenues through ticket sales (for example, film and music festivals such as Telluride and SXSW, or South by Southwest) and/or through the sales of other related products (such as gift shops in museums that also charge an entrance fee).[41,42] In addition, some nonprofit intermediaries raise philanthropic funds. Further, some intermediaries (including the Sundance Institute and many museums) obtain funds through some combination of these three revenue streams (that is, ticket sales, product sales, and donations). Earned revenues, however, cannot come from sales of the product itself; for example, a museum cannot sell the art it exhibits (although it can certainly sell prints, posters, or other products with images of the artwork), nor can a film festival retain a share of the distribution deal signed by a director at the festival.

AVOIDING CONFLICTS OF INTEREST

One could ask whether potential revenues from ticket sales influence a film festival's curators—might they select only those films that are likely to find a sizeable audience, which would significantly reduce the real and/or perceived objectivity of the festival or intermediary? Although this is theoretically possible, it is unlikely in practice for two reasons: it is difficult to reliably predict the type of films that will be popular among viewers, and a limited number of tickets are available. Relative to the impact of a stake in a distribution deal, therefore, any increase in revenue resulting from a manipulation of the programming roster to include crowd-pleasing films rather than objectively high-quality films would be miniscule. The potential conflict of interest in the case of ticket sales, therefore, is negligible.

Although ticket sales may not present a significant conflict, intermediaries do face other, more significant conflicts of interest. Although intermediaries do not have a *direct* economic stake in the sales of the goods for which they construct value, they do have an indirect interest in the market. In the case of *Vogue*, for example, strong sales of the goods (fashion apparel) that are the subject of its discourse are important to the financial health of the intermediary. Without strong sales in the fashion market, brands would not be able to purchase ad space in the magazine. Similarly, nonprofit organizations such as the Sundance Institute or the James Beard Foundation, which depend on sponsorships for revenue, need their sponsors (in the film and culinary industries, respectively) to do well financially to sustain their operations. Of course, not all intermediaries depend on advertisers or sponsors in the same industry in which they contribute to the value chain. For instance, although newspapers or general-interest magazines such as *The New Yorker* do depend on revenues from advertisements, the typical advertiser in these publications is not a particular restaurant, film studio, or publishing firm, but rather any brand that targets the same demographic as the publication. Similarly, luxury brands (in industries not directly related to art) pay high sponsorship fees to the organizers of Art Basel, the premier art fair in the world, in return for being seen and experienced by wealthy art collectors, who frequent these events in large numbers.[43]

Despite the absence of a direct vested interest in revenues, this indirect connection with revenue, especially in certain cases, could potentially affect the operations and value-constructing discourse of intermediaries. In the case of fashion magazines, readers have probably noticed that, unlike newspapers, which frequently publish negative reviews of books and/or films, magazines contain exceedingly few, if any, negative reviews of collections and/or designers. Consumers, therefore, can legitimately question the objectivity of the discourse produced by some intermediaries. Magazine editors typically explain away the lack of negative reviews by noting that although the published reviews are all positive, not being mentioned in the editorial content of the magazine is tantamount to a negative review (because a collection that consumers are not aware of will have little to no market value). Conversely, *Ms.*, the feminist magazine cofounded by Gloria Steinem and Dorothy Pitman Hughes, discovered that, because its target audience was women, most of its advertisers came from the beauty and fashion sectors, much to the dismay of both editors and readers, who wanted the magazine to adopt a critical feminist approach and perspective. The magazine began to accept advertisements from only a select few organizations whose ideologies were similar to those of the magazine's editors, an action that allowed the editors to maintain both their objectivity and their critical stance.[44] Such a step—limiting advertisers or sponsors—is, however, not always feasible, given its obvious negative effect on revenues and sustainability, but intermediaries have other means of preserving and emphasizing their independence and of maintaining strict objectivity in their discourse. Additional checks and balances that preserve the integrity of intermediaries and their discourse are discussed in the next two chapters.

MANAGING A DUAL IDENTITY

Doing business as an intermediary involves challenges beyond creating a revenue stream and avoiding conflicts of interest. The example of magazines and newspapers highlights another challenge: the dual identity with which market intermediaries often grapple. Although intermediaries do not sell cultural goods, they are still producers in a certain sense because they produce independent commentary, which the consumer buys. This role becomes clear when, using an industry lens, one thinks of an intermediary such as *W Magazine* as belonging to the "magazine industry," or *The New York Times* as belonging to the "newspaper industry," or MTV as belonging to the "TV entertainment industry." Along the same lines, Chanel and the restaurant French Laundry (both producers) could be said to belong to the "fashion" and "culinary" industries, respectively. However, *W Magazine* is also considered an intermediary in the context of the fashion industry. Similarly, a restaurant critic who writes for a newspaper is an intermediary in the restaurant industry, whereas the newspaper is a producer in the media industry (and the critic is a creator). Although there are some exceptions (for example, film festivals and museums), most intermediaries inhabit a dual identity—they are producers in the context of one industry but intermediaries when considered in the context of a different industry.

This dual identity leads to a particular weakness in the business model of intermediaries: the need to manage a very fragile balance between revenues and relevance, which has two specific implications for intermediaries and one for society as a whole. First, intermediaries must walk a fine line to produce discourse that is relevant to consumers (so consumers will buy the discourse) but at the same time does not anger producers, causing them to withdraw advertisements in retaliation. Balancing these two objectives is an ongoing struggle for intermediaries because consumers trust them to provide objective unbiased opinions about industry-specific goods, but providing such opinions may offend the producers of these goods, which are often also the advertisers that generate the bulk of intermediaries' revenues. Relative to magazines, newspapers are better protected against such volatile reactions or retaliation from producers because they have a broader mass audience. Thus, newspapers can attract advertisers from multiple industries rather than a limited set of firms within a single or a few closely related industries (as with magazines).

The second implication of the dual identity is that intermediaries have opportunities to increase revenues by taking kickbacks directly from producers (this situation is discussed in detail in the next two chapters), although, of course, doing so undermines their independence and objectivity, that is, their relevance in the market. Even though taking advantage of such opportunities might lead to greater revenues in the short term, in the long run it would reduce intermediaries' relevance and undermine their position in the value chain.

Because the discourse produced by intermediaries has broad influence, the challenge of balancing revenues and relevance is not only a business problem for intermediaries but also an important societal issue. Intermediaries benefit multiple constituencies: creators, producers, and consumers, of course, but also society more broadly. The extent of this influence is nicely illustrated by the example of the Pritzker Prize in architecture, which confers the highest honor on a single architect every year. In interviews, Pritzker laureates (the creators) describe both tangible and intangible benefits of winning the prize; not only do they (and their firms, that is, producers) obtain access to certain large and prestigious public architecture projects, but they also rise in stature so that their innovations are taken more seriously.[45] As a result, the discourse of intermediaries benefits the creative professions by raising their public profile and familiarizing laypersons with the work of each profession's high-quality practitioners. In addition, intermediaries can create long-term benefits for society more broadly by validating new ideas and making the avant-garde more acceptable, thus enabling the repeated cycle of disruption and creation that rejuvenates cultural and social life.

Do Intermediaries Act as Gatekeepers?

The potential for intermediaries' discourse to have such a wide-ranging and powerful impact forms the basis of the common perception that intermediaries—critics and reviewers, in particular—are gatekeepers who use their position to arbitrarily deny or allow artists and producers access to the marketplace. There is often a distinct negative connotation to this characterization, casting intermediaries as elite arbiters of quality with rarefied tastes that do not necessarily reflect the tastes and desires of the general consuming public. As a result of these supposedly elite tastes and high and esoteric standards, some people (both creators and consumers) feel that many simpler, more populist (and popular) works have been unfairly denigrated by highbrow critics. Countless artists, the argument goes, could have made a living if only critics had not dismissed their work and ruined their chances of reaching consumers and finding a market.

There is some truth to the belief that intermediaries act as gatekeepers; their very position and role in connecting consumers to creative works entails curation and other acts that control the connection. This capacity has meant that some artists and creators whose work did not receive sufficient attention from intermediaries have suffered from low market visibility and presence. Because it is difficult to prove the counterfactual (that these creators would have succeeded if only they had received the blessing of intermediaries), it is unclear whether the unfortunate fates of these creators were unwarranted given their quality. However, based on anecdotal evidence—certain artists are later understood as being "ahead of their time" and/or recognized only after their deaths—it seems plausible that intermediaries do restrict market access to some degree.

Take, for example, J. S. Bach, now regarded as one of the greatest classical composers to have ever lived. Bach's music was hardly known during his lifetime and did not achieve its current fame until composers such as Felix Mendelssohn and academic intermediaries, such as scholars in the (then new) field of musicology, initiated a "revival" in the nineteenth century.[46] Another musical example is Igor Stravinksy's well-known piece "The Rite of Spring," which was met with riots by the public and negative reviews from critics when it premiered in 1913 but has since become known as one of the highest-regarded musical masterpieces of the twentieth century.[47]

Two facts can possibly exonerate intermediaries from the gatekeeper accusation. First, there are some creators in every generation who do gain fame and fortune in their lifetimes, indicating that intermediaries do not block every artist at any given time and that at least some high-quality artists do gain both praise and an entry into the marketplace. The success of virtually any contemporary artist—Toni Morrison, Beyoncé, and Grayson Perry, to name a few—supports this observation. Second, the fact that some artists and creators who were unappreciated during their lifetimes eventually gain recognition and appreciation should raise questions about the application of the "gatekeepers" metaphor or, at the very least, recast the term in a more forgiving light. Clearly, these visionary artists *were* brought to the market at some point and were perceived as having meaning and value, presumably at least in part due to the actions of intermediaries. Consider the example of John Kennedy Toole's *A Confederacy of Dunces*, which was published more than a decade after Toole committed suicide and only as a result of the persistent efforts of Toole's mother and the commentary of author and college professor Walker Percy. More than 3.5 million copies of the book have been sold around the world, and the novel won the Pulitzer Prize in 1981, but, during his lifetime, Toole had no success finding a publisher.[48] The "gatekeeper" role is, therefore, an apt metaphor only in the short term; intermediaries may indeed shut the door in the face of some artists and/or works at some point in time, but other intermediaries may let the same artists and works into the marketplace at another time or in another place. Just as often as intermediaries' neglect or negativity keeps creators and their works *out* of markets, their attention and acclaim *create* markets for new categories of creative works. These latter intermediaries, who bring works to market that have previously been excluded, are the pioneer entrepreneurs and market makers, who, along with other entrepreneurial intermediaries, are the subject of the next section.

Intermediaries and Entrepreneurship

The social contract of an intermediary requires it to commit to objectivity and to the advocacy of new good ideas regardless of their commercial potential. As an intermediary, an individual or organization can engage in discourse that reinforces prevailing conceptions of appropriateness and value, or it can challenge and change these conceptions. Especially when intermediaries' discourse is employed to explain, evaluate, and value new categories of cultural goods, the second option can lead to market creation and cultural change—thus allowing an intermediary the opportunity to be a pioneer entrepreneur. However, intermediaries, especially new ventures or pioneer entrepreneurs, encounter obstacles in the process of achieving consumers' acceptance of their discourse as credible and impactful; they face difficulties and challenges due to the complex business models available to them. These obstacles are particularly problematic for pioneer intermediaries. The bulk of this section focuses on pioneer intermediaries to describe how discourse generated by firms (new or established) as well as individuals can create new markets, leaving the description of new intermediary ventures largely to the next two chapters, where more specific details about the role, operations, and features of intermediaries will be discussed.

PIONEER INTERMEDIARIES: DISCOURSE AND MARKET CREATION

Consider once again the example of the Sundance Institute and independent cinema.[49] When the Sundance Institute was founded in 1981, big-budget spectaculars were popular (that is, considered appropriate, acceptable, and desirable).[50] An entire ecosystem of producers and intermediaries existed, which brought these films to market and constructed their value based on an internally consistent system of evaluation and instruction that was pertinent to such films. Actor/director Robert Redford founded the institute to encourage an alternative cinema that emphasized storytelling, particularly from the point of view of underrepresented (at least in American cinema) populations. The institute initially provided grants to filmmakers with interesting ideas. Realizing that these films needed audiences, the institute then organized a recurring festival for independent films. Through the festival and its prizes, as well as the grants, the institute gradually created an implicit schema for understanding and evaluating independent cinema based on criteria and standards that differed from those used for big-budget studio films. This schema helped audiences appreciate, accept, and value these films, which were unlike the films they had seen before; in turn, audiences' appreciation of these films provided a platform for alternative narratives and stories that depicted a wide range of realities and expanded the emotional and cultural horizons of audiences. Gradually, as these standards for evaluating films became broadly accepted, Hollywood studios began to adopt some of the practices and conventions of independent cinema, leading to the rise of greater artistry in studio films intended for a broad audience.

More recently, the Prototype Festival in New York has, since 2013, actively encouraged innovative reconceptualizations of traditional operatic compositions to make these works more modern and experimental in a theatrical context.[51] The goal of the festival is cultural rejuvenation, but a desire to provide a stage to new, young composers also motivated the founding organizers. In essence, these ventures have redefined conceptions of what constitutes good art within a particular creative category (film and opera, respectively). In other words, they have changed the prevailing cultural norms that define what is appropriate and valuable. Through discourse, intermediaries thus bring about cultural change, making consumers less resistant to innovation and creating a market for innovative works.

INDIVIDUALS ACTING AS PIONEER INTERMEDIARIES

Incidentally, both the Sundance Institute and the Prototype Festival were new ventures, separate from other existing organizations. However, pioneer entrepreneurship can be undertaken by existing entities as well. This is the point at which the analytical distinction between individual intermediaries and organizational intermediaries becomes relevant. Often, singular individuals within existing large organizations are responsible for generating discourse that constructs the value of a new category of goods, even if their employer does not turn over all discourse to the new category. The intermediary function, therefore, enables a model of entrepreneurship that is qualitatively different than the usual models of entrepreneurial activity: individuals can engage in pioneer entrepreneurship from either within a firm or outside a firm.

Consider, for instance, the example of food critic Craig Claiborne, who popularized the concept of fine American cuisine as devised by chef James Beard. Via his discourse (articles and reviews), Claiborne contributed significantly to a nuanced understanding of the category among consumers and the consequent creation of a market while still being employed at *The New York Times*.[52] Similar contributions were made by academics and art historians employed at universities and/or museums, who played a central role in the creation of a market for twentieth-century art from India by recasting the category as a novel form of modern art that had been previously misunderstood and undervalued.[53,54] These individuals, despite not being founders of intermediary ventures, were, like all entrepreneurs, in possession of knowledge and skills that could create economic value (that is, enable the exchange of goods for money in the market). Thus, pioneer entrepreneurs can be not only founders or new firms, nor even just large opportunity-seeking firms or their chief executives, but also individuals who act in a freelance capacity or are employed (as critics and/or reviewers) and working within a larger organization.

An individual employed at an existing firm has two available options when engaging in value-constructing commentary for a new category: to engage in pioneering entrepreneurship from inside the structural confines of the firm or to leave and start a new venture that focuses on the novel category. The choice depends on the reputation and influence of both the individual and the larger entity with which he or she is affiliated. Being part of a larger enterprise has advantages in that the individual's new ideas are more likely to have a credible platform and to become widespread and accepted (that is, to become part of broader cultural norms). Although the reputation of an individual acting as an intermediary (outside a firm) engenders a disproportionate influence over consumers, this influence is not sufficient to generate the large-scale cultural change necessary for creating a large market for a new category. Thus, the risks involved in such commentary, coupled with the scarcity of quantifiable benefits, may explain why even individuals with a radical new vision and new perspective on a category may choose to remain employed at an intermediary firm rather than create their own enterprise.[55]

NEW VENTURES AS PIONEER-INTERMEDIARIES

In contrast, depending on their employer's openness to radical new ideas and to allowing employees to pursue new categories, individual critics or reviewers may have different levels of freedom to engage in discourse that endorses new ideas. A lack of such freedom may nullify their options and lead to a decision to exit to start a new venture, where they will have requisite freedom.[56] Thus, the limited vision of established organizations may motivate individuals to start new ventures that provide much-needed commentary and context for novel categories.

Such was the case when rap music was introduced in the United States in the early 1980s; although some established music critics took note of the new genre, it was an entirely new venture—*The Source*—that became the intermediary of record for all things related to rap and hip-hop.[57] Started in a Harvard dorm room by two students, *The Source* began as a cyclostyled sheet of paper that provided information about rap artists, events, and performances; it also described and explained rap lyrics and the context from which they emerged. The information in *The Source* was unavailable elsewhere, and thus the publication gained a following and loyal readership. Later, this early success and influence led to the production of a large glossy magazine that emerged as the leader in the category and served as an inspiration for other important magazines, such as *Vibe*, that almost exclusively covered hip-hop. By the time *Vibe* was founded, hip-hop had established a place in the market, and thus that magazine was an example of a new venture in an established category.

Consider also the example of the storytelling radio show and nonprofit organization, "The Moth." Founded in 1997 by poet and best-selling novelist George Dawes Green, "The Moth's" approach differed from that of any existing radio programs that offered stories through a cultivated journalistic lens (such as "This American Life"). Instead, the organization hosted "events" at which audience members shared stories on stage, delivered to live audiences, without notes; these events were recorded and broadcast unedited on the radio. Inspired by past summers spent in his home state of Georgia, where he and friends would gather on porches in the evenings and share stories, Green hosted the first "Moth" in his living room in New York with a few friends. He quickly recognized that there was a growing interest in guerilla-style storytelling and began hosting events elsewhere. Moth events are now hosted at cafés and clubs around the United States. Although "The Moth" is still the primary radio storytelling program, a number of other story jams have sprung up, hosted by other nonprofits as well as bars, cafés, clubs, and restaurants as a part of their weekly evening programming, thereby creating a creative ecosystem of storytelling entities.

The preceding discussion of intermediaries, particularly the fact that intermediaries do not actually stand to benefit economically from their work in constructing the value of a good and creating a market for that good, raises a question: What makes being an entrepreneur, pioneering or otherwise, in the intermediary role in the value chain, attractive at all? As in all entrepreneurial activities, nonpecuniary motivations play a large role in intermediaries' work in constructing the value of cultural goods, especially those in radical new categories. Rather than monetary gains, intermediaries stand to accrue status, reputations, and other intangible assets. These benefits, moreover, can explain why individuals may choose to undertake the arguably risky activity of explicating and endorsing a new category that is not familiar to consumers; when it works, this market-creating move has payoffs beyond the pecuniary.

Like many founders in other industries, such individuals are also likely less motivated by wealth, and more motivated by the prestige, self-actualization, and lasting impact on culture that accompanies the pursuit of such intellectual opportunities.

Summing Up and Looking Ahead

Without intermediaries, markets—particularly those for cultural goods—are unlikely to function smoothly. Further, markets for new categories have an especially strong need for intermediaries' evaluative and explicatory discourse. Given their lack of vested interest in the economic value of goods, intermediaries are more likely than creators or producers to influence consumers' perceptions of the appropriateness and value of the new category. Intermediaries are thus crucial to constructing value in markets. Yet, paradoxically, specifically because of their position as third parties—neither sellers nor buyers—in the market, intermediaries are fragile as business ventures because they cannot directly capture any of the economic value they create. Nevertheless, both individuals and firms continue to serve as intermediaries, and many intermediary firms survive and even thrive in the face of high odds. Moreover, intermediaries accrue intangible benefits: because they are vital to new and established markets and they influence consumption, intermediaries possess considerable power over the fates and fortunes of creators and producers, who place goods for sale in markets.

Discourse takes multiple forms in the context of creative industries, and accordingly different forms of intermediaries' discourse achieve different objectives. To develop a thorough understanding of how intermediaries operate as businesses and maintain their status as entities with market responsibility and accountability, it is important to systematically examine both the tasks they perform that render them essential and viable (by enabling them to earn revenues in exchange for their discourse) in the marketplace and the features that grant them authority over other actors in the value chain. The next two chapters do just this: Chapter 4 explains the specific functions of intermediaries, and Chapter 5 describes the features of intermediaries—the properties they must possess to legitimately occupy this significant role that carries power and influence.

DOING THEIR JOB

The Functions of Intermediaries

To see something as art requires something the eye cannot descry—an atmosphere of artistic theory, a knowledge of the history of art: an artworld.
—Arthur Danto[1]

In 2012, the board for the Pulitzer Prize announced that the prize for fiction would go unclaimed that year; the announcement generated outrage, disappointment, and frustration among publishers who, every year, counted on the prize to grant at least some publishing firms (and the short-listed authors) in the industry an opportunity to bolster both their prestige and their revenues.[2] Winning the Pulitzer increased the visibility of certain books and writers because consumers used the well-respected prize as a marker of excellence to guide their book choices and purchase decisions. This process occurs not just for books, nor only for prizes—other types of cultural goods are similarly affected by the discourse of a variety of intermediaries. For example, movie listings, reviews, and the Oscars all influence movie choices, both implicitly and explicitly. Although the specific entities vary (the Grammys instead of the Oscars, for example), this pattern of influence repeats itself in the case of music, fashion, art, and other creative industries. Consumers regularly utilize the discourse of intermediaries and depend on this discourse to shape and determine their consumption of cultural goods, although they may not even be aware of their participation in this process. This chapter sheds light on the specific functions performed by intermediaries in the service of constructing the value of cultural goods to enable market transactions and consumption, explaining how these functions relate to each other as well as to markets and entrepreneurship in creative industries.

The Value Construction Process

Comprehending and categorizing the multiple functions of intermediaries entails analyzing the specific properties of cultural goods and the features of creative industries in the broader context of the process of value construction. In the creative industries, the valuation process is complex, explicit, and essential due to the inherent symbolism of cultural goods and two other properties discussed in the previous chapter, proliferation and subjectivity. Taken together, these properties pose particular challenges for the consumption of cultural goods. Consumers are unable to keep track of the full range of goods available for consumption due to proliferation; further, on gaining information about the entire range of available goods, a lay consumer would have difficulty understanding their symbolism and discerning their quality because the evaluation of such goods is a highly subjective process. These three properties—high symbolic value, proliferation, and subjectivity—juxtaposed with the nature of the process of value construction (described next) determine the specific form that intermediaries' tasks take in the creative industries. The market for cultural goods must include intermediaries that present consumers with the entire catalogue/inventory of goods in a particular category, intermediaries that explain the symbolic worth of the goods to consumers, and intermediaries that distinguish between low- and high-quality goods (following widely accepted rules).

Broadly, scholars of economic sociology have long contended that markets are socially embedded[3] and that value is a socially constructed[4] rather than an inherent objective property of a good. This framework implies that the process of value construction occurs in all industries and for all varieties of goods—albeit to varying degrees depending on the comprehensibility, familiarity, and utility of the good—but is particularly intense in creative industries. Because the value of a good is constructed, it is also socially and temporally circumscribed; what is valued at a particular time and in a particular context may not be valued at another time or in another context. For example, the social, cultural, and economic value of diamonds changed drastically over time as it was elevated (largely) through advertising copy.[5] Value, therefore, is not entirely exogenous to markets, and neither are individual preferences; instead, both value and preferences are, to a large extent, endogenously determined by the *commentary* of constituents *within* the market[6] (advertisements in the example of diamonds). Such commentary (that is, discourse)—texts, events, and interactions—can originate from producers as well as intermediaries; this section of the book, however, focuses on the discourse of intermediaries. Thus, consumers' preferences (which influence their market transactions) for goods in the market (*commerce*) are affected considerably by the prevailing collective norms and beliefs—the *culture*—in society at large, or, at the very least, in their proximate social circle.[7] *Consumption* is driven by the perceived exchange value of the good, which, in the context of markets, is specifically defined by three valuation elements—category, criteria, and standards—that are ascribed to the good. The value of any good depends on the category to which it belongs or is assigned, how well it meets the evaluative criteria applicable to goods in that category, and the extent to which it meets standards of quality set for the category. The process of constructing the value of a good, therefore, involves generating, interpreting, and establishing these three elements of value.[8]

Assigning a good to a category—a cognitive group of objects/elements that are similar along some dimension—is the foundation for further assessment and valuation of the good.[9] The category to which a good belongs has a significant impact on its perceived value because some categories are perceived as more valuable than others. For instance, one category—say, fine art—may be perceived as inherently more valuable than another—say, decorative art—and thus the value of an object is higher if it is categorized as the former than if it is categorized as the latter.

Categorization enables audiences/consumers to understand the nature of the good as well as which objects constitute its comparison set. However, this information is obviously insufficient—consumers still do not know which of the goods' attributes are important and should be used to evaluate the good. Continuing with the example of fine art, for instance, consumers must know that "originality" is an important criterion of a work of modern art (which is a subcategory of fine art). Knowledge of the generally accepted criteria[10] (in this case, originality, style, school, medium, and size) for assessing the goods within a particular category provides consumers with a valuation rubric for a particular good.

Knowing that originality (or any other criterion) is valued, however, still does not allow consumers to locate the good on a hierarchy of relative quality or value. That step requires the generation and establishment of standards[11] that measure and establish the value of goods as a function of the extent to which the goods meet those standards. These standards define a hierarchy or rank order, in which, presumably, the goods at the top (that is, those that meet the highest standards) are the most valued. In modern art, certain artists, like Picasso, are thought to represent the highest standard of originality; the value of the works of other artists can then accordingly be assessed relative to that standard.

Intermediaries contribute to the commentary that establishes these valuation elements, which influence consumers as they make consumption decisions.[12] Accordingly, intermediaries' tasks can be described as generating and/or adding to a broadly accepted, shared understanding of the categorization of goods; honing the criteria for assessment and evaluation; and establishing and maintaining the standards for measuring and conveying quality and value. However, these tasks are neither tightly demarcated nor distinctly separated. Indeed, the three tasks often flow seamlessly from one to another: the process of categorization generates at least an initial set of possible criteria of evaluation, and the generation of criteria leads toward certain types of standards while precluding others.

To continue the previous example, classifying a work as fine art generates certain evaluative criteria (originality, technique) while excluding others (trendy colors, soothing shapes). Once intermediaries add to these initial criteria to create a full set, it is possible to anticipate certain standards (such as a wholly new treatment of a subject, as a measure of originality, versus a completely novel subject itself) that will likely be applied. The reverse holds true as well—the application of certain criteria generally understood to be reserved for a particular category can provide an indication of the categorization of the good, even in the absence of an explicit or distinct categorization process. This pattern is most clearly seen in cases when critics and/or academics apply fine art criteria and valuation routines to understand and evaluate objects typically viewed as traditional craft products—a deliberate action that can have the effect of elevating craft objects to the level of fine art with correspondingly higher value. This scenario illustrates why the discourse of intermediaries is so crucial to markets. Absent intermediaries, which do not have a vested economic interest in constructing and/or conveying an inflated value of a good, producers' attempts to reorient the valuation of goods for their own benefit would be unchecked, unverifiable, and ultimately deleterious to the fabric of markets and society.

Intersubjective knowledge about, agreement on, and acceptance of valuation discourse is crucial to the smooth functioning of markets. To be useful in the process of exchange in markets, valuation elements must be shared and broadly accepted; without agreement on these elements and their interpretation, they are of no use to the consuming public. Imagine a situation in which an individual uses the color red as an evaluative criterion for art, whereas other entities in the market evaluate art primarily on its originality. The seller of a deep red painting characterized by little or no originality, and therefore of little or no perceived value (at least to the seller), would, nevertheless be able to sell the painting to the individual who values red at quite a high price if the buyer's preferences and criteria of evaluation were known. But, absent such inside knowledge, the seller is unlikely to promote the painting, assuming that the buyer desires paintings that meet the criteria accepted and used by the rest of the market. Crafting the required broad consensus on appropriate valuation elements, which are essential to smooth market exchange, is the job of intermediaries.

The Functions of Intermediaries

Intermediaries perform three core functions—providing information, generating knowledge and shared understanding, and pronouncing judgments—that loosely correspond to the valuation activities of defining categories, criteria, and standards. Notably, although these functions are defined and described in a straightforward manner here, the real-life process of constructing and conveying the value of a good is neither linear nor straightforward.[13] Further, the boundaries between these functions are relatively fluid, with the potential for different stakeholders to perceive the same entity and the same output of the entity as performing different functions (irrespective of whether the multiplexity was intentional or planned). Because value is a *general* belief in the desirability and appropriateness of a good, the process of value construction, which is essentially a process of shaping beliefs, inevitably occurs in a diffuse and ongoing, sometimes even in an informal manner outside the market and is often unnoticed by consumers, even as it shapes their preferences. However, this chapter focuses only on the formal dimensions of intermediaries' discourse, which accomplishes the following ends. (See Table 4.1.)

INTRODUCTION: PROVIDING INFORMATION

Intermediaries render cultural goods visible by providing information about (that is, *introducing*) the entire set of cultural goods that are available for

TABLE 4.1.   Functions of intermediaries.

	Intermediaries that **include** (share judgment)		
Include	E/A*: Awards; Oprah's book list U**: People's Choice Awards; best-seller lists	Intermediaries that **instruct** (share knowledge)	
Instruct	E/A: Award citations; film festivals	E/A: Books and publications/ magazines/reviews U: How-to videos; blogs	Intermediaries that **introduce** (share information)
Introduce	E/A: Man Booker Prize; Pritzker Prize	E/A: Museums, educational institutions (general and trade)	E/A: MTV; fashion week, *Variety* U: Event listings; community boards

* Generated by experts and authorities.
** Generated by users (lay consumers).
Note: The functions are not separated perfectly owing to their very nature and form. For instance, it is to be expected that a film review that *instructs* also *introduces* that particular film to at least some readers, even though it is not a comprehensive list of all films available to consumers at that time.

potential consumption. This task is particularly important in markets for cultural goods because of the vast proliferation in the number and types of cultural goods produced. Not only are there multiple forms of cultural goods (for example, art, films, books, music), but, because individual creativity knows no bounds, there are also multiple instantiations of goods within each form. Even in contexts (such as publishing or music) where firms vet quality and cull a large proportion of created works, prolific numbers of goods (books and records) are produced and brought to market. For instance, 186,000 individuals self-identified as musicians, singers, and related workers in the United States in 2010,[14] and in 2013 approximately 1.7 billion music shipments were made to consumers from all music companies (although each shipment—a CD, record, cassette, or mp3 file—is not a separate, unique recording).[15] Further, in 2013, nearly 2.6 billion books (again, each book sold was not unique) were sold in the United States.[16]

This function of intermediaries—providing information—involves keeping track of producers and goods in a way that consumers, who have limited time and energy, cannot. A good has value in a market only if it is visible to potential consumers, but it is impossible for the lay consumer to stay abreast of the staggeringly high number of cultural goods. This inability among consumers necessitates the existence of specialized intermediaries that *introduce* goods to the consumer by providing information and generating awareness of the entire set of cultural goods that exist and are available for consumption in the market. Examples of intermediaries that perform this function include trade associations that organize events such as book fairs, art fairs, the twice-yearly fashion weeks held in various metropolises, and video game and comic book conventions. Simple listings, such as those published under titles such as "What's On [Broadway]" or the *TV Guide*, also perform this function, as did MTV in its early days.

The first function of intermediaries—providing information—corresponds to the value-construction task of categorization. Thus, in the apparel or fashion industry, individuals or firms who show their collections on the runways during fashion weeks are categorized as "high-end," or even simply "designers," whereas other apparel stores are not considered "designer" clothing stores. This distinction explains the attention and media coverage that mass-market apparel brands receive on the rare occasions they are included in formal fashion weeks, as occurred in the case of J. Crew, which presented a fashion show on the runway during New York fashion week in 2012 and has done so every year since.[17] In the eyes of consumers and other audiences, being part of New York fashion week elevated the retailer's status to the level of high-end fashion designers because the fashion week event was understood as catering to that category of firms.

In many ways, the function of providing information is straightforward because the only relevant criterion for doing the task well is comprehensiveness. Nonetheless, fulfilling this function is not a simple matter, for it is important that an intermediary introduce, or render visible, *every* cultural good in a category that is produced within certain geographical and/or temporal boundaries (such as every book published and available in the United States in a year). This goal implies, essentially, that there should be no filter applied in the performance of this function: an intermediary that introduces should merely *inform*—not analyze or restrict according to any specific criteria (such as quality, size, value) other than categorical alignment. For instance, a listing that is categorically and specifically intended to be for fiction books will, of course, exclude nonfiction books but should not exclude fiction books that are, say, shorter than 500 pages or are considered poor quality by the compiler of the list. Given that an intermediary that introduces goods must necessarily restrict its output to factual information and steer clear of any evaluation, rarely, if ever, does such an intermediary do more than provide information, that is, it rarely provides knowledge and/or judgment (see Table 4.1).

The process of providing information about the very large number of cultural goods in the market entails a trade-off between breadth and comprehensiveness. First, broad categorical listings tend not to be reliably comprehensive. Second, those listings that are in fact comprehensive tend to engage exclusively with narrow/niche categories (for example, short stories, or even short stories written by women); this trade-off (narrowing a category to achieve comprehensiveness) can lead to a proliferation of intermediaries that mirrors the proliferation of cultural goods. The existence of multiple listings, each of a narrow, manageable category—such as poetry, short stories, and novels (as opposed to simply fiction and nonfiction)—is quite common and such listings are naturally more likely to be comprehensive. The prevalence of narrow categorizations does beg the question regarding their utility: How are consumers to be expected to keep track of cultural goods if the intermediaries that are meant to do so are themselves prolific, each covering a narrow category? However, this is not particularly problematic because consumers have usually developed preferences for specific categories of cultural goods (as a result of the activities of nonmarket intermediaries) and tend to follow the developments only in those categories; for example, a consumer may attend to the actions of intermediaries focused on hip-hop but not those focused on opera or jazz.

A common form of intermediary that performs the function of introduction is the trade intermediary. Often manifested as industry directories or trade events, the discourse of trade intermediaries is meant primarily, as the name indicates, for "the trade" (that is, producers rather than consumers in the industry). Producers rely on trade intermediaries for information about creators, cultural products, and other producers, as well as industry knowledge. For instance, the trade paper *Variety*'s "Ten to Watch" feature, which showcases promising new actors and directors, is rumored to have a direct positive effect on the compensation negotiated for the listed actors by their agents.[18] Although the discourse of trade intermediaries is primarily aimed at providing information to industry insiders, trade discourse plays a role (albeit an indirect one) in constructing the value perceived by consumers because trade events are attended by other intermediaries, especially those that provide knowledge and share judgment, and these intermediaries directly influence consumers' preferences and consumption decisions.

For example, fashion week is a trade event, and end consumers rarely, if ever, attend these events, but fashion journalists from magazines and newspapers are present in abundance. The discourse of these writers and photographers, in turn, has a strong influence on consumers' understanding of style and trends, which then informs their preferences and therefore their buying decisions. This example highlights the porosity of the boundaries delineating the three functions/tasks of intermediaries. Although the runway shows at fashion weeks (the discourse of trade intermediaries) are the means by which styles and their designers become visible, they are effectively introduced to the consumer by a different set of intermediaries—fashion magazines such as *Vogue* or *W*—through articles and photo spreads that not only provide information but also provide knowledge and share judgment. Thus, for the consumer of fashion apparel, the articles in *Vogue* do introduce certain designers or, at the very least, certain new styles or fashions. However, this is a secondary function of *Vogue*, an unintended consequence of the complexity of the value construction process (see Table 4.1). The primary function of *Vogue*'s discourse is to describe and explicate the intangible and symbolic attributes and value of that designer and/or style, as described in the next section.

PROVIDING KNOWLEDGE: INSTRUCTION

The provision of knowledge is likely the function of intermediaries that is most familiar and useful to consumers, even though they may not consciously note the process. Cultural goods need the work of intermediaries that *instruct* consumers, that is, explain the meaning of the goods and decode their symbolism so that they can be understood and valued. Although the discourse of such intermediaries frequently includes a final evaluation of quality ("[. . .] is an excellent book/film/song" or "not worth your time"), these pronouncements are not necessarily the chief point of the discourse. This is because there is a significant element of education and explication that has come to be expected in the instructive discourse of intermediaries, so that it is not sufficient to tell consumers about the quality of the good without also providing not only a justification of that assessment but also contextual background and information. In some ways, then, discourse that fulfills this function of instruction also clarifies, disseminates, and establishes evaluative schema and quality criteria that consumers are able to apply when attempting to make sense of and evaluating goods in the future. Such embedded instruction through explication and contextualization enables intermediaries that *instruct* to play an influential role in defining tastes of consumers and in shaping broadly accepted norms and beliefs about what is appropriate and valuable. Intermediaries that perform this function are, not surprisingly, more common in the so-called high-culture sectors, where works are typically imbued with complex symbolism. Rarely, for instance, does one come across deep instructive critiques of Harlequin romances, pop ballads, or landscapes.

Instruction is a necessary function of intermediaries because of the social meaning and signals embedded in cultural consumption, which make consumers insecure and uncertain about their tastes and preferences—no one wants to appear misinformed or to be seen as lacking "good taste" within her or his social circle.[19] Instruction is also needed to create intersubjective agreement in the valuation process. By generating (especially in the case of schools and other educational institutions), disseminating, and reinforcing a common basis for understanding cultural goods, instruction by intermediaries ensures that a buyer's social circle is, figuratively speaking, "on the same page," enabling a widespread understanding and appreciation of the purchase, which, in turn, validates and/or reinforces the buyer's social position. Thus, instruction by intermediaries not only decodes the symbolism inherent in cultural goods and explains their meaning but also establishes the foundations of culture in a society.

Given its nature, instruction is often carried out by nonmarket intermediaries in addition to market entities. Nonmarket intermediaries, which are situated outside the purview of commerce, are more explicitly instructive because their discourse is not concerned with specific cultural goods produced for the market. This category includes institutions—schools and universities, for instance, and even museums to a certain extent—that have been anointed by society to establish and reinforce a "canon" of literature, music, art, and other works and thus act as keepers of the cultural heritage of a society. These institutions, especially schools, influence individuals' preferences well before they enter the commercial realm or encounter a specific cultural good available for consumption. Being explicitly involved in education and instruction, these institutional intermediaries also are responsible for: (1) providing individuals with frameworks and schemas for evaluation and (2) decoding and explaining the symbols and meanings in cultural goods.

For instance, almost everyone reads some of the works of Shakespeare in school because educators usually agree that a core set of authors and books are essential reading, and Shakespeare is one of those authors. These books are assigned to all students within a system and are then deconstructed and explicated in classrooms, providing students with a general framework for understanding literature and assessing its quality. Formal education and instruction influences individuals' preferences and tastes—in a nonlinear manner, often well before they enter the market for cultural goods—at the most elemental level (novels over poetry and Victorian novels over modern literature, for instance) and thus enables individuals to navigate and make sense of the thicket of specialized informational listings described in the previous section. This early development of tastes via nonmarket intermediaries also influences consumers' choice of instructional market intermediaries; critics and reviewers who share the evaluative schema of an individual are more likely to receive the attention of that consumer.

Instructional intermediaries such as critics and reviewers are integral to the market for cultural goods. Their discourse is limited to the sharing of knowledge about *specific* goods that are proffered in markets. As a result, their existence is an inbuilt consideration in producers' production and distribution systems, manifest, for instance, in the practice of earmarking a certain number of books as "reviewer's copies." Critics and reviewers exist in the commercial realm, and the "instruction" provided by these intermediaries is implicit relative to that of educational institutions; critiques and reviews are not meant to educate in the same manner as textbooks and classroom discussions.[20] Nevertheless, critics and reviewers do explicate evaluative criteria and contextualize specific works to help consumers understand *why* the work is good or bad, rather than merely stating that it is so. Lacking the formal authority of a school or other nonmarket intermediary, these instructional intermediaries can influence the preferences and consumption of consumers only by painstakingly developing a reputation as a knowledgeable expert. These reputations are acquired through proxies (for example, education), actual output (for example, quality of the discourse), and both idiosyncratic (how often the particular individual agrees with the critic's/reviewer's assessment) and intersubjective (how often there is broad agreement about the critic's/reviewer's assessment) characteristics of the intermediary's track record.

Finally, it is worth noting that instruction by market intermediaries as well as some nonmarket intermediaries (such as museums) may include introduction to a category or a particular good (see Table 4.1). For example, individuals with limited arts education may have been made aware of the broad category of "modern" art in school, but their first introduction to the nuanced categories of modern art—abstraction, expressionism, figurative—and specific creators may occur later in life, at a museum.

SHARING JUDGMENT: INCLUSION

Despite the instruction provided by intermediaries, the subjective features of cultural goods make it difficult for consumers to accurately and confidently judge the quality of a work for themselves. Even when value judgments are pronounced (as when reviewers explicitly recommend a particular book), this discourse does not specifically define standards of quality or establish hierarchies within categories of cultural goods; instead, goods are recommended or positively evaluated in isolation (that is, the statement that a particular book or film is good reveals little or nothing about its relative quality with respect to other books and films that are similar or part of the same category). This type of ranking of goods to create a hierarchy in which certain select goods in a category are unequivocally *included* in the upper echelons of quality is the task of intermediaries that pronounce judgment. Examples of such intermediaries are formal award-granting bodies as well as both individuals and (rarely) firms that have garnered the attention of the consuming public and thus can influence consumer's preferences and decisions by proclaiming that a particular good meets their high standards.

Quality judgments enable consumers to consume cultural goods judiciously, overcoming the challenges posed by the infinite variety in creative works and the subjective and experiential nature of their consumption. Explicit judgments provide direction to consumers, who are typically unsure of their ability to judge complex symbolic works. Finally, in a world where tastes are subjective, and yet the consumption of cultural goods carries social meaning and implications, unambiguous indicators of quality provide security and comfort by validating individuals' preferences and decisions. From the perspective of creators or producers, these rankings and hierarchies are particularly desirable and preferred to instructional discourse because the former constitute a definitive positive evaluation—unlike a review, which can be positive or negative, a high rank or an award is always a positive signal.[21] Such positive ramifications of awards are one of the main reasons for the very public nature of the announcements of nominees or short lists and the glamorous and often extravagant nature of award ceremonies.

The boundaries between inclusion and the two functions discussed earlier—introduction and instruction—are blurred (see Table 4.1). This is especially true in the case of books. Because so many books are written and published each year, it is exceedingly likely that the announcement of the Booker long list not only results in the inclusion of the listed books in the upper echelons of quality but also introduces some of the books on the list to many lay readers. The overlap with instruction is less obvious and more implicit in that consumers often arrive at conclusions regarding quality criteria for the evaluation of cultural goods through post hoc analysis of commonalities and patterns among nominees and awardees. However, sometimes an inclusion intermediary engages in more explicit instruction by contextualizing the contenders and explaining in the citation for the prize why they were chosen. This is an especially salient practice in the citations for the Nobel and Pritzker Prizes. In either case, only rarely does discourse that pronounces judgment do so exclusively without also providing some explicit or implicit interpretation and instruction and introducing some goods to at least a certain proportion of consumers.

Quality judgments come in two forms: the more formal imprimatur and the less formal endorsement that is accepted by consumers as valid on the basis of the *identity* or *ideology* of the intermediary. The formal judgment is the public acknowledgment and announcement of the superiority of a work over the other works in its category, through the granting of awards and prizes—that is, an imprimatur—by a group of individuals who are widely accepted as having the requisite knowledge and authority to create such hierarchies, pronounce judgments, and grant honors. There are imprimaturs aplenty in every creative field: the Academy Awards and the Cannes Palme d'Or in film, the Man Booker Prize and the National Book Award in books, the Grammy Awards in music, the Council of Fashion Designers of America (CFDA) Awards in fashion, the Turner Prize in art, the Pritzker Prize in architecture, and the James Beard Award and the Bocuse d'Or in food are just a few examples. Many of these awards are so prestigious that even being considered—nominated or short listed—for them is taken as an unequivocal signal of high quality; therefore, the list of nominees (as for the Academy Awards) or the short list (as in the Booker Prize or the National Book Award) is also much awaited and made public. Thus, these short lists function as imprimaturs too, helping consumers understand the hierarchy of quality in the field.

From the point of view of creators and producers, awards and imprimaturs are particularly valuable because their prestige can be transferred to future endeavors and creations; being formal recognitions of quality, awards (or nominations) are permanently associated with the specific winner (or nominee) and thus are also associated with any additional goods they produce. This is evident in publicity materials for works created subsequent to the receipt of an award or nomination, which unabashedly proclaim the formal credentials of the creators or producers: "Featuring Academy Award winner . . ." or "by Pulitzer Prize–winning author . . ." or "on the Booker Prize short list . . ." In this regard, imprimaturs are similar to educational qualifications or credentials in that individuals possess them for life. This parallel is perhaps not surprising given the formal and systematic way in which most prestigious imprimaturs operate; the award-granting bodies are perceived as having the requisite authority and expertise to consistently and fairly apply accepted criteria of quality to discern differences in quality and identify the entities that meet the highest evaluation standards.

In addition to imprimaturs and awards, other formal rankings also convey quality and therefore influence consumers' preferences for certain cultural goods. Best-seller and "Top 10" lists are rankings that are less exogenously determined but still influence consumers' preferences considerably, making them aware of what everyone else is buying and (presumably) enjoying and thus generating a desire to buy and enjoy the same goods.[22] However, these rankings influence consumers via a different mechanism than industry awards and imprimaturs. "Top 10" or best-seller lists increase consumption because of the social meaning underlying cultural goods—consumers tend to believe that the experience of consuming the same cultural goods as others in their community is an essential part of social existence. Such rankings must clearly indicate the nature of their criteria, either through their official names or in public information. In a way, such rankings, rather than being involved in the construction of the value of goods, are post hoc confirmations of their market value and are therefore not the same as the other formal imprimaturs. However, they do possess similar transitive properties (for creators and producers) and convey value and quality (albeit of a specific kind) to potential consumers.

The second and less formal means of providing quality judgments is the endorsement of goods by an intermediary that consumers trust to provide valid judgment because they identify with, or share an ideology with, the intermediary. Notably, these perceptions are not necessarily grounded in the intermediary's direct expertise in the field. An excellent example of such an identity-based system of judgment is Oprah Winfrey's book list, which is popular among consumers who identify with or aspire to be like her. Although Winfrey is not a qualified literature expert, she and many other entities like her (the actress Gwyneth Paltrow, or actress, comedienne, and talk-show host Ellen DeGeneres,[23] for instance), who strike a chord among a particular group of consumers, influence buying decisions because consumers see in these intermediaries sympathetic sensibilities and/or other desirable qualities and attributes. Other examples of this type of identity-based judgment are *W* magazine's annual art issue and a list of "Must-Watch Artists" published in *Vogue*. Consumers who view these magazines as fashion authorities and trust their judgment in that sector may well trust the magazines' pronouncements on art because of a sense of shared sensibilities and perspectives, even though these magazines are not intermediaries in the art world and lack the requisite expertise in art (although hired writers and editors may possess this expertise). Subgroups of consumers tend to have specific cornerstone intermediaries, whose identity or ideology they admire and/or align with; this alignment grants these intermediaries immense power to establish quality and value standards and influence the buying decisions of these segments of consumers.

VALUATION PROCESSES: THE PUZZLE IN THE PYRAMID

Although the nonlinearity of the valuation process precludes overly simplistic characterization, the idea of a value pyramid can be used to illustrate the relationship between the three functions of intermediaries and their outputs (see Figure 4.1). The base of the pyramid includes all the eligible goods in a category, which must be introduced to consumers. The middle section comprises a smaller set of goods that have been evaluated and explicated for consumers. The apex of the pyramid contains goods that have been selectively anointed as the best in their category based on their excellence with regard to certain predetermined evaluation criteria—these goods meet the highest standards of quality for the category. The goods at the apex, which have received a formal validation or informal endorsement of high quality from an intermediary, are generally considered to have the highest artistic/cultural and/or economic value in the category.

As an illustration, consider books, hundreds of thousands of which are published every year. Enormous book fairs are the first place where the vast

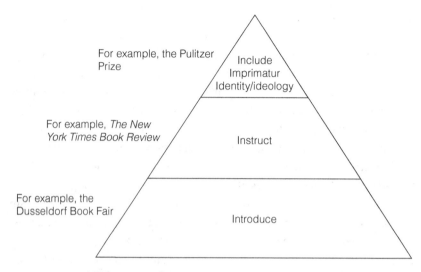

FIGURE 4.1. A Value pyramid.

majority of these books are initially encountered by/introduced to trade and consumer intermediaries. Some (but not all) of these books are then reviewed by critics and reviewers, who explain the book and elucidate why, if at all, it is worth reading. This instruction places those books that received a positive review into consumers' consideration set. Many consumers will indeed purchase those books, thus increasing the aggregate amount of revenues (value) accrued to those books. However, if one of those books wins an award (for example, the Pulitzer, the National Book Award, the Man Booker Prize), it gains further widespread recognition as belonging to a select group of works of exceptional quality and is now within the consideration set of consumers who may have previously ignored it. Thus, once intermediaries' discourse has placed the book at the apex of artistic value in the ecosystem, sales (that is, the aggregate economic value) of the award-winning book increase.

For consumers, a frustrating feature of the pyramid is that the correlation between endorsement and value is not always perfect, in the manner described in the preceding example. For instance, sometimes, bafflingly, even a bad review does not deter audiences;[24] as a corollary, high-quality award-winning goods earn less than goods that won no awards. Such incidents reveal the challenges posed by proliferation and the resulting lack of visibility for cultural goods and are also a useful example of the interpenetration of the functions of introduction and instruction; in a crowded marketplace with countless products, getting noticed, even without being praised, sometimes has benefits, even if only in the short term.

Similarly, some goods that are included in the select group at the apex do not accrue as much economic value as other goods that were not considered worthy of the imprimatur. In the film industry, for instance, the film that wins the Academy Award for Best Picture is rarely the highest grosser at the box office. Such instances should not be surprising given that all awards display "equivocality" because they "serve simultaneously as a means of recognizing an ostensibly higher, uniquely aesthetic form of value and as an arena in which such value often appears subject to the most businesslike system of production and exchange."[25] It is, therefore, to be expected that, in some instances, the balance tips toward either artistic value or exchange value, creating a discrepancy, so that, in a particular year, goods of artistic merit may win awards but not be popular blockbusters, whereas the situation may be reversed another year, and in a third year the artistic and economic value of awardees may converge. For example, in 2013, *12 Years a Slave* won Best Picture at the Academy Awards, despite being only the sixty-second highest grossing film domestically.[26] The highest-grossing film in 2013, *The Hunger Games: Catching Fire*, was not nominated for a single Oscar (although it was heavily nominated for and awarded popularity-based awards such as the Teen Choice Awards, People's Choice Awards, and MTV Movie Awards, whereas *12 Years a Slave* was nominated for and awarded very few of these awards).[27,28]

In the context of this book, particularly this chapter on the functions of intermediaries, the most pertinent, and perhaps most worrisome, disparity is the scenario in which the most exclusive, highest-quality goods, which are located at the apex in their category, may not benefit economically from the value construction conducted by intermediaries. There are two ways of understanding this seeming discrepancy. First, discrepancies are possible, if not probable, because to maintain validity, integrity, and prestige, formal awards and prizes must maintain a certain distance from purely commercial considerations and must adhere to broadly accepted criteria of quality. As the discussion in Chapter 3 of the Pritzker Prize emphasized, awards have multiple stakeholders and influence several significant aspects of civil society. An award that is in essence a popularity contest would quickly be perceived as such, and such excessive interpenetration of art and commerce would lead to a decline in the prestige and validity of the prize, rendering it relatively ineffective in constructing the value of goods in the future. As a result, such discrepancies are to be expected in cultural fields where heavy symbolism and complexity, which make goods intellectually taxing (and therefore probably not easily or widely liked by consumers), are considered markers of quality. Moreover, given that there is a place and need for acknowledging the popularity of certain goods, particular awards and imprimaturs (for example, People's Choice Awards, top 10/40/100 lists, best-seller lists) exist to explicitly recognize that dimension of value.

The second way of understanding this discrepancy is that, in all likelihood, artistically meritorious goods that join the exclusive group at the apex of the pyramid would have accrued even less economic value had they not received validation and endorsement. A comparison of the pre- and postwin sales of Booker Prize–winning books provides some evidence of this counterfactual: comparing the average weekly sales of the books before the prize was announced and the sales in the week the prize was announced (a 1,000 percent increase, on average) shows that, even when observing similar time frames, winning the prize has a significant impact on the fortunes of a book.[29]

Aside from considering the counterfactual to explain this discrepancy, it is useful to think of value construction as well as market participation (of creators and producers) as a repeated game and to give due consideration to the intangible aspects of perceived value that will persist in later cycles of this game. The transitive property of awards means that being at the zenith in one cycle brings creators and producers great benefits and value in future creation and production cycles. Entities that are new to the field reap the greatest benefits from this transitive property because a win or a nomination can bring significant attention and prestige, as well as economic benefits in the form of higher remuneration in future projects or the ability to charge higher prices in coming years. Thus, although the award may not boost the economic value of the awarded good itself, it confers honor and a badge of quality on the creators/producers, which contributes to the perceived value of their subsequent endeavors. Moreover, being noticed by respected intermediaries leads to the "Matthew Effect":[30,31] products from reputed and known creators and producers are more likely to be reviewed than products from unknown creators and producers. This effect creates a self-perpetuating cycle of renown as well as significant monetary benefits for a select few.

In summary, intermediaries fulfill three functions—introduction, instruction, and inclusion—and in so doing create a value pyramid of cultural goods. However, even though their functioning is crucial to the market in that they influence the market value of cultural goods through their discourse, intermediaries cannot directly capture that value. The next section examines how the functions already described factor into the business models of intermediaries.

Business Models and Entrepreneurship in the Context of Intermediaries' Functions

Intermediary entrepreneurs—pioneering or otherwise—must not only have knowledge of the functions of intermediaries but must also understand the available niches and differentiation strategies in the current ecosystem of the particular creative industry. The process is not simple or risk free—the (two-sided) business model is complex and slow to stabilize, and intermediaries must be seen as unequivocally objective and credible sources of information, instruction, or judgment. However, being an intermediary can be extremely rewarding because the position entails a significant potential to influence markets and society; the ability to have such an important impact is a likely reason that intermediary positions have proliferated in the value chains of various creative industries.

Intermediaries can be either individuals or firms; this distinction has certain effects on the way tasks are performed because individuals employed at a firm are constrained by the economic and political issues that are typical of all organizations,[32] and their fortunes are (to a certain extent) tied to the fortunes of the firm. At the same time, the corresponding freedom enjoyed by individuals operating on their own does have a downside. Because firms tend to have greater continuity and longevity than individuals, as intermediaries they often have greater impact than individuals, especially with regard to the functions of instruction (providing knowledge) and inclusion (sharing judgment). Any well-known and well-established newspaper or publication, such as *The Wall Street Journal, Washington Post, The New York Times,* or *The New York Review of Books*, provides a helpful illustration. The fact that a publication has existed for several decades and has built a reputation for integrity, excellence, and hiring talented professionals increases the potential impact of the individuals working at the publication, who can bask in its reflected glory. Therefore, although the specific individual reputations of, say, all the film critics at these papers may vary, each of them has the benefit of being able to influence the valuation process to a greater degree than a film critic working at a lesser-known and/or less-respected outlet. Working on their own, individuals would likely need significantly more time and effort to reach a similar level of influence.[33]

NEW INTERMEDIARY VENTURES

In some instances, an individual founds a firm that operates as an intermediary. In the early years, a new venture of this type will likely consist of not much more than the founder doing all the work; however, the enterprise may eventually become a full-blown firm. Robert Parker's *Wine Advocate* is a prototypical example of such a venture; from humble origins, the publication grew to be a reputed intermediary with immense influence in the U.S. wine market. In France, the film journal *Cahier du Cinéma*, started by André Bazin, Jacques Doniol-Valcroze, and Joseph-Marie Lo Duca in 1951, is another such example.

The eventual impact and success of these two intermediaries, their modest beginnings notwithstanding, indicate that a new venture operating within a well-established category (that is, not a pioneer entrepreneur) benefits from differentiating itself from extant intermediaries in that market. Unless the intermediary has a novel and unique way of collating comprehensive information on the universe of goods, the functions of instruction and selection offer the greatest opportunity for differentiation. Thus, for instance, a new venture could differentiate itself by taking a unique perspective or by providing a different point of view when critiquing particular cultural goods. In this way, the new venture will stand out in a crowded marketplace and gradually gain a following. Parker employed a new and unique perspective in *Wine Advocate*—he created a new, simpler, more intuitive, and customer-friendly way of evaluating and conveying the quality of wines in the market (a point system as opposed to the flowery language about terroir and bouquet typically used by wine critics). More recently, teenage fashion blogger Tavi Gevinson garnered attention for her unique and somewhat iconoclastic voice and take on fashion despite her youth and inexperience. The blog developed a loyal audience, which she was able to leverage when she subsequently launched *Rookie Magazine*. A somewhat extreme example of the value and viability of a clear and differentiated point of view is *Cabinet* magazine, which describes itself as an art periodical combined with a design magazine, with the features of a scholarly journal; *Cabinet* has won several awards since its founding in 2000.

Intermediaries can also differentiate themselves by occupying a particular niche, usually by covering specific categories or genres within an industry. Specialized magazines for rap, rock 'n' roll, country music, and other music genres are an example of intermediaries using this type of differentiation. Intermediaries that provide category-specific discourse are valuable because evaluative criteria and standards vary across categories. To describe and/or evaluate all existing genres of music under the same rubric is inherently un-fair and inadequate—rap cannot be judged by the same criteria as country music. Similarly, in the theater industry, the Tony Awards focus on Broadway productions whereas the Obie Awards focus on off-Broadway productions. Such differentiation can be carried too far, however. In the case of entities that perform the selection/inclusion function, for instance, the proliferation of new awards[34] has been much lamented by observers. The existence of too many awards can be deleterious because the valuation impact of each award is proportionately reduced due to narrow classifications, which imply fewer contenders, leading potentially to a "first among three" situation.

That said, a rap album that wins a specialized rap award but wins noth-ing at the broad category–spanning industry awards will likely accrue greater value than if the specialized award had not existed at all. Further, within-category comparisons, which are regarded as having greater integrity, often lead to higher-quality assessment and evaluation than cross-category com-parisons. The starker the distinctions between genres and the higher the number of genres, the greater the need for within-category rather than cross-category comparisons; thus, specialized awards make more sense in some in-dustries (music, for example) than others. For instance, in literature, there are two main categories—fiction and nonfiction—and although there are some subcategories within nonfiction (memoir, political writing, essay, and so on), due to the obvious differences in writing style and format, it is rare to find subcategories in fiction awards beyond the simple classification based on length (novel and short story) or type of story (science fiction, historical fic-tion, and the like), with the Man Booker being a notable exception and there-fore a pioneer intermediary. Starting a new intermediary that performs the inclusion function, then, is likely more relevant and valid in the former kind of industries.

Specialization is a viable entrepreneurial strategy for intermediaries also because it fulfills a consumer need. Discourse that is specialized by cat-egory is valuable to consumers because it enables them to streamline their decision-making process by allowing them to focus only on the categories that interest them. Especially in the case of intermediaries that instruct, specialization may also permit premium pricing (on both sides of the platform) because ardent fans of the genre make for loyal customers, thus ensuring a better stream of revenues. Beyond loyalty, certain categories are attractive in and of themselves for various reasons. Consider the case of an intermediary focused on opera: it would be able to attract the best individual contributors in the specialized field of opera, as well as opera lovers as consumers; thus, in turn, this intermediary could attract highly lucrative advertisers or sponsors. These advertisers and sponsors, believing that the opera lovers are a high net worth segment of the population, would be willing to pay higher advertising rates. A virtuous cycle of high revenues could thus ensue if the intermediary invests some of its revenues in further improving its content, which would bring more readers, due to which advertisers and sponsors may be charged a higher rate.

Specialized discourse and targeting has become increasingly attractive and feasible for new intermediary ventures because the Internet provides an affordable medium for the dissemination of such discourse (much cheaper, for example, than publishing a print magazine for a small niche group of readers). Blogs that provide commentary on very specific topics and categories of goods are perhaps the best example of this proliferation. These blogs often adopt a differentiation strategy that combines narrow specialization with a unique perspective or novel way of instructing consumers regarding the goods (as Tavi Gevinson did). Many of these specialized blogs are written by lay consumers rather than professional intermediaries, but this turn toward discourse generated by users (commonly known as "user-generated content") is not entirely new (look again at Table 4.1). The Internet, with its democratizing platform that allows widespread contribution to the commentary from users with whom mainstream consumers can identify, has allowed the emergence of a large number of new intermediaries that reinforce the social meaning of cultural goods. Aside from facilitating the rise of individual blogs, the digital medium also provides a platform for crowd-sourced lists and particularly for consumer reviews (as opposed to reviews by professional critics/reviewers). Such sites—Yelp.com, Fandango.com, Goodreads.com, and others—and the reviews available there appear, on the surface, to fulfill the same function as any other traditional intermediary that instructs, but there are differences (good and bad) that are addressed in later chapters of the book.

Worth noting here is that consumer reviews and user-generated content, like best-seller lists, usually provide post hoc commentary.

PIONEER-INTERMEDIARIES

Some intermediaries choose to go down the risky path of engaging in valuation discourse for a novel category of goods to create new markets. By definition, this process must happen almost concurrently with the production of new goods. Intermediaries' discourse explains the ideas underlying the unfamiliar and often initially unattractive products and makes those ideas seem less threatening, more acceptable, and more valuable. Pioneer intermediaries can be either new ventures or individuals within existing ventures, but, in the context of the functions of intermediaries, the two types do not entail very different situations or challenges.

Given the novelty of new categories of goods and consumers' unfamiliarity with the relevant producers and goods, pioneer intermediaries must often engage in more than one of the functions already described (introduction, instruction, and inclusion). As the new category matures and a larger number of creators and/or producers enter the field, these functions usually become more complex and thus are more likely to be performed by separate entities. Taken together, these changes are markers of the establishment and legitimacy of the new market and pave the way for further entrepreneurial activity of the type already described, particularly specialization. Independent cinema and rap are two examples of such evolution. Once the independent cinema category was well established and understood, due largely to the efforts of the Sundance Institute, the number of annual independent film festivals held in the United States grew to more than 1,000 by 2015.[35] Similarly, the rap genre has witnessed a proliferation of intermediaries that perform one of the three functions in the years since the first rap single was released.

Although performing multiple functions may be a necessity for pioneer intermediaries, the best way for such entities to draw attention to an overlooked or undervalued category is to adjudicate standards and expose consumers to those category prototypes that in their view represent the best the category has to offer. In other words, engaging in the inclusion function by creating an award that grants formal imprimatur is an influential first step in establishing the worth of the new category. The Threadneedle Prize, initiated in Britain in 2009, is a useful example.[36] In an attempt to establish the value of contemporary representational art in an art world where nontraditional media hold sway, the Threadneedle Prize short list comprises primarily paint-ings and sculptures. The Obies, spearheaded in 1955 by Jeffrey Tallmer, a the-ater critic at *The Village Voice*, were also intended to encourage, support, and celebrate an overlooked subfield of a broader sphere of art, in this case the off-Broadway theater movement, which was just beginning to take root at the time.[37] Because awards and prizes capture the public's imagination,[38,39] set standards, and generate an understanding of both the category and its evalu-ation criteria, they offer a useful and efficient way to initiate discourse about a new category.[40]

Instructional discourse is the next best path to market creation because understanding the embedded meanings and symbolism of cultural goods is crucial to overcoming hostility or resistance toward their consumption; the example of *The Source* as a market creator for rap has already been discussed. In another instance, the founders of Performa, a nonprofit arts organization that seeks to increase awareness of performance art, employ a multipronged instructional approach to achieve this goal; the approach includes a think tank, an annual conference, and an online magazine, as well as a biennial that straddles the introduction and instruction functions.[41] Finally, pioneer intermediaries can also introduce novel products or categories; for example, the Codex Book Fair and Symposium, which was developed by the Codex Foundation to preserve the art of handmade books, introduces consumers to goods. The category of goods existed, but, in the absence of a clear cat-egorical definition of the product and a place where artists and creators could gain visibility, fine handmade books had a limited market. However, even in this case, when there is broad preexisting knowledge about the category, the event includes a symposium featuring lectures by key figures and artists in the field—in other words, this intermediary also performs the instruction func-tion. Indeed, it is difficult to imagine an effective pioneer intermediary that only provides information and offers no instruction; merely seeing new goods in a de novo category and understanding the boundary definitions of the new category are unlikely to be sufficient to overcome the resistance that new cul-tural goods face.

Summing Up and Looking Ahead

Intermediaries fulfill three discursive functions: introduction (generating and sharing information), instruction (spreading knowledge), and inclusion (sharing judgment regarding cultural goods). These three functions overlap to a certain extent and are characterized by a nonlinear relationship. By fulfilling these functions, intermediaries play a significant role in constructing the value of, and creating markets for, both new categories of goods and new goods introduced within existing categories. The need for multiple valuation functions in the market creates several niches and opportunities where intermediaries operate and where entrepreneurs can venture. The effective performance of each of the three functions requires slightly different strategies and approaches. Moreover, the functions are differentially conducive to entrepreneurial entry and variably important in pioneering market creation.

The functions of intermediaries affect entrepreneurship and original creation among producers and creators because producers (and to an extent, consumers) rely on intermediaries to "level the playing field" in terms of which creators and goods are reviewed, evaluated, and certified for quality and value. By discerning between creative works solely on the basis of quality, intermediaries ensure that radically novel cultural goods have a fair chance of being introduced to a market and that these new unknown works and/or creators or producers of excellent quality can compete against well-known and established players. If intermediaries were removed from the system, their functions would be left to producers, who lack the third-party position and prerequisites needed to influence consumers' decisions.

Thus, although producers in the market depend on intermediaries for revenues, the market functions as it ought to only when intermediaries occupy appropriate independent structural positions, lack a direct economic stake in the value of the goods in the market, and perform their functions accordingly. The resulting tension among producers' interests, market dynamics, and the role of intermediaries is key to understanding the attributes and features that are required of an effective intermediary. The next chapter describes the prerequisite properties of intermediaries and examines their implications for entrepreneurship among both intermediaries and producers.

MAXIMIZING INFLUENCE

The Features of Intermediaries

The honest critic must be content to find very little contemporary work
worth serious attention, but he must be ready to recognize that little . . .

—Ezra Pound[1]

Intermediaries run the gamut in both form and function, from MTV (a TV
channel), to *The New York Times* (a newspaper), to the Academy Awards (an
event/ceremony and a material object). Further, even within a single category
of cultural goods, there are often multiple intermediaries—manifest in either
similar or dissimilar forms—performing the same function. Despite this proliferation, rarely do any two intermediaries have an identical (actual or perceived) influence. This variation in format and influence raises the questions:
What features make an intermediary and maximize its influence? For example, the website Yelp.com collates the reviews of restaurants (and other types
of businesses) written by lay consumers who have visited the establishments.
Do such websites and user-generated content qualify as (the discourse of) intermediaries like the ones listed here? The answer is a qualified "yes," and,
to understand both the qualification and the affirmation, this chapter turns
to the properties that intermediaries must possess to perform their functions adequately and responsibly, thereby maximizing their influence on the
market for cultural goods. In other words, this chapter addresses *why* certain
intermediaries are granted such extensive power to shape consumers' value
perceptions and influence the consequent impact of products in the market
and in society more broadly.

Properties of Intermediaries

Beyond intermediaries' structural status as a third party in the market, two qualities—independence and expertise—are essential for intermediaries to perform their functions successfully. Intermediaries with independence and expertise can have an impact on the perceived value of a cultural good and influence the market for that good because consumers place a great deal of importance on the discourse of such intermediaries. For example, film viewers tend to trust reviews written by impartial critics who have not been pressured by a studio to write a favorable review. Moreover, consumers will trust a review when they believe the critic is knowledgeable about cinema and therefore describes and evaluates films according to broadly accepted and established criteria rather than personal preferences. In this example, independence and expertise offer obvious benefits to consumers but seem to disadvantage producers by placing market outcomes outside their strategic control and in the hands of independent expert entities who can be neither corrupted nor fooled. However, this chapter will show that the independence and expertise of intermediaries are, in fact, also beneficial to producers. Finally, these two properties have significant implications also for culture and society more broadly, especially in the context of pioneer entrepreneurship by intermediaries.

INDEPENDENCE

By definition, intermediaries have no direct economic stake in the sale of the cultural goods they evaluate and discuss; this absence of vested interests is crucial to the ability of intermediaries' commentary to sway consumers' beliefs about the value of goods. Independence, however, goes beyond the mere absence of economic incentives to construct a high value for goods. As emphasized in the editorial policy of *Variety* magazine,[2] independence also entails that intermediaries are both able and willing to withstand pressure from producers and/or creators, and that the discourse of intermediaries is unbiased. Independence underpins consumers' trust in intermediaries' discourse and is thus critical to their successful operation. In the absence of this trust, intermediaries' commentary would trigger coping mechanisms[3] and discounting among consumers just as the commentary of producers (that is, marketing material) does. Therefore, intermediaries expend a great deal of effort to not only maintain their independence but also ensure that consumers recognize it (that is, intermediaries must not only be independent but also be perceived as such).[4]

Acquiring, Demonstrating, and Maintaining Independence

Intermediaries' independence comprises structural, economic, and cognitive dimensions, which are interdependent and interlinked. Structural independence (that is, their position as a third party, neither seller nor buyer, in the market) is, as explained earlier, inherent to the intermediary role. Economic independence can be maintained through organizational aspects of discourse creation, as when intermediary work is conducted by firms and entities (such as the publishers of *Consumer Reports* or *Good Housekeeping*) that are both explicitly distinct from producers and unconnected to them. Further, economic independence is also maintained within intermediary organizations in two ways, one direct and one indirect. First, intermediaries must never receive direct commissions for generating a sale. Second, self-imposed conventions and norms (for example, in the case of magazines and newspapers) stipulate strict separation between the editorial and advertising departments;[5] at most newspapers and magazines, disclosure rules also apply to all reviewers and feature writers. In an example directly pertinent to creative industries, food critics at reputed publications pay for their meals at the restaurants they review. To further protect intermediaries from pressure to adjust their discourse, the expression of opinions by legitimate reviewers is accorded legal protection in most countries. Finally, independence has a cognitive dimension. Although the self-imposed norms, which exist in deference to an implicit contract that has evolved over the years between a publication and its readers, are internal to an organization and are assumed by consumers to exist, independence also has to be observed and recognized by consumers. Cognitive indicators that convey independence include disclosures[6] as well as direct evidence in the form of a track record of, for instance, not shying away from negative reviews or criticisms of goods sold by obviously powerful producers.

In general, consumers' marketplace metacognition[7] keeps them mindful of intermediaries' vulnerability to influence and therefore alert to signs that an intermediary has been co-opted by producers. Mere suspicion of co-optation, let alone proof, will lead consumers to discount the intermediary's commentary, much as they would that of a producer. Repeated or consistent infractions of this nature amount to a breach of the social contract between intermediary and consumer, and the reputation of the intermediary will be significantly and permanently damaged, likely leading to its failure in the long run; therefore, intermediaries' reputational concerns help maintain their independence in situations when legal protections are either not applicable or unavailable. Moreover, any breach of the implicit contract between consumers and intermediaries causes a stir and leads to recriminations as well as long-term negative effects on revenues (and even viability and survival) that usually more than offset any short-term economic gains. In fact, FCC (Federal Communications Commission) regulations that cover transgressions of this implicit contract were the direct result of such a violation: the "payola" scandal that occurred in the late 1950s in the United States, when it emerged that disc jockeys (DJs) on American radio stations were being paid by record labels to repeatedly play songs produced by those labels.[8] About 200 DJs, including well-known radio personalities such as Alan Freed, admitted to taking bribes, and Dick Clark of *American Bandstand* was found to have invested in thirty-three record labels, whose songs he played on the show. Although Clark was cleared of any malpractice (partly because he divested his shares before appearing in court) and went on to have a very successful career, Freed was unable to find work anywhere after the hearings. Payola was eventually criminalized in 1960; accordingly, under current U.S. federal law, nondisclosure (on air) of payments received in exchange for broadcasting any material is an offense punishable by fines or one year in prison.

Given the ease of potential corruption, it is valid to ask how consumers can be sure that intermediaries do not succumb to tangible and intangible pressures from producers. In addition to the existence of voluntary norms and codes of conduct that define the ideal situation of independence and integrity, the reputations of certain types of intermediaries also protect them from potential advances and corrupting influences of producers. For example, an auction house or a collector would most likely be quite reluctant to try to blatantly influence or manipulate a large and highly respected public institution such as the Metropolitan Museum of Art in New York (the "Met") to affect the value of an artwork. Nevertheless, even in these settings, some specific norms exist to prevent manipulation of markets by unscrupulous individuals. For instance, because the loan of an artwork to a reputed museum such as the Met can significantly increase its value as well as that of the lender's/donor's collection if the artwork is subsequently sold, reputed museums do not accept such loans and gifts unless all or a significant portion of the collection is pledged.[9] In another example, the value of independence has led to concerns in the art world about the recent emergence of private museums—such as Alice Walton's Crystal Bridges—that display personal collections. Art market insiders fear that collectors will start private museums to boost the value of their personal collections rather than simply to share their artwork with a broad audience.[10]

Intermediaries can also employ tactical means of conveying and maintaining independence. The foundation that grants the Pritzker Prize, often referred to as the Nobel for architecture, conveys its incorruptibility in various ways. The jury for the prize not only changes every few years but also includes individuals who are not part of the architecture profession to ensure that professional rivalries or political considerations play a limited role in deliberations.[11] Moreover, the Pritzker family, which has real estate interests that could be interpreted as causing a conflict of interest, stays out of the jury selection process as well as the nominations and discussions of the architects being considered.

Despite being a crucial property of intermediaries, independence is neither easy to signal (to consumers) nor easy to uphold consistently, as the history of *Variety* demonstrates. *Variety*'s founding editor, Sime Silverman, publicly announced his choice to make "honesty and independence" the cornerstones of his competitive strategy.[12] At the time of its founding, *Variety*'s policy was an anomaly in a world of entertainment publications that prohibited writers from writing negatively about shows that spent substantial money on advertising or pulled negative reviews when threatened with the loss of advertising revenues. Although these previous publications placed greater importance on the financial bottom line than on fulfilling their function of providing useful information/instruction to the public, consumers at the time had not expressed a desire for greater independence among magazines; instead, consumers were resigned to the status quo or perhaps unaware of the benefits of independent, unbiased reviews. Silverman nevertheless pledged in *Variety*'s opening issue to always prioritize readers' interests and to publish the honest opinion of the paper, regardless of advertising revenues.[13] This policy meant that producers who spent large sums of money on advertisements in *Variety* were subject to the same stringent criteria and strict evaluation as those who spent little money, and wealthy producers could no longer be assured of a good review and its attendant monetary and reputational benefits. However, producers did not initially take the policy seriously and persisted in trying to influence reviews in the publication. The task of clearly establishing (among readers and producers alike) that its independence was not for sale was not a straightforward one for *Variety*, and sincere announcements regarding their intent were not sufficient; repeated demonstrations of independence from powerful interests are far more impactful than even the most emphatic proclamations. In more recent times, this practice of conveying their incorruptibility is evident in the set response of *Variety* editors, when they receive a request/invitation to review a work—"Are you sure?" they ask.[14] The question is meant as a warning that per company policy the paper's reviewers will be honest and objective; anyone can submit his or her work (it is a level playing field), but producers and creators should be prepared for the possibility that the review may be far from positive.

In addition to being difficult to uphold and signal, independence is also expensive to maintain: it took *Variety* twenty-five years to become profitable.[15] Of course, the policy of editorial independence was likely not the sole cause of the poor performance of the publication—Silverman was a notoriously bad businessman. However, the publication might have become profitable sooner had it not repeatedly lost significant amounts of advertising revenues from irate producers who had received a negative review; in fact, this situation was anticipated in the publication's prospectus, which, after laying out the editorial policy, asked, "Is honesty the best policy? We shall see." That said, like most assets, once acquired, independence provides sustained benefits in the marketplace. Once readers learned that they could implicitly trust *Variety* to provide an honest assessment of a film or play, the publication's standing in the marketplace became such that no producer, however irate, could afford to ignore it.

Independence and Functions of Intermediaries

When it comes to understanding the importance of independence for intermediaries, it may seem that the *introduction* function (the one performed by the radio DJs involved in the payola scandal), which merely involves the compilation of information, is the least likely of the three functions to be negatively affected by the absence of independence from vested interests. Further, it may seem that, even if corruption does occur, it will have few effects on consumers—an intermediary's intentional removal or addition, under duress, of a cultural good from a listing should not make a significant difference to consumers. However, if anything, resisting the influencing tactics of powerful producers may be more important to this function than to instruction or inclusion. Independence in introduction is essential for every creator/producer—large or small, new or established, famous or unknown—to have an equal chance of being noticed and evaluated, which is the whole point of the introduction function (ideally, intermediaries should provide comprehensive information). Without intermediaries' independence, powerful and resource-rich producers and/or creators would be able to crowd out others and maintain an advantage. This ability would result in limited discovery of new ideas and goods for consumers.

The importance of independence to intermediaries that perform the other two functions is more straightforward. Unbiased reviews and objective endorsements—*instruction* and *inclusion*, respectively—have an obvious value for consumers. Despite this value, producers still attempt to influence intermediaries' evaluations, as exemplified by two practices, companies gifting "samples" to magazine editors and movie studios' rampant pre–Academy Award campaigning. However, these practices must adhere to the common principles applicable to any promotional activities (no bribery or false representation, for instance). Yet, the prevalence of such excessive persuasion tactics employed by producers is the precise reason for intermediaries to maintain their independence and bolster consumers' perceptions of it; they must do so to properly perform their functions and discharge their duties to society.

Independence is clearly crucial to the existence and functioning of intermediaries. Yet, even when explicit and implicit indicators attest to their independence, not all intermediaries have an equal influence on consumers' beliefs. This variation in influence is driven by perceived expertise, the second prerequisite of intermediaries.

EXPERTISE

To maintain credibility among consumers, intermediaries must possess not only independence but also expertise—the necessary knowledge to comment on cultural goods, which are typically difficult to understand and evaluate. Professional intermediaries are individuals who have deep knowledge of the history of ideas and the contextual granularities in their field and are charged with the responsibility of bringing notice and recognition to ideas and works that are novel, critical of prevailing societal norms, or simply incomprehensible (*Ulysses* and, more recently, *Infinite Jest* by David Foster Wallace are examples in the publishing industry). Moreover, in line with Ezra Pound's exhortation, it is the duty of critics to illuminate and endorse the new, the provocative, and even the subversive, so consumers can come to understand these works and accept their underlying ideas, changing their thinking in the process.

Only credible intermediaries can be entrusted with this weighty responsibility of changing minds. The credibility of intermediaries derives from trustworthiness, which is a function of both factors: the knowledge the source is believed to possess (expertise), and the belief that the communication of this knowledge will be done accurately and truthfully (independence).[16] Whereas independence facilitates the truthful transmission of knowledge or evaluation, expertise ensures the accuracy of the knowledge. The expertise of intermediaries is thus closely and almost recursively related to their independence; an entity that is not independent is unlikely to be perceived as an expert or authority in evaluation, and vice versa,[17] rendering both equally necessary to functioning as an intermediary.

Acquiring, Demonstrating, and Maintaining Expertise

Expertise is usually demonstrated via formal credentials and/or an intermediary's track record; however, individuals who lack formal training or certifications can demonstrate their expertise through related accomplishments. Thus, for instance, restaurant inspectors at the *Michelin Guide* are often former chefs or writers with a passion for food. Similarly, award juries often comprise past awardees and other well-respected individuals in the field. In fact, awards granted by industry/trade associations are typically the most reputed and coveted by creators and producers because it is easy to accept that judges appointed by industry associations are deeply knowledgeable about the industry, its criteria for quality, and the standards to apply while judging a good.

Intermediaries that do not in this manner inherently possess credibility as expert evaluators must develop and demonstrate it instead. The Pritzker Prize, given by a private foundation, has, for example, become extremely influential even though it is not an industry award. The Pritzker Foundation appointed well-known and expert jurors who, over time, established a track record of choosing laureates who were universally accepted as deserving of the prize. The foundation thus borrowed the credibility of the jurors and benefited from early selections of praiseworthy laureates. Too many bad and/or controversial awardees, especially in the early years, would have cast doubt on the expertise of the foundation and therefore would have undermined the value of the prize itself.

Expertise and Functions of Intermediaries

Expertise is more important for intermediaries that *instruct* and/or *include* than for those that introduce. That said, in some situations, perceived expertise grants an intermediary acceptance among (and therefore access to) an otherwise esoteric field of creators, enabling comprehensive coverage not possible for others to achieve. For instance, celebrities and/or well-known critics may be able to tap into a unique network of creators who send them their work, largely in hopes of gaining visibility from their association with such intermediaries. In general, however, *instruction* and *inclusion* are more closely intertwined with expertise, owing to the greater level of engagement with the product that is required of the intermediaries that perform these evaluative functions. Given that these functions involve knowledge and judgment, rather than simply information, the discourse of intermediaries in these roles is more nuanced and has greater impact on value construction. For these two types of intermediaries, therefore, credentials have a strong influence on the extent of their effect on consumers' preferences and purchases.

Exceptions to the Rule: Situations when Expertise Is Not a Requirement

Intermediaries that facilitate identity- or ideology-driven *inclusion* (such as Oprah Winfrey and her book club) are an exception to the general requirement for expertise. Given that one of the defining characteristics of this type of intermediary is the absence of credentials that are directly relevant to the category of the cultural good, their level of influence is higher than would be expected. One of the defining characteristics of this type of intermediary is the absence of credentials that are directly relevant to the category of the cultural good. However, the indubitable market influence of these nonexpert intermediaries is not entirely inconsistent with the importance of expertise because there is a third element (in addition to independence and knowledge) that contributes to credibility—social value.[18] The attractiveness of the personality of the commentator, his or her perceived social status, and, above all, his or her similarity to the audience all contribute to social value, which is an important source of credibility. Thus, the perceived social value of intermediaries such as Oprah Winfrey is an important driver of their influence in markets, even in the absence of formal (or even informal) indicators of their expertise in the particular area. Producers embrace such nonexpert intermediaries. A recent announcement by Mark Zuckerberg, the founder of Facebook, that he would start listing ten excellent books he thought were worth reading, was met with excitement among the publishing industry, which was anxious to find a replacement for Winfrey's book club (which ended with her TV show in 2011, although a version still exists on her website, Oprah .com).[19] The hope among those in the book business is that Zuckerberg's iconic status as a young and innovative billionaire entrepreneur will inspire a following among admiring youth who aspire to be like him, thus boosting the sales of the books on his list, even though Zuckerberg is not known as an expert on literary topics.[20]

In addition to the case of intermediaries with social value, expert opinion may not be necessary in certain situations and/or for certain product categories; consumers may simply want to know what other consumers think about the product. The impact of this type of post hoc discourse, such as best-seller lists or people's choice awards, is evidence of the desire to be part of a social process of consumption. This is especially true in the case of products that have less symbolic content and complexity and those that are sought out largely for entertainment value and for the pleasure of social or collective consumption. Crime procedurals, mystery novels, decorative artworks, mass fashion apparel, and pop music are some examples. When looking for a pleasant evening out at the movies with friends or for a book to read on the beach during a vacation, consumers are amply served by other consumers' reactions to and opinions about a film or a book. Similarly, knowing that a particular TV show is popular and therefore likely to be the topic of discussion at one's workplace or any social gathering is impetus enough to cause an individual to watch it rather than risk being a social outsider. However, even when a consumer is seeking guidance on entertaining and less complex works from other consumers, it probably is advisable to rely on information from informal intermediaries such as one's personal network, whose preferences and biases are known and can be accounted for, rather than complete strangers.

These exceptions to the need for expert intermediaries do not, however, suggest that lay consumers, writing on sites such as Yelp.com that aggregate user-generated content, always have the same potential for impact as formal, expert intermediaries. In the context of the first exception, it is clear that lay reviewers do not possess the celebrity/identity that would grant them social value. As for the second case, more complex cultural sectors such as art, architecture, and literature virtually always require the discourse of professional critics and reviewers with the requisite expert qualifications. Consumption of these goods both requires consumers to commit significant amounts of time and money and has significant implications for the reputation and social standing of the consumer. These consumption decisions are, therefore, best not based on the commentary of lay consumers.

At times, a segment of lay consumers (who have nothing to lose by highlighting innovation and/or work that challenges established norms[21]) may be more willing than formal critics (whose status and power may be embedded in maintaining status quo) to accept innovative goods and raise their visibility. Certainly, in some instances critics and "the establishment" have been slow to recognize the value of certain new ideas that were nevertheless embraced by laypersons: the rap genre is a fairly recent example of this phenomenon. This and other similar instances demonstrate the inherent limitations of experts. However, the acceptance of these works by established critics and intermediaries is quite essential to the *mainstream* adoption of new categories. Thus, although lay consumers may take to innovations quickly, professional expertise and formal structure comes with a level of experience and objectivity that is, in the long run, an important aspect of intermediary work.

Just as Weberian bureaucracy and its attendant professional objectivity created a more democratic and meritocratic organization that was independent of social class and status,[22] formal training and professional norms among critics enable them to transcend social prejudices and preconceived notions more fully than laypersons, who are more likely to adopt an idiosyncratic and subjective method of evaluation. Expertise is especially important in the case of cultural goods because of their highly symbolic and complex content. For example, although a user-generated review of a vacuum cleaner is plausibly accurate and valuable (because the functionality of the product is the most important aspect of the review), someone who has worn a skirt[23] is not necessarily qualified to write about that particular skirt or about fashion more broadly.[24] Further, at least during the transition period after the introduction of novel products, when old and new worlds coexist and both expert and user intermediary voices reach the mainstream, a formal critic's evaluation is likely more influential and widespread than the evaluation of lay critics. In that sense, then, expert intermediaries are more likely to create a broad market for novel products. Meanwhile, user intermediaries often have most clout within their own limited communities of like-minded people, perhaps leading to the creation of niche markets.

As with independence, expertise is beneficial not only to consumers but also to producers. Expertise likely brings an open-mindedness that benefits new and young producers. Domain expertise, long hours of practice and experience, professional norms, and formal training all enable expert intermediaries to steer consumers toward new and original ideas from innovative creators and producers that might otherwise languish in anonymity. This effect becomes clearer in the next section.

THE SOCIETAL IMPORTANCE OF INDEPENDENT AND EXPERT INTERMEDIARIES

Independence and expertise also have broader implications—beyond the market influence exerted by intermediaries—for culture and society. An indirect but very important effect of the work of intermediaries is to enable the rejuvenation of culture and society through the introduction and endorsement of novel ideas; independence and expertise enhance this effect. Independence increases the probability that an intermediary will not shy away from novelty or controversy just because such engagement entails risk (reputational and/or financial), whereas expertise increases the likelihood that an intermediary will understand the specifics of the radical innovation and will subsequently explicate and frame the innovation in a way that appeals to risk-averse consumers. For instance, at a time when big blockbusters were popular, the Sundance Institute generated discourse that portrayed small-budget humanistic films as a desirable and valuable alternative to mainstream films and thus allowed new and diverse stories and narratives to reach a wider audience. Had Sundance instead chosen to mirror the prevailing culture and reinforce the promotional commentary of Hollywood studios for pecuniary benefit (that is, if they were not independent), audiences' access to a new, eye-opening, and mind-broadening cultural good and experience would have been delayed, if not denied. In another example of broader repercussions, the Denver Art Museum, by being among the first few intermediaries to attribute Native American artworks to individuals, rather than tribes, deployed its expertise to reframe works that (would) have been consigned to the broad category of "tribal" or "folk" art as modern, original, and individualistic.[25] In doing so, the museum and its curators applied conventions of modern art to change the perceived value of the artistic expression of an entire social group, rendering the works more understandable by presenting them in a manner familiar to consumers.

Although independence and expertise are crucial to the success—and indeed the very survival—of intermediaries, they are built only slowly, produce returns on the investment only after an extended period of time, and thus may seem to be financial burdens; however, in the context of the right business model, these features are assets that facilitate the collection of revenues.

Independence and Expertise as Assets in the Business of Intermediaries

Independence and expertise are the chief assets of intermediaries. Being crucial to their operation, these properties must be accounted for and built into the design, operation, and management of intermediaries' work. The business models of intermediaries, in turn, must enhance these assets, a process that is neither simple nor straightforward, largely owing to the fact that the bulk of intermediaries' revenues come from producers that advertise or provide sponsorship, rendering intermediaries vulnerable to pressures from producers.

To understand how intermediaries manage these two requirements, it is useful to appreciate how the two-sided business model works. Clearly, advertisers and sponsors subsidize the discourse of intermediaries (for example, magazines, festivals) to reach consumers and persuade them to buy (the producer's) products. Advertising revenues would disappear in the absence of sufficient and/or sufficiently attractive subscribers. Therefore, an intermediary cannot collect significant advertising revenues unless its discourse strongly appeals to a large enough group of attractive potential consumers. As a result, independence and expertise become essential aspects of intermediaries' business models. If their discourse lacks impartiality or does not manifest expertise, it will not be appealing to readers, who may flee, causing an exodus of advertisers and a decline in revenue.

Because independence is so important, nonprofit business models are common in the intermediary sector in the creative industries. In particular, key intermediaries, such as museums, are structured as public institutions that operate as nonprofits so as to be (perceived as) above reproach and beyond the direct influence of producers. Being untouched by such influence is especially relevant when an institution is viewed as having the responsibility to safeguard the heritage of a society, as museums often are. Similarly, many award-granting industry associations are nonprofit organizations, although there are a substantial number of for-profit award-granting organizations as well, such as the Tribeca Film Festival and the SXSW Festival. All else being equal, consumers perceive nonprofit intermediaries as having greater integrity because they know that such entities will not take shortcuts or make decisions that compromise their independence to earn a profit.

In the for-profit world, the mutually reinforcing relationship between independence and expertise helps build reputations such that even established and prestigious producers and creators lay great store by positive evaluations from prestigious intermediaries (like *The New York Times*), although, at the same time, not attempting to overtly influence it. Expertise—the other main asset of intermediaries—is easier to convey and maintain but more difficult to strategically incorporate into a business model as an asset that yields returns or direct revenues. It is a cost, a sine qua non, of doing business as an intermediary. Consumers' perceptions of intermediaries' expertise are typically influenced by their credentials and reputation, and these can be neither manipulated nor built up quickly. Thus, high-quality expert discourse is expensive to generate and disseminate. Nevertheless, unless the intermediary's expertise is recognized beyond question, the discourse will have limited impact on markets and limited appeal among consumers, owing to suspicion and skepticism about the intermediary's authority to evaluate and pass judgment. Such a lack of interest in the discourse will likely set into motion the vicious cycle described earlier, which leads to a decline in revenues. This cycle is clearly observed in the case of the *Guide Michelin*, which is published by the French tire manufacturer Michelin. Originally published as an informational pamphlet to encourage people to drive long distances in France, the *Guide* soon developed a strong cadre of expert food critics, known as inspectors. Although the expertise of the inspectors granted the iconic Michelin stars legitimacy and status, making them highly coveted by chefs in Europe, the United Kingdom, and Asia, consumers in the U.S. market, where the *Guide*'s inspectors were not perceived as having relevant expertise, have been reluctant to pay for the discourse.[26]

The prerequisite properties of intermediaries thus have significant long-term implications for a business model because maintaining independence, in particular, places constraints on potential streams of revenue as well as on growth. Unlike producers, which can grow organically or via acquisitions by simply producing greater volumes and/or a wider range of goods or can increase their profitability by reducing costs through vertical integration, intermediaries have few available options for growth and expansion. If an intermediary takes steps to capture a portion of the market value created by its discourse, it forsakes its independence and loses the trust of consumers, thus losing future revenues. However, such a move may increase revenues in the short term. Therefore, individuals in intermediary organizations must be introspective—they must determine whether they wish to achieve sustained relevance and cultural impact (which may or may not lead to financial sustainability) or make a large amount of money quickly but be unsustainable in the long run because they lose relevance. Although these two goals are not completely antithetical, there are trade-offs in maximizing one over the other.

At this crossroads, intermediaries' nonpecuniary motivations and their desire to have a cultural impact become more relevant. Although it is not impossible to grow revenues and/or profitability as an intermediary, it takes time and care to do so in a manner that does not dilute or destroy one of the chief assets (that is, independence). Keeping the potential for cultural impact in sight can make the process seem less arduous, more worthwhile, and more significant. Thus, when faced with the need to grow revenues, one option for intermediaries is to generate discourse for a novel idea or category of goods (that is, engage in pioneer entrepreneurship, discussed next) to attract a new set of subscribers/members. For instance, the Sundance Institute could potentially broaden its impact by creating a market for humanistic films in and from countries without a strong existing film culture. Similarly, *Vogue* has expanded its operations as well as its cultural impact by publishing an edition in India, which focuses on the newly established fashion market in that country. This type of expansion is not a straightforward path to growth because establishing a foothold in a new category entails the time-consuming and difficult process of building a reputation for expertise and credibility in this category (recall the earlier Michelin example). However, an intermediary driven by the desire to possess broader cultural influence will find the process fulfilling and mission critical, even if not directly rewarding in the financial sense. Moreover, staying focused on the mission at hand ensures consumers (and producers) of the intermediary's relevance in the long run, which, in turn, facilitates financial sustainability.

The nature of independence and expertise and the complexity of incorporating these properties into the business models of intermediaries have implications for both types of entrepreneurs, pioneering and otherwise. In particular, new intermediaries are at a significant disadvantage in terms of gaining a foothold in the ecosystem of creative industries. Finally, these two prerequisites also have significant relevance to the success of new creators and entrepreneurial and pioneer producers. These topics are detailed next.

INDEPENDENCE AND EXPERTISE: IMPLICATIONS FOR ENTREPRENEURSHIP

Pioneer Intermediaries

As already described, independence and expertise are difficult to acquire, demonstrate, and maintain, a fact that puts resource-poor entrepreneurial intermediaries at a disadvantage. However, the very same properties are also especially relevant to the success of pioneer intermediaries, for their independence and expertise ensure the credibility of the discourse that creates a market for a new category of cultural goods. The independence of pioneer intermediaries grants legitimacy to their value-constructing discourse and increases their influence, particularly relative to pioneer producers. Moreover, because new categories of goods generally face resistance among consumers, intermediaries' expertise allows them to provide much-needed knowledge to consumers and ease consumers' anxieties about the new goods. Their expertise not only allows intermediaries to authoritatively discuss and explicate radical new innovations but also amplifies the market impact of their independent discourse. For instance, the Sundance Institute produced nuanced discourse, delineating the boundaries and definitions of the category (independent cinema in the United States) as well as its attributes. These definitions and attributes then evolved into the criteria used to evaluate the quality of independent films. Finally, the institute clarified the standards of quality through the highly selective curatorial process at the festival. By relying on this discourse, consumers were able to better understand and appreciate the new category of independent cinema. Such institutional work by expert intermediaries creates a sustained intersubjective understanding of the category, which is beneficial for producers and consumers alike.[27]

Given the importance of credibility to pioneer intermediaries, and the difficulty of establishing this credibility, established and already respected and trusted entities make for more effective pioneer entrepreneurs in creating a market for a new category of goods. When *The New York Times* writes about producers trying to elevate the status of pornographic films from an earlier era to art,[28] the claim seems far more legitimate and acceptable to consumers than if it had come from a marginal publication or an individual. However, extreme novelty sometimes threatens intermediaries embedded in an existing system of understanding and evaluation. In such situations, new entities may be the only intermediaries that identify the cultural and societal relevance of the innovation (that is, pioneer intermediaries); in general, entities that are peripheral to the powerful core of society and have nothing to lose by accepting and endorsing a good that deviates from norms are often more hospitable toward radical innovations. For example, *The Source*, which was started out of a dorm by two college students, was the provider of discourse that expounded rap, a musical form that was almost threatening in its radical unconventionality. Of course, a new venture in a new category would likely face greater challenges in establishing and maintaining its independence and expertise, further exacerbating the challenges in creating a market for a new good.[29]

Notwithstanding these problems, the work of a pioneer intermediary has the potential to be very satisfying, owing to the immense potential for cultural impact. In fact, much like creators and producers, many intermediaries are often driven by nonpecuniary motivations and a desire to be close to new ideas and the products of artistic imagination. These nonpecuniary motivations are crucial because they enable individuals to continue even when faced with economic difficulties, which, as in the case of *Variety*, are almost inevitable.

New Intermediary Ventures

The same nonpecuniary motivations are also salient in the founding of new intermediary ventures, even those that are not pioneers. The main question facing new intermediaries (and these issues are only sharper and thornier in the case of newly founded pioneer intermediaries) concerns how the requisite credibility can be acquired. There is no ready answer to this question. Credibility is a function of expertise and independence, and there are no shortcuts to acquiring these properties. In particular, expertise is crucial to having influence, and even seemingly straightforward to demonstrate (through the means of qualifications and erudite discourse), and yet its business benefits are quite elusive. Intermediaries must engage in discourse, submit to market scrutiny, and wait for the reaction from consumers, gradually building traction on the basis of the initial reactions. There are limited, if any, simple frameworks, solutions, or prescriptions for success, a situation that puts new intermediaries at a significant disadvantage.

New Intermediary Ventures in the Online World

In recent decades, the Internet has had a dramatic impact on entrepreneurship in the intermediary sector. The costs of starting a new intermediary have decreased significantly due to the ease of publishing online. As a consequence, entrepreneurial opportunities have proliferated for individuals wishing to perform one or more of the intermediary functions, as is evident from the abundance of online event listings, how-to videos, and opinions on and reviews of every type of cultural product imaginable. The existence and sheer number of such online start-ups has threatened the very survival of their older and costlier physical counterparts and predecessors. The success of these new business models seems to indicate that establishing a new intermediary venture may gradually become less difficult; nevertheless, the need for independence and expertise will still create challenges for such ventures.

Aside from allowing easy and low-cost dissemination of discourse online, the Internet has also altered the very way in which intermediaries fulfill their functions. Notably, the roles of consumers and intermediaries have interpenetrated online due to the use of user-generated content in value-constructing discourse. The high cost of acquiring expertise has led to an increase in new online ventures that attempt to harness the wisdom of crowds through "user reviews" or by marrying social media platforms with user reviews, which are obtained at no cost to the firm.

Another new form of digital discourse is the algorithmic process of collaborative filtering, which generates lists of recommendations to consumers based on their own and others' past purchases (commonly seen as lists with the heading "You May Also Like" or "Consumers Who Bought This Also Bought"). These, or other algorithmic means of generating interest in goods, are inexpensive substitutes for the discourse of professionals and experts. In the current social and cultural context, when consumers seem to value informal discourse and lay opinions as much as, if not more than those of formal expert evaluators and endorsers, one seeming advantage of the use of algorithms is that they grant a degree of freedom from both the perceived hegemony of experts and the subjective evaluations of bias-prone human beings. In addition, these engines serve as a means of discovering new goods, and a highly personalized one at that; in the world of online retail, where the almost infinite number of goods make discoverability a real challenge, this method of introduction can reap major benefits.

Yet both the user-dependent and the algorithm-dependent models beget problems in terms of building and demonstrating the necessary properties of intermediaries. Obviously, neither model credibly conveys any domain expertise on the part of the intermediary itself. Further, both models are more vulnerable (than the discourse of traditional intermediaries) to manipulation that weakens their independence. For instance, user-generated discourse is often copresent at the point of sale (such as on Amazon.com), a situation that destroys the structural and economic independence of instructional discourse. Even when user reviews are collated on a separate site, as on Yelp.com, it is difficult if not impossible for consumers to know with confidence that the user reviews were truly independent and objective—whereas the existence of negative reviews may seem to signal objectivity, consumers cannot be sure that the negative comments were not posted by a competitor. Similarly, automation and algorithms render the process vulnerable because small changes can have big repercussions; a single tweak to the way an algorithm takes certain attributes into account or to the hierarchy of attributes considered can change the output of the algorithm significantly, leading to very different recommendations.[30,31] With respect to the discovery of novel goods, this vulnerability to manipulation and the influence of small changes might be desirable, leading consumers to step out of their comfort zone and sample entirely new goods. However, consumers have no control over these tweaks and changes and therefore have no idea of the basis on which these changes are made; changes in algorithms could, for instance, have been made to favor a particular producer or creator in exchange for payment. Moreover, the ease of tweaking these algorithms raises the possibility of firms' changing them in response to pecuniary or other pressures from producers or competitors. Given that "cooperative promotion" payments, for instance, already allow book publishers and other producers to pay Amazon.com (an online producer) in return for prominent placement on the online retailer's home page, it is not difficult to imagine an online intermediary changing its algorithms to favor certain goods and/or producers in exchange for a payment.

Such vulnerability to manipulation is certainly not unimaginable or impossible in the case of traditional individual intermediaries. There are, however, several potential points of failure in the process of persuading book reviewers or film critics to alter the way in which they evaluate and discuss goods. Fine-tuning an algorithm is more impersonal and straightforward, making it easier to execute and therefore more likely to occur. Moreover, regulations require the disclosure of any inducements offered to individual critics and reviewers, and even if critics did not disclose the relationship (an unlikely scenario), the detailed and nuanced nature of critical discourse means that any drastic changes in opinion or style, or departures from the usual, would be evident to consumers. Imagine, for instance, how surprising it would be if the film critic for *The New Yorker*, Anthony Lane, were to praise an inane movie that contained terrible dialogue and lacked any nuance. In contrast, the opaque nature of algorithms—consumers usually have little knowledge about the parameters under which they function and how they produce results—as well as the nature of their results, which are presented as simple lists without much rich detail, render such changes less evident to consumers.

In addition to undermining the perceived expertise of intermediaries through user-generated content or algorithmic filtering, the business models of online intermediaries are also particularly prone to the blending of third-party discourse and commerce, which leads to reduced independence. Digital publication and the sophistication of online commerce make it possible for magazines to benefit from their discourse and reputation by embedding either an explicit "Buy Now" link or an implicit invitation to buy in the form of a link to the online store, next to or embedded within editorial copy; if the reader clicks the link and makes a purchase, the intermediary stands to gain revenues in the form of affiliate commissions. This practice is particularly common in the fashion industry, where magazines such as *Allure* and *Vogue* have embraced the affiliate revenue model:[32] for example, a reader who fancies the lipstick or dress favorably reviewed by the magazine is now able to buy the product directly from the magazine's website. Firms often justify this revenue model by claiming it is necessary to counter the threat from online publishing and dwindling advertising revenues. In addition, established magazines address criticism of the new model by pointing toward their long history of independence and expertise to mitigate allegations of favoritism or reciprocity. However, the use of the affiliate revenue model is slippery territory, particularly in the case of new ventures.

The seamless way in which hyperlinks can be embedded into digital discourse and narrative has enabled more and more new purely digital intermediaries to augment advertising revenues with commissions. But, for these new ventures (blogs, online magazines, YouTube channels, and others), their lack of a track record may mean that such a business model is far riskier than it is for established magazines, which point to their previous record to defend their credibility. These digital intermediaries thus face a Catch-22, wherein they need revenues to survive and build a reputation, but advertising revenues are limited and/or slow to accrue because of their newness, and other revenue streams (such as sales commissions) prove to be inimical to the very goal of building a reputation.[33] For entrepreneurs who choose not to gain revenues from commissions, being purely ad supported in the online world is a daunting task, given the difficulty of being discovered and building a steady base of followers that, in turn, attracts advertisers. Therefore, small, new organizations (for example, blogs, review sites) facing economic hardships are less likely to have the fortitude to resist the pressures exerted by advertisers than are larger well-established magazines and newspapers, which benefit from the added security of legal and professional protection.

Another threat to the independence of blogs is the attractiveness of lucrative affiliations and partnerships with large producers, which have an incentive to co-opt popular blogs. A recent example of this type of relationship (that could be perceived as co-optation) is the collaboration between Estée Lauder and Cupcakes & Cashmere, a blog created by Emily Schuman, who, since the collaboration was announced in 2012, has been contributing to the Estée Lauder blog, acting as a brand ambassador for the firm, featuring Estée Lauder products in her blog, and running Estée Lauder ads on the site. Although the collaboration was announced publicly and Schuman gets paid separately for her work on behalf of Estée Lauder, this scenario could be perceived as blurring the boundaries of the Cupcakes & Cashmere site and reducing Schuman's independence.

Finally, maintaining independence is especially difficult in the virtual world because there are no generally accepted sectorwide professional ethics and standards—one shortsighted miscreant who does not abide by disclosure conventions or receives cash or in-kind gifts such as samples and tickets in implicit exchange for a favorable review could bring down the entire sector and ruin the credibility of all such ventures. Many bloggers and other online entities are aware of such problems, and those in the industry are taking steps to create safeguards and develop principles and norms similar to those that guide traditional intermediaries. But until such principles and norms become widely accepted and adopted, the issue of credibility will persist.

The Effects of Intermediaries'
Properties on Producers

The properties of intermediaries have significant impacts on producers, chief among which is that producers have limited, if any, influence over the discourse of intermediaries. Scandals such as payola or other forms of corruption negatively affect the offending producers as well as the intermediary, resulting in lasting damage to their reputation in the marketplace and potentially tainting the public's perception of their products, even if the product is, in fact, of high quality. Therefore, producers should and, for the most part, do refrain from direct and blatant attempts to influence intermediaries' discourse, tempting though it may be to try and ensure a positive review or endorsement from an intermediary. As a result, producers and creators have no option but to submit their goods to scrutiny in the market and hope they meet the criteria and standards of quality applied by intermediaries and thus garner a mention or, even better, a favorable review.

Intermediaries' independence is crucial even to producers' long-term success, particularly for new and/or innovative creators and producers, who, in the absence of a level playing field maintained by impartial intermediaries, would be crowded out of listings and vanish into oblivion. For instance, in 1983 when soul and funk Super Freak artist Rick James charged MTV with intentionally shutting out black artists, he said, "I figure if they [MTV] played my video I could probably sell hundreds of thousands more records than I do now."[34] By this time, MTV, which had begun broadcasting two years earlier, had established its role in the music industry as the mainstream population's point of first contact with musicians, and the channel's significant impact on album sales was widely acknowledged.

When intermediaries that *introduce* succumb to economic pressures from incumbents (by either engaging in payola or purposefully excluding certain producers from their lists), it has a negative impact on the fortunes of small, new, or innovative creators. Similarly, because of the Matthew Effect (described in Chapter 4), new producers or creators who are able to pay for placement on an introductory list gain longer-term benefits that are not always deserved. Owing to uncertainty and a lack of control over the outcome, coupled with the significant positive effect of favorable commentary, new creators and producers are often tempted and advised to seek guaranteed endorsements or favorable reviews from influential entities in exchange for payment (even though being paid for their endorsement of a product by definition precludes such endorsers from being considered "pure" intermediaries). Most new ventures, however, are strapped for resources and must spend wisely the resources they do have; therefore, paying for endorsements may not be the most efficient or even the most effective way of gaining visibility and revenues.

All producers benefit significantly from the presence of strong independent intermediaries in all three functions, although such intermediaries are especially beneficial for new creators and producers. For these new producers and creators, the existence of independent intermediaries provides an equal chance of being seen, evaluated, and (if they are of high quality) praised and endorsed. In the absence of independence among intermediaries, producers/creators with novel, unfamiliar, provocative, or subversive creations and products would face considerable challenges in trying to find a market. More specifically, if the discourse of intermediaries praised only the highest bidder, the most prestigious producers, or the least controversial producers, new ventures would be unable to obtain favorable coverage and would be considered unworthy of mention.

Receiving a mention—particularly a favorable evaluation—in the discourse of an intermediary known for independence and expertise has a strong positive impact on a producer or creator. Thus, the existence of independent intermediaries that take their functions seriously and are committed to granting visibility to high-quality goods is an advantage for entrepreneurs; in terms of long-term sustainability, dedicating resources to improving the quality of their good so that intermediaries are impelled to take notice of it is likely a more viable strategy (than influencing an intermediary with a financial incentive). For new producers, another advantage is that intermediaries' independence also ensures their imperviousness to incumbents' status, reputation, and prestige, or economic pressures, which, in turn, levels the playing field for new producers, which typically lack these assets. Finally, but not trivially, the expertise of intermediaries also has advantages for new producers, especially those in novel categories. Expertise and the attendant critical abilities of intermediaries, although intimidating for a new producer, may, in fact, be crucial in identifying, understanding, and promoting novel ideas and originality, if accompanied by open-mindedness of the type exhorted by Pound (whose commentary in support of Joyce's *Ulysses* exemplifies the positive impact on market creation of expert intermediaries) in the quotation at the opening of this chapter.

Summing Up and Looking Ahead

Intermediaries confront unique challenges to business success. These challenges are the result of their structural position, as well as the difficulty inherent in developing the prerequisite assets of independence and expertise. Therefore, intermediaries must be zealously committed to their work and fully able to grasp its unique importance: the potential to influence the creation of markets for new cultural goods, provoking cultural change in the process. This promise of a future impact is, without question, a strong motivator for pioneer intermediaries and is primarily responsible for driving individuals toward this role, despite its myriad challenges.

Because intermediaries' discourse wields such influence over consumers' purchasing decisions, producers' fortunes are shaped, and to some extent even controlled by, intermediaries. Yet, producers must not be seen attempting to influence the reactions of intermediaries. This complex interdependence between these two types of entities affects the operations of producers, which are the central topic of Part III of this book. Producers (and creators, to a degree) in creative industries straddle the twin (and contradictory) realms of culture and commerce and are therefore subject to the often conflicting and contradictory principles and conventions of the two worlds. Producers must address the inherent tension between the cultural and financial imperatives they face. The next section describes the specifics of producers' existence, the challenges they face due to the structure of creative industries and the nature of cultural goods, and the various ways in which producers attempt to achieve the delicate balance between cultural value and financial viability.

Part III

PRODUCING CULTURE

Producers in Creative Industries

CREATORS AND PRODUCERS

Making Art, Making Markets

Once private citizens began to be seriously engaged in the cultural
market, works of art became, more than ever, a commodity. . . .
Businessmen of culture offered and sold artistic products, whether
dramas, drawings, or volumes of poetry, [and] with the same
gesture, advanced the aesthetic cultivation of the buying public.

—Peter Gay[1]

At the turn of the twentieth century in Britain, books and literature were
serious matters; the format in which they came—formidable, leather-bound
tomes—duly conveyed the gravitas and importance of the object.[2] Created as
means of edification and instruction of the elite, these expensive and erudite
books were materially (financially) as well as symbolically inaccessible to the
masses. With the rise of the middle class and the expansion of literacy, however, publishers began to produce inexpensive, entertaining novels, which the
elites promptly derided as not worthy of inclusion in the ranks of literature.[3]
In 1935, when London-based publisher Penguin Books released its first series
of ten literary classics in paperback versions, available for sixpence each, the
publishing industry democratized reading for good.[4] No longer did one have
to be wealthy to enjoy the works of literature that were previously available
to only a small section of society. Penguin, under the guidance of its founder
Allen Lane, published, distributed, and sold the works and ideas of authors to
a larger audience than had any previous publisher.

Literature is no longer inaccessible to the majority of the literate population, and Penguin and other publishers are the primary entities responsible
for providing and maintaining consumers' access to books (both good and
bad ones). Publishers—along with gallery owners, film studios, record companies, restaurants, retailers and department stores, and other counterparts
in the various creative industries—are *producers*; these entities bring cultural
goods such as books to consumers/audiences through a process governed by

the market mechanism. Producers comprise all the entities involved in the production, distribution, and/or sale of art, music, fashion, film, books, and food (or any other cultural good) to consumers. In contrast to intermediaries, producers have a *direct* economic stake in the value of cultural goods; successfully increasing the perceived value, and consequently the market price, of a good through discourse and other methods produces financial gains for the entity. Producers, therefore, have a vested interest in facilitating maximum consumer access to cultural goods and in ensuring that these goods are valued and purchased by consumers.

In their role as firms that produce, distribute, and sell cultural goods, producers have arguably been the greatest democratizing force in the history of society's interactions with art and artists; even when groups of individuals came together to create music or stage plays, before the emergence of producers and the creative industries, the creations were accessible to only a limited number of people in the vicinity of the creative groups. Before the modern era, easy and reliable access to artworks was limited to royalty, nobility, and the wealthy through a deeply complicated system of patronage,[5] which not only shaped the nature and content of the art created but also determined the dissemination of artworks and the audiences for artists. Laypersons had virtually no contact with artists or exposure to artworks unless munificent patrons sponsored the installation of sculptures or other works in public spaces, such as churches, or funded concerts or performances that were open to the public. Over the course of history, various individuals and families had gained a reputation for providing strong financial and other support to artists and certain forms of artistic creation, and during the reigns of such families, the arts thrived, albeit only among rarefied groups belonging to the patrons' social class. With the decline, if not the outright disappearance, of large-scale formal patronage arrangements, however, the market mechanism and market-oriented firms have stepped in as de facto patrons of artists and creative works, a change that has had wide-ranging effects on the arts as well as the broader society. Driven to increase revenues, either by selling goods at higher prices or by selling a higher volume of goods, producers are motivated to disseminate works at high prices to a limited number of consumers or at a price that makes the works attractive to many to reach the largest possible audience. As a result, lay consumers' access to all manner and forms of artistic creation has reached unprecedented levels, and the general population's awareness of and knowledge about cultural goods—especially once-esoteric forms of cultural production such as classical music, high fashion, dance, or architecture—has undergone a sea change.[6]

The existence of today's producers and their role in the cultural ecosystem, however, is not always viewed as an unqualified success for society or artists. Markets are perceived as venues of rational economic exchange, in which objective evaluation and commensurability of goods are the keys to seamless transactions and smooth functioning.[7] In contrast, artistic endeavors have been characterized as a means of transforming measurable and calculable material items into cultural goods of subjective and symbolic worth that, many believe, cannot be measured in economic terms alone.[8] Several cultural commentators, therefore, have lamented the direct interpenetration of art and commerce that is common today among producers in creative industries, rather than hailing it as a victory for modern society and its citizens. The current state of affairs, these critics warn, entails grave risks, and society should either actively try to prevent such interpenetration or, at the very least, minimize its debilitating effect on artistic integrity and quality. Given that creators' work and creations must be funded in some way, however, a certain degree of interdependence between business and art seems inevitable, as does the accompanying tension—which is unique to the creative industries—between the world of creators and the world of producers. This section of the book deals with producers, who substantially embody this tension and without whom the creative industries would, in fact, not exist in their current form. Chapters 6, 7, and 8 examine the features of producers and then explore whether these features are indeed cause for concern and how, if at all, such concerns may be minimized.

Producers: Bridging Two Worlds

Given the differences between the art and market realms, producers occupy a precarious position at the cusp of culture and commerce. Producing firms are therefore subject to the institutional logics (the set of material and symbolic practices that define any institution by establishing sources of legitimacy and authority, defining identities, and otherwise clarifying norms within the institutional order)[9] of both realms. All organizations operate under an institutional logic, and most operate under several logics simultaneously,[10] which can result in tensions of identity, legitimacy, and alignment as the organization struggles to meet the requirements of logics that are sometimes contradictory.

In creative industries, the two chief logics that generate this tension are those of the market/commercial institution and the cultural/artistic institution. These two fields[11]—art with its aesthetic paradigm and business entailing the market paradigm—are typically represented as different and often contradictory institutions that are inhabited by radically different organizations and individuals, with different orders of worth,[12] different means of measuring value, and, subsequently, different economies[13]—in other words, they possess distinctly different logics.[14] However different the two fields may be, they coexist and intersect in the creative industries, where producers, which have an economic stake in the sales of creative works, are (unsurprisingly) particularly vulnerable to the conflicts and contradictions between the two logics.

One of the chief reasons for the unique tension between art and commerce is the fact that creators can create works on their own, without necessarily requiring the infrastructure and support of a firm (this is especially true of book writing, painting and sculpture, and music composition). As a result, most cultural goods embody the personal drive of creators to express themselves and create art that aligns with their own intellectual and aesthetic preferences;[15] therefore, these creative works are often far removed from the market and the needs and desires of consumers. In such cases, because the strong creative urge among artists is actualized by the mere creation of the work rather than its sale, artists almost always create works far outside the realm of the marketplace long before firms and consumers come to know of them. These artistic creations are therefore rarely, if ever, the product of studied market research or consumer knowledge.[16] It is not clear, at the time of creation, whether the work will appeal to anyone other than the artist, let alone find a sizeable or profitable market. This is not to say that artists and creators do not wish to ever sell their works or make a living via their art but only that the market and consumers' tastes and preferences are not the driving force behind their works. Moreover, most artists who intend to sell their works are wary of the pressures that the market entails and the corresponding potential for negative impact on their artistic expression. This scenario has problematic implications for producers because work that is not intended or designed to conform to society's known desires and preferences is unlikely to find a market easily.

Although there are, of course, some creators who generate works that are meant to amuse, entertain, and please and could be said to create with an audience in mind, the art–business tension still comes into play in their case, albeit indirectly. Writers of genre fiction, pop musicians, and makers of star-studded action films or romantic comedies are all aware that their creations provide an escape from the humdrum of everyday life and are not meant to be complex or laden with abstruse symbolism that would require consumers to "work" to enjoy them; nevertheless, they do not create formulaic works, reverse engineered to fit consumers' tastes. Creators who repeatedly engage in the "paint-by-numbers" approach that reverse engineering entails would lose the respect of intermediaries and consumers at some point[17] and ironically would not inevitably achieve commercial success because consumers' tastes and reactions to cultural goods and their attributes are highly subjective and highly uncertain and therefore difficult if not impossible to predict.[18,19] Finally, creators cannot create solely to please an audience or a market, despite the financial security of such a path, if they want their fellow creators and/or reputed critics, reviewers, and other intermediaries to take them seriously. Even in the case of creators who choose to create populist works, admitting to reverse engineering a formula or following a set recipe for success is tantamount to admitting failure as an artist, and such creators are characterized as sellouts.[20]

The distinction between creators and producers and their disparate motivations has two main practical implications: first, managers of firms that produce cultural goods often have to actively create a market for creative works because they are not necessarily created with a consumer or a market in mind; second, these managers must be aware of the creator–producer duality and the conflict between the two worlds and manage firms in ways that balance both artistic and financial success.

TYPES OF PRODUCERS

Producer Firms and Creator Firms

There are two models of producers, the producer firm and the creator firm. In most creative industries, creators do not take their creations directly to market through their own ventures; instead, firms—referred to as producer firms in this book—are responsible for collating the creations of many creators and presenting them to consumers. For example, in the music and publishing industries, record labels and publishing firms are both producer firms that aggregate the works of a large number of individual creators. Producer firms, being removed from the creator and having to navigate the market terrain, are likely more objective evaluators of the creators' works than are the creators themselves—because producer firms seek to increase revenues, they acquire only (what they perceive are) high-quality works from the best creators. Accordingly, there is a general belief that producer firms serve to vet the quality of creators and creative works.[21] An association with a reputed producer firm, therefore, is often seen by intermediaries, and consequently consumers, as a signal of the quality and value of a creator and the creative work. By the same logic, the generally negative connotation of the term *self-published author*, for instance, stems from the belief that the absence of an association with a reputable producer firm is an indicator of the limited ability, talent, and appeal of the writer.[22]

The structure of other industries, such as fashion and food, allows creators themselves to found firms (referred to as creator firms in this book) to bring their creations to market. It is not entirely clear why some industries favor producer firms and others allow for creator firms. Why, for example, is it virtually unheard of for a writer to found a publishing *firm* (with at least a few employees) to publish her books exclusively, whereas it's not uncommon for a chef to start a restaurant in which only her recipes are prepared and served?[23]

One possible explanation for this phenomenon is that the creative processes in these separate artistic realms, as well as the career paths of young creators in these industries, are quite different. For instance, both designers and chefs typically start work in other design firms and restaurants, respectively, as members of a team of apprentices to the chief designer or head chef, moving up in the organization as they hone their skills. Being immersed in a team within an organizational setting helps these creators better understand the process of running a firm. At the same time, the advantages of being the head designer or chef in a firm—the space and freedom to work on one's own ideas—are visible to all subordinate creators in the firm. Not surprisingly, then, talented assistant designers and sous-chefs aspire to start firms to realize their own ideas, rather than play second fiddle to another creator. Writing a book, painting, sculpting, and making music—in contrast to working as a chef or designer—are all relatively solitary endeavors that do not require assistants engaged in the actual creation process. Therefore, a young aspiring creator in one of these fields does not need to start a firm to have full creative freedom. Further, individuals in this latter group are never socialized in an organizational setting because being part of an organizational infrastructure on a daily basis does not provide them any significant benefits or aid their creative process in any way. The benefits of starting a firm and managing it, therefore, are minimal.

Filmmakers are unique in that they occupy the middle of the spectrum of producer firms and creator firms. Filmmakers must necessarily work with (often large) teams of individuals, including assistants or apprentices, much as chefs and designers do. And yet, not all large film studios are creator firms. The explanation for this discrepancy likely has something to do with the high cost of producing and distributing films, relative to the initial investment required to start a restaurant or fashion firm. Moreover, both restaurants and fashion designers can directly reach and serve their customers at the venue where creation occurs, which is not true of films. Some creator firms do exist in the industry, for example Dreamworks[24] (founded by director Steven Spielberg) and Section Eight[25] (founded by director Steven Soderbergh but shut down in 2006), but creator-founded studios are typically started late in a director's career and only by extremely well-known and financially successful directors. Further, similar to publishing firms and other film studios, director-founded studios produce the works of many directors, not only the founding creator's (director's) works (unlike a restaurant founded by a prominent chef).

Given that business (firms) and art (creators) reside in two separate worlds with distinct governing logics, a creator firm seems to be a contradiction in terms. Further, there is a widespread assumption that artists do not make good businesspeople. Whether or not artists make good business managers, most have limited, if any, interest in disrupting their creative work to worry about the market, sales, and running a firm. Although creators enjoy having complete creative freedom—a very attractive situation—within their own firms, the business implications of availing oneself of this freedom are unappealing to creators, and business is not their area of expertise. This scenario often leads to the need for a codependent partnership in creator firms; most firms founded or run by creators are cofounded and/or comanaged by business managers.[26] Although consumers are often only aware of the creator in creator firms—for example, almost everybody is familiar with Yves St. Laurent, the founding designer of the eponymous firm, but few, if any, individuals outside the industry have heard of Pierre Bergé, his founding partner—the business manager is, and should be, considered the creator's equal partner for all practical purposes related to the firm. Due to the complementary skills of the two individuals and the purpose of the firm—bringing cultural goods to the market—each partner is necessary but not sufficient. Without the creator, there would be no product to sell or distribute; without the business manager, the creator would have to expend too much time and effort engaged in activities that are not related to creation of goods. Neither of these scenarios is favorable to the firm.

Supply-Chain Firms

The creative industries are also home to a third type of firm, supply-chain firms. These firms—distributors and retailers, for instance—earn revenues in a variety of ways, but each involves payment in exchange for physically moving the product along to the consumer. Distributors and/or wholesalers collect fees for managing the logistical aspects of the exchange process, whereas retailers receive a portion of the price (the retailer's margin or markup) charged to the customer. The number of stages in the supply chain differs across the various creative industries. For instance, an artwork passes through at most two other producers before arriving at a gallery (the art market equivalent of retailers in the fashion industry), whereas an item of clothing typically passes through many more steps between the fashion designer and the retail store. Additionally, garments are likely to have originated at a creator firm, whereas most artworks originate from an individual creator. As a result of these differences, the fashion industry is more formally structured and seemingly more organized than the art market. In the art market, the success and impact of galleries depend on the ability of gallery owners to establish and maintain personal relationships with artists and to discover new, original, and talented artists. In contrast, the more formally structured industries such as fashion (and to some extent film) comprise a group of entities whose number and transactional relationships considerably reduce, if not preclude, the need for deep personal relationships.

Agents and Talent Scouts

The art market is somewhat of an anomaly with respect to its continued need for direct personal relationships between producer firms (especially galleries, which interact directly with consumers) and creators. In other industries dominated by producer firms (for example, publishing, film, and music) entities that mediate the relationship between creators and producers have arisen to make the process smoother. These actors—agents and talent scouts—are sometimes single individuals operating on their own but are often firms, ranging from small literary agencies to extremely large organizations such as Creative Artists Agency (CAA), a talent agency with global reach. Although many of these agents and agencies work on the creator's behalf, they also have a financial stake in the value of the creative work in the market and therefore a vested interest in the creator's artistic and financial success, which brings them revenues through commissions (a percentage of the payment made by the producer to the creator).[27]

Like gallery owners, agents and talent scouts must both maintain relationships with individual creators (current clients) and be on the lookout for new talent to add to their client list. Like all other producers, agents and scouts engage in discourse that conveys the value of their clients and the clients' work. Further, they also face the same challenge as other producers: their vested (financial) interest in growing their clients' stature and economic value lowers the credibility of their valuation and endorsement.[28] That said, the relationship between literary agents and editors at publishing houses is rather similar to the relationship between galleries and art collectors; because the pair are engaged in a repeated game relationship, it is in the best interests of the agent to build a strong foundation of trust and to avoid advocating for creators with limited talent, despite the potential for short-term financial gain from such misrepresentation. Given the subjectivity of assessment and the high degree of uncertainty inherent in cultural goods, therefore, personal relationships matter because they mitigate the lack of credibility in producers' discourse.

As shown in the previous chapters, the discourse of intermediaries, especially trade intermediaries, provides an additional set of checks and balances to ensure the trust in these relationships is not misplaced or misused. Not only do industry-specific intermediaries play a role in introducing new creators to relevant agents and/or producers, but their discourse also serves as a credible independent source of verification of, for instance, an agent's claims about the quality and talent of a creator. *Variety*, the trade paper for the entertainment industry (primarily TV, film, and music), for instance, is practically required reading for employees at the CAA, as well as employees of TV networks or film studios. A positive mention of a creative artist in the trade paper can bring both the agent and producers to the negotiating table, creating greater interest on the part of the producers and allowing the agent to boost the market value of the client.[29] In both spheres, *Variety* serves almost as a monitor, ensuring that both parties in a producer–agent relationship behave in a way that maximizes trust, and therefore economic value, in the long run. In fact,

Variety itself portrays its mission as achieving a "balance of terror" in the entertainment industry.[30]

The Business Implications of Bridging Two Worlds

Fundamentally, all producers must straddle the cultural world and the commercial world, trying to achieve success in both by producing cultural goods of high quality and making money in the market, respectively. Although the business model of producers is straightforward (relative to that of intermediaries)—revenues are made (grown) by engaging in (increasing) economic transactions that bring cultural goods to consumers—there are nevertheless challenges inherent to being a producer.

THE CHALLENGE OF MARKET-MAKING

First and foremost, although an artist can create without regard to consumers and markets, producers do not have that luxury. As a result, producers in creative industries, more than in any other context, are required to engage in *market making*, rather than merely marketing.[31] To understand what that means for actual operations, recall that markets are not just about providing a supply of goods to fulfill the demand for them but also about understanding how customers' preferences can be influenced so that they appreciate the value of goods in the market. In the case of cultural goods in particular, the process of influencing consumer preferences is crucial because creators are not creating works with consumers' existing preferences in mind. Thus, as mentioned in Chapter 2, markets must be created anew for nearly every new cultural good, even if it is not a radical innovation. The works of known and reputed creators will naturally be fraught with less uncertainty and possess an advantage over those of new and unknown creators. However, even these works require fresh market making; for example, publishers send well-known best-selling authors such as Margaret Atwood on book tours, and studios spend a lot of money on generating publicity for, and promoting the generation of, commentary by intermediaries on even films made by directors who have previously delivered hits.

Producers are right to expend such extensive efforts to create markets for every new iteration of a cultural good. The uncertainty regarding the reception of cultural goods is evident in the lukewarm and sometimes downright cold reviews that works by creators previously acknowledged as high quality sometimes receive. Reviewers widely criticized *A Long Way Down*, the fourth novel by well-known writer Nick Hornby, with one reviewer describing it as a "cringe-making excuse for a novel" with a premise that "feels like a formulaic idea for a cheesy made-for-television movie," even though, as the reviewer admitted earlier in the review, Hornby's first book had been full of "wonderfully acute observations of pop culture" that made it a "rollicking delight to read."[32] Critical and consumer success in one instance may establish a creator as someone worthy of consideration and appraisal, but it certainly does not guarantee a positive evaluation of every subsequent work. Producers in the creative industries, therefore, take on the risk of a work not finding a market each time they engage in the production, distribution, or selling of a good. This situation differs from the production of other kinds of goods such as appliances, which, being different only in surface attributes (color, size, and so on), if not entirely identical, do not require the same extent of market-creation activity for every new product. Of course, this risk is not entirely due to creators' lack of regard for consumers' preferences. The subjectivity inherent in individuals' assessment of cultural goods exacerbates the situation.[33] The uncertainty faced by producers, therefore, is two sided. First, creators often create a work that is far removed from consumers' tastes; second, even a work that is not offensive or strange may not easily or immediately appeal to sufficient numbers of consumers. Because of this dual uncertainty, intermediaries and their value-constructing discourse are essential to producers in creative industries.[34] Within the firm, too, this market uncertainty and the tensions between norms of the market and the art world lead to a delicate but mutually dependent relationship between managers and creators in producer as well as creator firms.

THE CHALLENGE OF BUILDING TRUST BETWEEN MANAGERS AND CREATORS

The relationship between art and business is less strained in creator firms because creators who choose to work in a creator firm cannot afford to ignore the norms of the market, whatever their artistic orientation. For example, although Karl Lagerfeld, creative director at the iconic fashion firm Chanel, brooks no interference from management when it comes to the design process, he is not oblivious to the reality that he is a designer—not a conceptual artist—and is therefore fully cognizant of the fact that his creations are meant to be worn by women and *not* exhibited in museums (that is, they must sell).[35] Chanel management is also aware of this consciousness in Lagerfeld, which provides a strong enough sense of security for the firm to give him free rein in the design of clothes; management does not feel the need to impose directives intended to restrict Lagerfeld to creating goods that will sell more easily.[36] Such strong mutual trust between a creator and a business manager is essential to the success of creator firms. This trust allows managers to shield the creator from market pressures, while simultaneously being reasonably sure that the protection and freedom will not cost the firm needed revenues.

The need to build and maintain this type of mutual trust is crucial to managers, even in producer firms where they interact with multiple individual creators. Managers must shield creators to allow them to create their best work and, further, must understand and support the idiosyncratic and unpredictable process of creation. Thus, managers (founders or nonfounder principals) who understand the psychology of creators and value their work for its artistic integrity regardless of market dynamics have an advantage in the cultural marketplace. Such understanding also affords managers another, more strategic, advantage: a level of credibility among creators, which motivates the most talented ones to work with the firm. The close relationship that emerges when an author feels that her editor "understands" her, for instance, is considered a key competitive advantage of the editor because, when such a relationship exists, the author will often remain with the editor even as the editor changes employers or transitions to a new position. Good managers know this and treat these relationships accordingly, as assets that need to be protected against short-term business interests. For instance, speaking of publisher Sherry Arden on her death, a senior editor said, "One of her greatest gifts was knowing how to interpret acquisition editors and their creative writers to the conservative, bottom-line business types who control the money."[37]

Notably, there is a difference in the degree to which creators in various industries need to acknowledge market norms; in some cases, like the art market, creators can afford to ignore market norms more so than in other cases—fashion, some sectors of publishing, music, and films. In the art market, for instance, both collectors and society as a whole attach a somewhat romantic sheen to the concept of the solitary artistic genius creating masterpieces without regard to the market; as a result, producers (such as gallery owners) place less importance on market awareness among artists. Similarly, for reasons explained later in the book, producer firms, which are affiliated with several creators, do not depend as much on the market awareness of each individual creator with whom they work.

The preceding discussion notwithstanding, the distinction between creators and managers in firms, although very real and pertinent within the context of producers, may be somewhat artificial and exaggerated in this type of academic examination. Managers are indeed primarily tasked with and focused on protecting the firm's business interests and ensuring that the firm remains financially viable. This assignment and the resulting motivation suggest to critics of the system that managers are only interested in artistic creation that is likely to be commercially successful. To this end, popular and well-accepted conceptions of the functioning of markets for creative goods are grounded in the belief that poor-quality works are produced only because managers restrict production to the type of work they believe will appeal to the mass market (sometimes referred to as the "lowest common denominator"), thus making the most money for the firm. To a certain extent, this is an accurate characterization of the determinants of which cultural goods are brought to market. However, these works *are* created by creators, which implies that, for at least some creators, popularity and mass appeal may be a desired outcome of undertaking the process of creation. Entire categories of modern-day cultural goods (vampire novels, romantic comedies, and reality TV shows, for instance) are constituted of populist, entertaining, exciting content, which, despite most critics' and even some consumers' abhorrence, exists and is consumed. It is unlikely that these categories are populated solely by creators who have been forced to succumb to market pressures by their managers at production firms; a more likely scenario is that many of these creators actively seek to appeal to the masses via their creations. The most successful managers are those who understand that creators have varying talents, abilities, and proclivities and that artistic talent is not a general-purpose tool or skill that can be applied to a variety of tasks; in other words, a talented writer of literary fiction cannot be asked to write a spy thriller simply because the latter category of books sells better, nor can or should a pop singer be asked to perform an aria.[38]

THE CHALLENGE OF BUILDING AND MAINTAINING A REPUTATION

Another consequence of producers' need to bridge two worlds is that reputation matters considerably to the operations of producers. Producers' reputations are important for two main reasons. First, especially in the case of producer firms, reputation is the primary intangible marker of the value of the product they bring to market because consumers believe that good producer firms vet the talent and quality of creators and their works. Second, for both creator firms and producer firms, a good reputation allows their valuation discourse to have a greater impact because consumers are less likely to discount the discourse. Although this mitigating effect is most evident in the case of direct, personal interactions and relationships between consumers and producers (as in the earlier example of galleries), the importance of producers' reputations is also apparent in the case of more impersonal transactions (for example, purchases made at a fashion retailer or department store). Unlike galleries, which often deal with a small number of collectors out of both necessity and choice,[39] department stores must appeal and sell to thousands of customers at dozens or even hundreds of locations. Despite this large consumer base, the reputation of a department store still affects consumers' perceptions of the value of a designer and/or the actual designs; this process is somewhat similar to the way that being signed by a reputed publisher has a positive effect on a writer's value. A Bergdorf Goodman (department store) or a Farrar, Strauss and Giroux (publishing firm)—a consumer reasons—is unlikely to squander its hard-earned reputation for taste and discernment on a designer or writer, respectively, who does not possess a certain level of talent. In other words, both creators and consumers view such producer firms as vetting agents or quality filters and interpret an association with these reputed producers as a signal of quality and value.

In addition to judging producers based on their reputations, consumers view producers that operate on a not-for-profit basis as more credible evaluators of quality and value than those that seek to make a profit (as discussed in Chapter 5). Because their mission is to serve artists or society (or both) rather than shareholders, such producers are perceived as bringing only high-quality creative and cultural goods to the market. As a result, creators who are affiliated with not-for-profit producers benefit disproportionately from these relationships. Of course, these creators may not enjoy economic success as a direct result of these affiliations, but the recognition and validation they receive can be parlayed in the future into market success and wealth.

The particular uncertainties about markets, creators, and reputation faced by producers make entrepreneurship as a producer in creative industries especially challenging, given that entrepreneurship in any industry is a context of uncertainty. However, entrepreneurs—pioneering and others—do not seem to be deterred from the producer role in creative industries, with several possible versions of entrepreneurship as a producer existing due to the differences between creator firms and producer firms, and the kinds of innovations they can pursue.

Entrepreneurship in the Producer Role

The preceding section indicates that because producers face a dual uncertainty (the work of creators is often far afield from consumer's tastes, and even work that is not so unusual may not appeal to a sufficient numbers of consumers), the business of producers is generally quite challenging, and the business of entrepreneurship as a producer is particularly so. Being an entrepreneur in the producer role is more challenging than either being an entrepreneur in another context or being an established producer in the creative industries. The uncertainty inherent in being a new venture or a pioneer venture exacerbates, and is exacerbated by, the tensions and trade-offs caused by the creator producer duality and the differences in the artistic and commercial logics.

NEW VENTURES IN ESTABLISHED CATEGORIES

New Creator Firms

In the case of new creator firms, because creators are so important but often lack interest in business issues, firms founded by a team of creative and business partners are more likely to survive and grow than those founded by only creative or only business individuals.[40] Almost all successful creator firms have relied on the leadership and talent of both a creative executive and a business-minded one; in the preceding section, the example of Yves Saint-Laurent and Pierre Bergé illustrates the benefits of such a partnership. A more recent example is the partnership of innovative Danish chef René Redzepi and restaurateur Claus Meyer at Noma, a trailblazing haute cuisine restaurant in Copenhagen that created and established the category of New Nordic cuisine in the culinary world. Given the nature of the product, which is a physical manifestation of the creator's talent, the creator is more central to the success of the firm. Thus, the departure of the founding creator has a stronger negative effect on the firm's likelihood of survival than does the departure of the founding business manager.[41] However, the role of the business manager—"shielding" the creator from market issues, leaving that person free to pursue excellence in her or his creative work—is also extremely important. Further, a creator who is completely oblivious to consumers and lost in artistic reverie does not make a good founder. Just as Karl Lagerfeld is cognizant of current business issues at the House of Chanel, Coco Chanel, too, was acutely aware of the market and her customers. In Chanel's mind, her customers were women like herself—she explained, "I design clothes that I want to wear." She did not believe that selling her creations tarnished her status as a creator in any way.

New Producer Firms

Although not being creators themselves, founders of producer firms nevertheless possess an empathetic spirit that allows them to engage with and champion creators and creative works. For instance, Penguin founder Allen Lane was a book lover who firmly believed in the power of the written word and the importance of making it accessible to all strata of society,[42] and Evan Ratliff, the founder of digital publishing firm Atavist, is a former journalist and thus is sympathetic toward the writers whose work he publishes.[43] Similarly, actress Meryl Streep has said of producer Harvey Weinstein (who has professed to be in love with movies), "He can be really hard on people . . . But it's always, always, in the service of what he sees as the best interests of the film, commercially or artistically."[44] Such artistic empathy and passion for the art itself is a particularly essential characteristic for managers employed in, or founders of, pioneer producers, as will become clear in the following discussion.

PIONEER ENTREPRENEURSHIP IN THE PRODUCER ROLE

The difficulties in finding a market for creative works are further intensified in the case of radically innovative products. Given that radically new cultural goods are often received with wariness or hostility by a large segment of consumers,[45] pioneer producers, whose continued existence depends on consumers' acceptance and purchase of the goods they produce, place the entire firm at risk of failure when they engage in bringing such goods to market. Although maverick creators may create—without regard to consumers' tastes—goods that are not easily understood or accepted by consumers, producers do not have this luxury. By definition, producers must engage with the rational-economic norms of the market and therefore must, in general, be more pragmatic when it comes to selecting and offering progressive or avant-garde content. Thus, creators who create goods that depart radically from prevailing norms may not find producers willing to take a risk on their work. These creators may then found their own firms, but if so they face the challenges described earlier in this chapter: their success depends on finding a business partner who is as energized as they are by the work and whose partnership will leave the creator free to focus on creation. Such a partner may be only slightly less rare than a manager at an existing producer firm willing to take a risk on the new category. Moreover, managers in extant producer firms that do take on the risk of pioneering a category (by producing and selling a product that is unlikely to easily find a large market) must possess a sense of purpose that goes beyond profit and other economic objectives. In this way, such managers are not unlike artists, who are driven by more than pecuniary motives.

Pioneer producers, therefore, undertake the challenging task of market creation because they appreciate the art and believe in their ability to make others see the value of the new work. Managers in firms in the creative industries must possess some of the same characteristics that mark great creators—vision, confidence, and drive. Further, they must appreciate and understand creators and promote their work with authenticity to overcome resistance to and questions about the value of innovative works and, subsequently, create a market. These efforts are not always successful given the significant degree of uncertainty regarding the appeal of radically novel works that subvert the status quo, which is exacerbated by the fact that producers have limited influence on consumers' evaluation of the goods and, moreover, cannot influence the independent evaluations and discourse of intermediaries.

Despite this considerable risk, cultural innovations in the market occur repeatedly, if not frequently. The nature of the individuals attracted to the creative industries underlies this paradox. Much like the creators whose works they bring to market, the managers at firms in creative industries are also often driven by more than pecuniary motivations and, moreover, have often entered the field out of love and appreciation for the art. It is rare, for instance, to see a music company executive who dislikes music or a manager in a film studio who cannot appreciate a good film. These managers may not have the same tastes as creators or critics, but they have a sense of being involved in something more important than monetary considerations. Thus, for instance, when managers in creative industries are criticized for not being supportive of creators, a deeper look at their actions more often than not reveals that they are simply focused on a long-term strategy: balancing financial considerations against artistic motivations so that the more avant-garde creative works can be sustainably supported.[46,47]

Kinds of Radical Innovations That Need Pioneer Entrepreneurship

The disregard for audience reaction and marketability among artists leads creators and creator firms to pursue different innovations than producer firms. By their very nature, creators are more likely than producers to generate novel content, that is, an expression of a new idea, such as rap music (Sugar Hill Gang), cubism (Pablo Picasso), or modern literature (James Joyce). The creative and expressive drive that goads artists to "make it new,"[48] regardless of the potential for alienating audiences and consumers, means that creators are more likely to be at the frontier of generating novel but risky (from a business point of view) ideas. That said, some producers are willing to take a risk on such content, as Sugar Hill Records did with the first rap single, "Rapper's Delight,"[49] or as Picasso's dealers did and publishers have done with books such as *Ulysses*. Each of these innovations was first viewed as unseemly, strange, or even seditious and/or profane by consumers but was later embraced by audiences and revisited and claimed as a classic by progressive contemporaries and future generations. Thus, although producers may not themselves generate expressive or content innovations, they are nevertheless necessary for bringing these innovations to the market.

Producers that are interested in reaching the widest possible market and the largest number of consumers often create new ways of providing consumers access to creative works. Such innovations include the paperback book, Penguin's inexpensive vehicle for delivering books to a wider swath of society,[50] Saffronart's use of the Internet to sell twentieth-century art from India to potential collectors across the globe,[51] and, more recently, the innovative attempt to broadcast performances from the Metropolitan Opera or Broadway musicals from New York City to multiplexes across the United States.[52] The advent of the Internet has generated new opportunities for such distribution innovations and, therefore, for producer entrepreneurship. By lowering the cost of doing business, especially in the case of retail operations, the Internet has allowed producers to create, distribute, scale quickly, and, in some cases, to disrupt traditional industry structure. The large numbers of online fashion stores and the multiple online startups in the art space indicate that entrepreneurs are taking advantage of these opportunities.

As a medium for disseminating content, electronic formats and the Internet have generated entrepreneurial opportunities but have also posed great challenges to producers, especially in the spheres of music, film, and books. Producers have had to figure out everything from copyright protection to the intricacies of producing and distributing goods in a new format. Here, too, entrepreneurial initiatives have focused on distribution (for example, Netflix, e-book readers, Pandora) rather than content (startups such as Atavist are exceptions to this pattern, and Netflix has recently entered the arena of original programming). The main issue posed by the ubiquity and low cost of the digital medium is the potential for creators to reach audiences directly without needing the assistance of producers such as book publishers. However, as discussed previously, that path entails its own problems for creators, and it remains to be seen how far it will take those artists willing to undertake the commercial and marketing responsibilities that necessarily accompany this option. In rare cases, producers offer dual innovations—novel content delivered via a new vehicle. The recent example of Atavist—a publisher of digitally enhanced narrative long-form nonfiction—is a notable instance (the content is new, although some would argue it is not a new category of expression but rather falls within the category of narrative long-form nonfiction).[53]

These various innovations are accompanied by different risks. Given consumers' resistance to new ideas that challenge prevailing conceptions of appropriateness and/or value, content innovations (the expressions of new concepts or ideas) are the most difficult to sell and therefore the riskiest. In most situations, an innovative distribution mechanism merely requires behavioral change rather than ideological change and thus is easier to "sell" than a content innovation. Introducing a dual innovation—novel content via a novel delivery system—involves facing both ideological and behavioral challenges and therefore is extremely risky for a producer.

The process of entrepreneurship, especially pioneer entrepreneurship, as a producer is challenging due to the features of the process of creating cultural goods—individualistic, idiosyncratic, and not requiring the infrastructure of a firm. However, in this weakness lies the strength of the creative industries. The situation that creators can exist and create without producers, and that producers are separate from creators, offers some clear advantages for society. If creative industries did not allow artists to remain removed from the market, society would risk never being exposed to anything new because most consumers are perfectly satisfied to consume goods that meet their predetermined preferences and criteria of appropriateness, desirability, and value. Were it not for producers that devise strategies to balance the artistic and business realms in the process of creating markets for the artistic works created by artists, consumers would not be exposed to new ideas and expressions, and innovative artists would likely not be able to earn a living. Further, if creators and producers were not distinct entities with different means and goals, consumers might be exposed only to crowd-pleasing works that are perfectly adequate but do not in any way challenge the status quo.

Summing Up and Looking Ahead

The world of producers in creative industries is rife with contradictions. Although not essential to the creation of artistic works, they are, nevertheless, crucial to the process of bringing those works to appropriate audiences and consumers. They are sometimes reviled for ("crass") commercialism and populist pandering and other times acknowledged by both artists and society as saviors of the arts and culture. Caught in a complex web of meaning and value, they place their fortunes at the whims of subjective tastes but cannot overtly or excessively attempt to predict and/or manipulate these tastes, nor, definitively, the tastemakers. Business as usual in the case of producers in the creative industries involves managing these contradictions to maintain a remarkably tenuous balance. However, the existence of producers who attempt to overcome the challenges of market creation is very important to society, for these producers have essentially democratized access to artistic creations, which were once reserved for the enjoyment and edification of a privileged few. Moreover, in their willingness to take on the risk of bringing radical new categories of cultural goods to the market, producers have played an important role in pushing the boundaries of thought and expression at the societal level. The next two chapters in this section delve into the practical implications of these contradictions between culture and commerce, the pressures and the challenges they pose for producers, and the strategies that producers implement to address and overcome these challenges.

POWER AND UNPREDICTABILITY

Key Challenges Facing Producers

A new star—or new stars—may emerge. That's not only unpredictable; it's somewhat out of [their] hands. All they can do is put the best people in position and let them do their jobs. Good things are very likely to follow.

—Margaret Sullivan[1]

Gabrielle "Coco" Chanel, the iconic founder of the House of Chanel, created what are now considered the classic fixtures of a modern woman's wardrobe—the little black dress, Chanel No. 5 perfume, and the cardigan jacket—all of which were dramatic departures from the norms of women's fashion during the first half of the twentieth century when these designs were first introduced.[2] Despite the revolutionary nature of her designs, Chanel's work prevailed to such an extent that, when she passed away in 1971, her firm had been successful and well known for more than fifty years. Her aesthetic—modern, simple but stylish, and minimalist—changed the way women dressed in the twentieth century. Both customers and fashion writers heaped lavish admiration on her designs, which spawned many imitations.

Although the firm was in a reasonably healthy financial state at the time of Chanel's death, ten years later in 1981 the House of Chanel was struggling to regain its cultural dominance and financial strength. Certainly, it is natural for a fashion firm to lose its direction to a certain extent after the founding designer leaves, especially when the founder is someone of Coco Chanel's stature. However, it is notable that even a firm with a very strong reputation and good designers at its helm struggled after losing its original iconic designer. Despite the firm's long-term success and cultural impact, after Chanel's death it received little to no benefit of the doubt from stakeholders—including consumers and fashion journalists/reviewers—on account of its association with the acclaimed Coco Chanel. Its brand and reputation may have kept the firm alive, but they were insufficient to support the thriving success to which the firm was accustomed.

The case of Coco Chanel and her firm exemplifies the challenges that are common to all producers in creative industries. Due to the nature of creative industries and creators, the characteristics of (markets for) cultural goods, and consumers' resistance to novel cultural goods, producers operate in environments of extreme uncertainty and must typically forego substantial control over their destinies. Of course, firms in other industries also face constrained agency and limited influence over how they are perceived and evaluated by audiences and stakeholders, including customers. In the creative industries, however, the constraints are particularly severe because (among other factors) consumer tastes are inherently volatile and subjective,[3] intermediaries have a strong effect on markets for cultural goods but are beyond the influence of producers,[4] and cultural products have high symbolic value.[5] Fundamentally (as described in Chapter 6), producers in creative industries are subject to challenges that result from their position at the cusp of the cultural and commercial worlds, which are in tension with each other.[6]

Because the realms of culture and commerce have distinct conventions of worth and therefore different criteria for quality and success, actions that are appropriate in one realm are not necessarily acceptable in the other. Creators and producers in creative industries, as a result, inhabit an institutional system in which cultural capital and economic capital are seemingly at odds with each other, if not in full and direct opposition.[7] For example, writers (creators) and publishers (producers) of "popular" books that sell well in the mass market are frequently and rather disdainfully perceived as "sellouts" by their counterparts who produce literary or avant-garde works and receive critical acclaim and awards but generally do not make large amounts of money from their "highbrow" works, which are not widely popular. This phenomenon extends beyond books and the publishing industry; consider the disparity between the social status and financial wealth of opera singers and pop icons, or movie stars and stage thespians. As clarified in Chapter 6, producers, especially, cannot afford to lose sight of the fact that their very existence involves dealing with creators and their artistic works in juxtaposition with the vagaries of the marketplace. Operating at the edge of two worlds—culture and commerce—that are driven by contradictory institutional logics, producers must try to satisfy the requirements of both realms to maintain their standing as firms in the market for cultural goods. Producers, therefore, face constant dilemmas regarding which demands they should attempt to meet, what trade-offs their decisions will entail, and whether those trade-offs can be mitigated in any way. For reasons described next, the locus of these tensions is the product—the cultural good at the core of producers' existence, the selling of which is producers' raison d'être.

Managing the demands of both the cultural and commercial worlds entails paying close attention to broader societal norms of value, appropriateness, and desirability and how these play out in markets, both of which are significantly shaped and defined by intermediaries. Thus, intermediaries have significant control over producers' access to both cultural and financial resources, and this power imbalance is at the core of the tensions and challenges that producers face. Because the reactions and assessments of intermediaries are unpredictable, producers have a lot at stake every time they bring a product to market. Accordingly, producers must offer products of only the highest quality, created by the most talented creators. Thus, producers (and their profits) are perennially subject to the unpredictability generated by the power of three external forces—norms, intermediaries, and creators—that lead to the operational challenges that are outlined in this chapter.

Producers: Constrained by the Power of Norms, Intermediaries, and Creators

THE POWER OF NORMS

To understand the power of norms, it is necessary to revisit the elements of market creation (discussed in Chapter 1)—*commerce, commentary, culture,* and *consumption.* The framework emphasizes that prevailing cultural norms, which define the appropriateness and desirability of cultural goods, play a large role in shaping consumer preferences and, therefore, their purchase decisions. However, cultural goods are expressions of spontaneous, novel ideas or concepts that may or may not fit well within the current norms of society—the creativity and vision of artists sometimes leads them to express thoughts and ideas that may not be fully accepted or even understood by society. For example, imagine producers in the 1950s screening a (hypothetical) film depicting same-sex relationships in a positive light. Because such a film would not mesh with the social norms regarding appropriateness at the time, producers would likely find it difficult to gain a sizeable audience; that is, the film would not perform well in the market, earning limited, if any, revenues. Executives at a film studio could adopt one of two approaches to such a project: they could pass on the film, recognizing that it would face hostility and resistance and perform poorly in the market, or they could produce the film, knowingly sacrificing the prospect of making a profit but hoping to shape people's thinking about homosexuality and marriage.[8] As illustrated by this example, because innovative creative works often contradict prevailing norms, they are unlikely to fulfill the financial goals of firms, and thus they pit the cultural imperative against the business imperative. This opposition creates a dilemma for producers: always choosing to produce crowd-pleasing works makes sound business sense but will likely lower producers' prestige and status in the cultural world; at the same time, persistently producing cutting-edge artistic works could well put the firm out of business if consumers are not ready to favorably receive such works.[9]

At the core of a producer's dilemma is the reality that artists hold a mirror (or prism) up to society to respectively produce either works that reflect prevailing cultural norms or works that redirect these norms toward a new perspective.[10] In response, producers must decide whether to pursue a product strategy determined by the pull of markets (based on consumers' prevailing tastes and societal norms) or one determined by the push of the singular vision of the creator. A producer that chooses to do the former and *reflect* prevailing norms is safe from a business perspective because this strategy ensures that the work produced by the firm will be easily accepted by the market and society. The producer can, therefore, expect to earn revenues from sales. In contrast, producers that choose to *redirect* norms assume the risk of minimal consumer acceptance of the firm's creative works. This choice may lead to recognition, prestige, and/or awards but does not ensure revenues.[11]

This trade-off is best demonstrated by examples from the film industry. Mainstream movies seemingly hew to a known formula for popularity and audience acceptance, incorporating elements that are predictable crowd pleasers. In contrast, so-called independent films made by individuals with a singular vision and voice and little regard for audience tastes may shift societal beliefs and norms in new directions but usually make far less money. Reflection and redirection of norms are not binary extremes, however, but rather exist on a continuum, and the two can sometimes overlap (as described in the following paragraph). Firms should never produce goods that neither reflect nor redirect societal norms, because such goods would bring neither cultural prestige nor financial viability.

Products that both reflect and redirect cultural norms sound paradoxical, but firms can balance reflection and redirection within the same product by redirecting norms in a more palatable and less aggressive manner. In other words, a firm can present unconventional ideas in a conventional manner in the hopes of lowering audiences' resistance to the new ideas. This strategy is particularly visible in network TV shows in the United States; hits such as *Will & Grace* and *Friends*, although often criticized for their reliance on unimaginative sitcom tropes, have been acknowledged, in some circles, as particularly impactful vehicles that, precisely because of these nonthreatening tropes, managed to normalize socially marginal and taboo issues such as homosexuality, out-of-wedlock childbearing, and fertility treatments.[12]

This dual approach is similar to the framing strategy of pioneer entrepreneurs described in Chapter 2 (portraying a product as novel enough to stimulate consumers' interest but familiar enough to quell their anxiety).[13] Of course, as with optimal framing, the use of this approach raises the issue of managers potentially interfering with the creator's creative process. However, such manipulations are often performed by creators themselves, as in the example of Indian fashion designers (described in Chapter 2). Filmmakers, too, like creators of television shows, may adopt such balancing tactics, aware that audiences are not particularly keen on watching movies or TV series that are raw and disturbing but are more willing to accept radical ideas presented in small, possibly sugarcoated doses. Importantly, there is a fine line between explicitly reverse engineering or manipulating a creative work to meet imagined consumer preferences and empowering a creator to optimally balance conventional and unconventional elements of the work. Although stories abound of studio executives clashing with directors over the treatment of a particular film idea or story element, and it is true that some give-and-take is possible and necessary, there are also heroic examples of creators having stood their ground and managers having had the wisdom to let them present their ideas in the way they want to.[14] The latter approach allows a creator to produce high-quality work that both pushes artistic boundaries and has a substantial cultural and financial impact.

Another way producers can balance the reflection and redirection of norms is to focus on a conventional idea but with an unconventional treatment (for example, a traditional love story that features a homosexual couple rather than a heterosexual couple or a mainstream film with a strong female heroine). Such products may make some profits, but their audience will likely be small. Finally, sometimes creators focus only on redirecting norms—they present an unconventional idea in an unconventional manner. This type of cultural good entails the most financial risk because potential consumers may not be able to overcome their anxieties about a product that challenges their worldview. However, even though creators of such works may struggle to gain economic capital, they often have a strong influence on other creators (for example, such creators are often described in terms such as "a directors' director" or "a writers' writer").

THE POWER OF INTERMEDIARIES

The norms that exert power over producers are defined and intersubjectively disseminated chiefly via the discourse of market and nonmarket intermediaries. As a result, intermediaries exert considerable influence over producers' strategies and fortunes. Without the value-constructing discourse of intermediaries, producers would most likely be unable to effectively reach the consumer market and achieve financial viability. Although producers' advertisements, brochures, catalogs, press releases, and other publicity-seeking activities can and do emphasize the quality and value of the goods producers are selling, their transparent economic interest in amplifying the monetary value of their goods reduces the impact of their discourse.[15] For instance, many filmgoers have learned that "no movie is as good as its trailer," and therefore, when consumers make a decision about whether to watch a film, the trailer is less influential than a positive review by an independent and trusted film critic. As mentioned in Chapter 6, producers are aware of the importance of intermediaries' discourse, as shown by their frequent use of excerpts from reviews in film posters and trailers. Problematically, however, producers can neither accurately predict the reactions of intermediaries nor influence intermediaries to say positive things about the product. At most, producers can use intermediaries' discourse creatively within their promotional materials, for example, by quoting laudatory words or phrases from reviews out of context. In the end, producers have no option but to accept intermediaries' evaluations of their products.

The power of intermediaries is most visible and most extensive in the so-called highbrow sectors of the creative industries such as modern art, literary fiction, and opera. The reasons for this are twofold. First, creative works in these categories are more complex and are imbued with greater symbolism than works that are typically considered entertaining and simple—"popular" novels, mainstream "genre" films with crowd-pleasing formulas, "pop" music, and so forth. Thus, consumers rely more heavily on critical discourse to interpret complex cultural goods than to understand "popular" goods.[16] These putative lowbrow works are easily understood and appreciated by individuals because the works meet consumers' need for entertainment and/or escape from quotidian troubles and concerns. These works do not need to be decoded or explicated by *market* intermediaries; instead, the consumption of these cultural goods is guided by individuals' tastes and dispositions, which are based on the discourse of nonmarket intermediaries such as teachers and informal influencers like friends.[17]

The second reason intermediaries have such extensive power in the so-called highbrow sectors is that creators themselves usually crave cultural recognition from reputed critics, and they are aware that such recognition is typically not forthcoming for crowd-pleasing populist works. The case of Jennifer Weiner demonstrates as much. A writer of light-hearted romances, Weiner has enjoyed much commercial success as well as the adulation of female readers but has not been taken very seriously by the literary community or critics. This lack of consideration has led her to publicly allege that female writers are not given commensurate respect because the topics they write about, although important to their readers, are not considered weighty enough for consideration by serious intellectuals.[18] Thus, both consumers and creators grant intermediaries a significant degree of power, and producers bear the brunt of it.

In this situation, producers face certain trade-offs as they decide how to appeal to potential consumers. To circumvent intermediaries and maintain an advantageous business position, producers can appeal directly to consumers by producing popular goods that provide consumers with amusing diversions and do not require the instruction provided by expert intermediaries. By choosing this approach, however, producers may lose their credibility and status in the cultural realm, even as they may maintain a highly favorable financial position. Society's contrasting impressions of independent and mainstream filmmakers reflect this duality: the former are generally considered "artists" or "auteurs" (with these labels carrying positive connotations) whereas the latter are viewed as "entertainers." Producers, therefore, determine their priorities and goals based on the motivations of the firms' founders and/or managers and act accordingly.

Even if creators and/or producers of less complex cultural goods do not care about artistic prestige or the approval of reputed critics and award-granting organizations (that is, intermediaries that instruct and include), they are still likely to need intermediaries that provide information (that is, intermediaries that introduce) to introduce their products to consumers. The offerings of these producers might, however, be subject to fewer evaluations, especially if the works are brought to market as part of a series (such as the *Twilight* novels or James Patterson's crime procedurals featuring Alex Cross) that has an established following. Similarly, adaptations of already beloved works for another medium—film adaptations of books, for instance, or theatrical adaptations of films—have ready-made audiences; even though the adaptation may be unfavorably compared to the original, it is likely to attain reasonable commercial success without needing much help from intermediaries.[19]

Fundamentally, the powerful position of intermediaries means that producers in creative industries can neither harbor nor create illusions about the quality of their products. If producers wish to ensure the approval of intermediaries, they must strive to produce goods of excellent quality and hope that these goods secure the attention and approval of intermediaries while avoiding any blatant attempts to curry favor with influential intermediaries. The only way to secure intermediaries' approval is by offering goods that merit it—it is difficult to game a properly functioning system. Further, producers cannot anticipate the reactions of intermediaries or produce only goods that align with intermediaries' past revealed preferences, both because those preferences may change and because skillful and principled creators will not create works that meet specific requirements, that is, create "to specs."[20] High quality, then, is the only recourse for producers hoping to generate cultural approval (which, in turn, could lead to higher revenues); as a result, good taste (as defined by the prevailing cultural discourse) is a critical qualification for individuals who make decisions regarding the goods to be produced.[21]

THE POWER OF CREATORS

The quality of the product, which is the direct manifestation of the creator's creativity and talent, is as important (or more important) to a creative firm's success as branding, marketing, and advertising—hence the adage about being only as good as one's last (created or produced) work of art.[22] To produce goods of excellent quality that will earn intermediaries' approval, producers must have access to highly talented creators. Thus, creators possess a certain degree of power in their interactions with producers.

The few creators with a known track record of skill and a good reputation among intermediaries are extremely valuable to producers, which contributes to the "winner takes all" nature[23] of creative fields. These creators are in a much better position than the average creator (or new unknown creators) with respect to negotiating with producer firms; consider, for example, the travails of new writers, whose completed manuscripts land in the slush piles of editors at major publishing houses, in contrast to the multimillion dollar advances offered to established writers for their as-yet-unwritten books. The majority of creators, in contrast, have little to no power in the creator producer relationship (if the winner takes all, the losers have nothing), first because they almost always need producer firms to bring their works to an audience[24] and second because creators are numerous, which lowers their bargaining power.

Creators within Creator Firms

In creator firms, creators bring their own creations to market by founding a firm with a business partner. The case of the House of Chanel's dependence on Coco Chanel, the creator and founder of the firm, demonstrates a problem common to all creator firms: although a founder's departure often leaves firms somewhat adrift, the situation is exacerbated in the case of creator firms in creative industries.[25] Despite Chanel's excellent reputation and the wide reach of the firm's promotional materials, the designs from the House of Chanel— and therefore its revenues—suffered in the absence of the firm's founder. Creator firms such as fashion houses typically face the challenge of associating with high-quality creators only on the occasion of succession, that is, when either the founding creator or her or his successor must be replaced by another individual.[26] Although the infrequency of succession may suggest that the need to associate with high-quality creators is less challenging for creator firms, these firms' near-complete dependence on a single individual can make succession events potentially fatal. The difficulty of such a transition is exacerbated by two somewhat contradictory needs: the firm must remain true to both the quality of the work and the image of the firm established and nurtured by the departing founder/creator but must avoid installing a "clone" of the previous creative director. The need to balance these opposing objectives is another consequence of the importance of intermediaries, who typically do not hesitate to critique firms for either producing stale noninnovative works that rehash the tried-and-tested ideas of the previous creator or for departing (too) far from the ideas and work that made the previous creator successful—especially if the firm's innovations are hollow ideas with only shock value.

The following passage provides a clear example of these points; the excerpt is from an article about the two designers—Maria Grazia Chiuri and Pierpaolo Piccioli—at the helm of the design firm Valentino, named after its founding designer, Valentino Garavani:[27]

> When they first took over the collection, Ms. Chiuri and Mr. Piccioli were described as "very Valentino," which was meant as a compliment, at least in the eyes of Mr. Garavani's loyalists, if not critics who wanted to see something new. There was red, there was lace, there were cocktail dresses. Having designed accessories for Valentino for a decade, they understood, perhaps better than anyone, the codes of his house. Alesandra Facchinetti, a former Gucci designer, had immediately succeeded Mr. Garavani, but she was fired after two seasons of going too far in her own direction. (Ms. Facchinetti has recently joined Tod's as creative director.) Replacing any designer is like walking a tightrope; replacing Mr. Garavani is like walking on a thread. Ms. Chiuri and Mr. Piccioli have managed to do that better than anyone might have imagined, and they are now coming into their own. Their most recent collections have included designs that are often regal and conservative in appearance, like church dresses, with high collars, but with lively filigree or floral lace patterns. It looks nothing like Valentino of old, and no one has complained.

The excerpt also shows that when firms search for a replacement for the chief creator, they tend to interpret certain traits or characteristics of a creator/creative product as indicators of talent or quality. Some of these indicators include the reputation of the creator, past sales performance of the creator's works as well as the works of similar others, and the creator's alignment with prevailing tastes and norms (or in the case of truly innovative work, the "appetite" among intermediaries and consumers and the potential for market creation). As a consequence, creators with a track record of critical acclaim and/or consumer appeal are highly sought after by producers and can often be the subject of feuds among rival producers. Such fighting over creators occurs in both creator firms, as when fashion designers move between firms, and (as described next) producer firms, as when publishers or agents engage in a bidding war in pursuit of a sought-after author. For instance, when the phenomenally successful writer J. K. Rowling, author of the famed Harry Potter series, announced her intent to switch agents in 2011, there was extensive speculation as to who would be the new agent,[28] with many vying to occupy the spot.[29]

Creators in Producer Firms

Although creator firms usually need to establish a partnership with a high-quality creator only on succession, producer firms face the challenge of associating with and acquiring the works of talented creators on an almost constant basis. Further, unlike creator firms, which sell only the products of the founding creator, producer firms sell the products of creators of their choice. Although this scenario may seem more advantageous than that of creator firms, producer firms must also take on content risk—the risk that a work that the firm acquires (at some not insignificant cost) will not sell. Because the demand for creative works is uncertain, it is difficult for producers to assess this risk ex ante, and thus it is important for them to have access to as many creators as possible in order to mitigate such content risk.

Producers must avoid both false positive and false negative assessments of potential in their quest for talented creators. In the former case, producers are liable to lose the money spent on discovering and supporting the creator and marketing the creative work if the creator's work is not respected or appreciated by intermediaries and/or consumers. Further, they may lose a certain degree of credibility as identifiers of (popular or critical) winners. However, as long as their reputation as a discerning producer is not permanently damaged, most producers are willing to incur this risk and chalk up any losses as the cost of doing business. The latter mistake is more serious; it occurs when a producer assesses the potential of a creator's work as negligible when it is actually substantial, thus losing the revenues that the creator's work would have produced. A well-known example of a false negative assessment is the case of J. K. Rowling, who was reportedly turned down by twelve publishing houses before Bloomsbury (UK) decided to take a chance on her book *Harry Potter and the Philosopher's Stone*, which eventually became the foundation of the Harry Potter series, the biggest publishing success in history.[30] Although Rowling's case is an extreme example, a quick comparison of the costs of publishing a book to the total revenues from the sales of a typical *New York Times* best seller (not counting additional potential revenue streams such as licensing for films or merchandise) demonstrates why producers are far more worried about false negative assessments than false positives. Producers often use structural means, such as having a strategically diverse portfolio of creators and/or works (Chapter 8 explores this strategy in detail), to mitigate their dependence on talented creators and lower the cost of mistakes.

The Process of Finding High-Quality Creators

As a consequence of their extreme reliance on creators, producers strive to identify indicators of quality. However, absent a clear track record or objective measures of quality, such indicators are difficult to detect or even define. To successfully identify high-quality creators, managers in the creative industries—particularly those that form the interface between the market/firm and the creator, such as editors (at publishing houses), A&R (artists and repertoire) managers (at music firms), and creative executives (at film or TV studios)—must have superb discernment and taste. These individuals must also be able to nurture, support, and communicate seamlessly with creators. Because these skills are difficult to teach, skillful managers are critical assets of the firm who, much like creators, must be nurtured and supported. When their tenure at the firm ends, replacing such managers is almost as challenging as replacing the creative head of a firm.

In creative industries, the replacement of key creative individuals is often accomplished via different means than in other industries—creator firms tend to prefer hiring a replacement from within the firm, choosing someone who was trained and mentored by the departing creator. However, although a successful editor or manager is just as important as a successful creator, replacements for these positions are often hired from outside the firm. This outside hiring strategy is the result of hiring practices in the creative industries and the inherent competitive pressures. A typical career path in the creative industries involves a long "apprenticeship," during which, ostensibly, a young employee is mentored and hones the intangible skills needed for the job. Because there are no clear markers of the required abilities, firms employ a brutal elimination process; firms tend to hire more people than necessary at the lowest levels with the intention of culling those who do not demonstrate the required abilities over time. Given this lengthy and expensive process of skill development and assessment, someone trained at a reputed firm, under the supervision of a respected editor or manager, is extremely valuable to firms that are striving to catch up with the industry leader. Such well-trained individuals, therefore, have an advantage over others if and when they decide to look for another job; this eventual advantage is a major reason young employees are willing to suffer ignominy and uncertainty in the early years of their career. Moreover, the lengthy process these apprentices endure and the paucity of the monetary compensation or nonmonetary appreciation they receive make it easy for other firms to lure them away with the promise of a promotion. When that happens, the apprentice's original firm may look outside the firm for a replacement, thus setting in motion a chain of events that ripples through the entire industry.[31]

The resulting cross-fertilization across firms may have certain benefits: best practices are transferred, ideas are pressure-tested in new environments and subsequently refined, and fresh perspectives are introduced, with a resulting net positive outcome for firms, creators, and society. Naturally, these benefits are much more significant for creator firms, where the movement of the main creative talent across firms leads to more direct cross-fertilization as the creative abilities of a new creator are juxtaposed against the "house style." The movement of creators across producer firms, often denigrated as "talent poaching," is more likely to generate unnecessary switching costs, both tangible and intangible, for all parties involved.

Each of these challenges created by the power imbalance between producers and the forces that shape their fortunes—norms, intermediaries, and creators—is exacerbated in the case of entrepreneurial ventures, whether pioneering a new category or not, especially new producers because they are typically quite powerless at the time of founding. At the same time, as described next, the situation may be reversed in the context of entrepreneurship in one instance: the power that intermediaries possess in market making can, in fact, turn out to be beneficial to entrepreneurs in the producer role, especially in the case of pioneer producers.

Entrepreneurship in an Environment of Power Imbalances

NEW PRODUCER FIRMS: THE CHALLENGE OF GAINING ACCESS TO CREATORS

All new ventures are at a considerable disadvantage relative to existing firms, especially in terms of the tangible and intangible resources that are necessary for success. In the case of new producer firms in creative industries, the most pressing concern is gaining access to creators. Newly founded producer firms operating in existing categories of cultural goods (a new publisher of romance novels, for example) must compete with larger, more powerful incumbents that have plentiful resources, most important being a reputation that attracts the best creators and the most visibility in the marketplace. Most new producer firms, therefore, much like new ventures in other industries, can hope only to dance between elephants' feet, which is to say that they can and should attempt to occupy niches in the marketplace where consumers, creators, or both are underserved. For instance, despite significant concentration in the publishing industry, which consists of five very large firms ("The Big Five," previously "The Big Six" before the merger of Random House and Penguin), there are scores of independent publishers.[32,33]

For society, a diverse set of organizations that bring a similarly diverse range of ideas to the marketplace is a central cause (and effect) of a vibrant and open culture that allows dialogue and debate (even if the new producers are not pioneering a new category). This is true across creative industries; consider, for example, the importance of independent film studios or small avantgarde galleries or theater companies, which take risks on ideas and works that have uncertain and unproven demand. Large producers with much more to lose might be unwilling or unlikely to take such chances, leaving the door open for new adventurous firms (that thusly "dance between elephants' feet"). Many of these risky ventures eventually contribute to mainstream culture, as in the case of the American Repertory Theater (A.R.T.) in Cambridge, Massachusetts, whose innovative productions have found their way to Broadway and the Tony Awards.[34] Independent producers that are new and/or small, therefore, often serve as research laboratories for larger, more risk-averse producers, precisely because these firms, in their quest to start up and survive, occupy the interstices in the ecosystem.

The difficulty of gaining access to talented creators puts new producer firms at an extreme disadvantage, relative even to new ventures in other industries, which, at the very least, have some control over the anticipated quality and production of the goods they sell. In noncreative industries, this modicum of control helps new ventures develop an overall strategy to avoid a head-on confrontation with incumbent firms in the marketplace. New producer firms in creative industries, in contrast, can do little in the way of strategic planning, other than to be different and hope to discover talented creators that have gone unnoticed for reasons other than the quality of their work. Small boutiques, independent music and book publishers, film studios, and new galleries all base their business plans on their founders' confidence in their discernment and ability to spot and groom talent. These firms start by signing agreements or contracts with a few creators whose work they admire and believe consumers will admire and appreciate too. Problematically, however, the reputation of producer firms matters considerably, not only to consumers but also to creators, who stand to benefit from an affiliation with a reputed producer firm. Further, well-known and/or high-quality creators are unlikely to choose to work with a new and relatively unknown producer firm. New ventures are therefore frequently left with no choice but to work with new and lesser-known artists, whose works are of uncertain quality and value, leading to the need for market-creating efforts.

Although gaining access to creators is a significant operational challenge for new producers, the power of intermediaries can prove to be a boon to these firms. Because both the creator and the producer firm are relatively unknown, the products brought to market by new ventures would have a low chance of being noticed and/or evaluated were it not for the independence of intermediaries. Independent intermediaries pay attention to producers and products without regard to status, reputation, market power, or resources and therefore help to level the playing field and consequently promote innovation and entrepreneurship in creative industries. Further, expert intermediaries remain open minded about new creations, evaluate and explicate their quality, and sometimes offer an endorsement. Thus, the existence of such intermediaries, although sometimes a source of uncertainty and fear, is simultaneously a benefaction for new producer firms. That said, new ventures do not get a free pass—being reviewed does not necessarily mean getting a good review. Therefore, the talent of a new firm's partner creators and the quality of the produced work are extremely important to the longevity and success of new producers.

THE UNIQUE SITUATION OF NEW CREATOR FIRMS

New creator firms inhabit a somewhat different situation than new producer firms. The problem of gaining access to quality creators is less pronounced. In addition, such firms do not choose which goods to offer by identifying an overlooked niche but rather are founded largely because individual creators with a particular vision wish to bring their products to market while retaining the freedom to create without intervention. To be sure, business partners of creators often frame the firm's products in language that implies strategic thinking and design on the part of the creator, making assertions such as (hypothetically), "We noticed there was a gap in the market; there are no stylish, unique, but affordable professional clothes for women aged twenty-five to forty," or, "What we saw was a need for a fresh Continental take on Southern cuisine, in which the chef specializes." This type of commentary, which is often a post hoc rationalization of the product the creator wanted to create anyway, is an instance of market making, in which creators' business partners must engage.

Although creator firms do not face the problem of finding creators as a new venture, growth can be difficult for creator firms for a couple of reasons. A single individual (the creator founder) can produce only a certain volume of goods (whereas a producer firm can grow by working with more creators). In addition, the creator's vision is so central to the product's desirability in the eyes of consumers that scaling output by hiring other individuals must be undertaken with great caution, if at all. Further, the creator's imagination and creativity may act as a bottleneck—the firm may be unable to produce additional new goods until the creator is further inspired. Even if the ideas come rapidly and plentifully, the process of manifesting these ideas in a painting, poem, novel, film, song, or other product cannot be forcibly accelerated.[35]

PIONEER PRODUCERS

Pioneer producers (whether new or existing firms), face a somewhat different set of obstacles than new producers in established categories. Because the works they bring to market neither fit into existing categories of goods nor align with prevailing cultural norms, pioneer producers experience norms as all-important, controlling, and constraining. In contrast, the power of creators is a nonissue for pioneer producers; whether they are creator firms or producer firms, for pioneers the creator is a known entity and the product is a foregone conclusion. However, the quality of the product is still important—novelty, even radical novelty, if unaccompanied by superior quality is not sufficient to gain the respect and favor of intermediaries.

Because norms are so important for pioneer producers, intermediaries—who have the power to change norms—play a central role in shaping the success of pioneer producers. Pioneer producers must engage in more value-constructing discourse than other producers while also engaging in strategic actions (detailed in the first two chapters of the book) to generate an optimal understanding of the product among consumers. However, even if pioneer producers successfully generate an optimal understanding of the new cultural good, they still need intermediaries to create the market; therefore, intermediaries are very useful to pioneer producers and very powerful. Creating a market for a new category of goods requires independent intermediaries, especially expert ones; only intermediaries with both the expertise necessary to contextualize an innovation that is unlike anything seen before and the independence necessary to avoid any vested interests and withstand any pressure can adequately convey the meaning and value of new cultural goods to consumers and other stakeholders in the ecosystem.

Paradoxically, however, there may not be any appropriate intermediaries. Intermediaries that have expertise in the new category might not exist yet, and existing intermediaries may be unwilling, for a variety of reasons, to generate any valuation discourse for the new good. Thus, as in the case of hip-hop as a category, pioneer producers often need corresponding pioneer intermediaries to succeed in creating a market, which only strengthens the power imbalance between intermediaries and pioneer producers.

For pioneer producers that do not target lay consumers (for example. literary agents), trade intermediaries play a more influential role than consumer intermediaries. These pioneers typically have greater agency and control, largely due to the interpersonal nature of their transactions. Instead of changing the minds of scores of dispersed consumers, literary agents, for instance, need only to convince an editor at a publishing house to give the (potentially strange and/or incomprehensible) new manuscript a fair read. The agent's track record or the strength of the relationship between the editor and the agent can ease the interaction and thus the innovative novel or other work may face less resistance. Although the editor may still turn the book down, the job of the agent is less fraught and more manageable than that facing the publisher (should the editor accept the book).[36] Importantly, the success of these pioneers (agents and brokers) is still governed to a certain extent by the discourse of nonmarket intermediaries even if this influence is not directly visible in their specific market transactions. Because schools and other venues of instruction that reside outside the market provide individuals with a general understanding of various kinds of cultural goods and establish a set of foundational criteria for quality, editors and literary agents often agree on whether a new style of writing or a new idea, although seemingly strange, is nevertheless of high quality. Intermediaries, both within and beyond the market, therefore, have a very real and important influence on pioneer producers.

Summing Up and Looking Ahead

Being a producer in the creative industries is not easy. Although the business model of producers is straightforward (relative to that of intermediaries), and examples abound of strong and financially successful producers in all of the creative industries, producers may not feel all that powerful on a day-to-day basis. Producers are constrained in their operations by the power wielded over them and their fortunes by cultural norms, intermediaries, and creators. The primary operational challenges faced by producers in creative industries are the result of the fundamental tension between the cultural and commercial worlds. Society has always placed artistic expression on a pedestal of social impact, believing art to be the stimulus for and/or consequence of new ideas or viewpoints, the engine driving social and cultural change, and the conscience of society (ensuring that society is not completely controlled by the self-interested participants in markets, and politics). And, yet, today most production and consumption of art and creative works occur within the confines and rules of the market and are governed by firms that engage in economic transactions. The main question facing managers in firms, therefore, is how to meet the opposing demands placed on them by stakeholders who expect them to uphold both their fiduciary and artistic duties. Chapter 8 examines the specific strategies producers adopt to balance the cultural and financial imperatives they face.

PURPOSE AND PROFIT

Strategies for Balancing Cultural
and Financial Imperatives

The artist who hopes to market work that is the realization of his
gifts cannot begin with the market. . . . First, the artist . . . make[s]
some peace with the market . . . once the work is made he allows
himself some contact with the market. . . . if he is successful in the
marketplace, he . . . contributes his earnings to the support of his art.
                                                      —Lewis Hyde[1]

In 2001, a controversy erupted when author Jonathan Franzen publicly declared, "She has picked enough schmaltzy, one-dimensional [books] that I
cringe," and further asserted, ". . . [my] novel is a hard book for that audience." Franzen was referring to Oprah Winfrey's 2001 selection of his novel
The Corrections for her book list, an annual compilation of books she had
enjoyed and was recommending to her millions of viewers. Franzen's public
displeasure and refusal to acknowledge his selection as an honor led Winfrey to retract an invitation to appear on her television show.[2] Winfrey was, at
the time, an eminent intermediary, her influence on the market the result of
many consumers aspiring to be like her or identifying with her persona (see
Chapter 4 for a full description of this type of identity-based inclusion). The
inclusion of a book on her book list had been known to result in a significant
increase in the sales figures for that book.[3] Oprah's book list was, as a consequence, closely watched by publishers, and a spot on the list was highly coveted. Franzen reacted dismissively to being selected, despite these advantages,
largely because most individuals working within the creative industries believe there is a dramatic dissonance (and almost no overlap) between artistic
success and commercial success. His remarks suggest that Franzen worried
that being on the list, which was known for featuring crowd-pleasing novels,
would adversely affect his standing as a serious writer among the critics and
peers he respected. This conflict between art and commerce affects all of the

actors—creators, producers, and intermediaries—that constitute the creative industries and is at the core of the issues covered in this chapter.

The creative industries bridge the seemingly antipodal worlds of art and business and the entities within these industries are therefore regularly pulled in opposite directions. Nowhere is this tension felt more strongly than within firms engaged in bringing creative works to the market. These firms—the producers (both creator firms and producer firms)—have a direct economic interest in ensuring that the works sell well and therefore must play by the rules of the commercial world of business and the market. At the same time, producers must understand and align with the world of artists and their values to gain access to works for the market. Although intermediaries also endure these countervailing forces, they do not have a direct financial imperative to sell creative works themselves, and thus this tension is less salient to them and its economic implications less harmful than in the case of producers.

Given that producers' stated goal and the primary focus of their role in the creative industries is to sell creative works, it seems surprising that high sales and commercial success can be a source of concern and conflict for this group. However, a firm that resides and succeeds purely in the commercial world, with no *locus standi* in the cultural world, risks losing its status as a cultural producer; therefore producers must maintain a fine balance between the demands of both worlds. The primary cause of the artistic–commercial tension is the differences in institutional logics—the rules and norms of behavior that govern entities operating in any self-contained world—of art and business. These two institutional logics are based on different understandings of the market economy and the cultural world and thus embrace different, almost oppositional metrics of worth. (See Chapter 6 for a detailed discussion of institutional logics.) Being a producer in the creative industries entails dealing with the logics of both worlds and following the creeds of both by acquiring cultural and artistic value as well as financial viability.

Although producers are the entities most challenged by the contradictions between the art and market worlds, creators also experience these opposing forces, though in a slightly different way. In his controversial statement, Franzen verbalized precisely these contradictions—he rejected the promise of economic capital to retain cultural capital. As discussed previously, the currency of creators is not only, and not even predominantly, monetary;[4] rather, artists trade (and revel) in self-expression and self-actualization in the form of works that receive praise from expert critics.[5] Both scholars and consumers, therefore, understand the cultural world and the economic world as pursuing opposing goals;[6] further, the esoteric, penurious artist who creates deep, multifaceted, intricate works is granted much higher status than a significantly wealthier artist who creates light, entertaining fare that is liked, consumed, and paid for by many consumers. Hence, Franzen's dismissal of a book list that, by association, placed him in the latter category of artists (because Oprah Winfrey's influence was based not on literary expertise or the ability to validate literary innovation and quality but rather her social value among a large portion of the population) despite the economic benefits of such inclusion. In their day-to-day activities, creators constantly make this type of trade-off between the desire to create and the necessity of earning a living, and successful artists use a specific set of strategies to achieve this balance.

Creators' Strategies for Practicing Art in a Market-Oriented World

Creators use three strategies—selling artwork, working in an adjacent creative realm, and working in an unrelated field—to navigate the tricky terrain at the intersection of art and business.[7] These strategies can be explained in terms of the degree to which the cultural and financial worlds of a creator overlap.

THE IDEAL: SELLING ARTWORK

First, some artists make a living directly from creating art (that is, by selling art); in this strategy, there is no separation between the artistic and market spheres. Whether the artist sets up a storefront or a website to sell the works or approaches a producer firm to do the same, adopting this strategy means the artwork must sell and sell at prices sufficient to meet the artist's financial needs. This strategy is not without risk because it is unclear what will appeal to consumers. Further, as Hyde admonishes (in the epigraph at the beginning of this chapter), an artist cannot and should not "start with the market"[8] because doing so will result not in art but rather in anodyne crowd-pleasers. The financial risk is still present, albeit somewhat alleviated, when a producer is involved in creating a market for the work. The artist must still (as described in Chapter 6) "sell" the work to the producer, if not to the final consumer. Despite the inherent financial risk, most creative individuals' first choice is to earn a living via sales of their work.[9] Adopting this strategy has always been the prerogative of only the very best and most talented creators; moreover, by all accounts, this has become more difficult to implement over time.

A COMPROMISE: WORKING IN AN ADJACENT CREATIVE REALM

A second strategy available to individual creators is working in an adjacent creative realm that is more commercial, and thus more financially viable, than the putative "pure/fine arts." Examples of such arrangements abound: the abstract artist who works in an advertising agency, the novelist who writes tourism brochures or blurbs in catalogs, the modern dancer who auditions for commercials, the composer who writes film scores or advertising jingles, and so on. In these examples, individuals attempt to minimize the financial risk inherent to the first tactic while still utilizing their painstakingly honed artistic abilities. Many artists who choose this path continue to practice their own art in their free time. Their "pure" art and its commercial counterpart can even benefit from each other, so that the separation between the two facets of their lives—their day job and their art making—is not complete.

ONLY IF NECESSARY: WORKING IN AN UNRELATED FIELD

In the final strategy—typically adopted out of necessity rather than choice—artists work in an entirely unrelated field. For example, nineteenth-century British novelist Anthony Trollope worked as a postal employee for much of his early life but still dedicated three hours each day to his writing.[10] Certainly, some artists may intentionally decide to work in an unrelated field to maximize either tangible or intangible benefits and will select the field accordingly. For instance, a painter may opt to become an investment banker to make enough money to retire early and pursue painting as a full-time profession. Similarly, a writer may become a security guard or a chauffeur/cab driver to maximize both flexibility and the amount of free time available for writing.

For artists who pursue this strategy, the separation between their creative life and their financial life is temporal ("I'll paint after I retire"), cognitive ("I'll write the great American novel in between ferrying passengers in my cab"), or sometimes both. Artists often take on unrelated jobs while they wait to break into the creative field of their choice. Large urban centers for creative industries—New York, London, Paris, Los Angeles, Hong Kong—are typically teeming with, for example, baristas who want to be writers, and bartenders and wait staff who audition for roles in plays or films during their free time.

This method of managing both worlds can be overwhelming and is both emotionally and physically difficult, as any artist who has experienced this life can testify. Artists should therefore take this path only if the two strategies described previously are not viable options for them for various reasons.

Parallel Strategies for Producers

The strategies that creators adopt at the individual level can be executed by producers at the organizational level. The three primary producer strategies are blending the cultural and commercial worlds, loose coupling/building a portfolio, and decoupling (the two worlds). These strategies can be understood as falling along a continuum of the extent of the overlap of the cultural and commercial spheres.[11]

BLENDING THE CULTURAL AND COMMERCIAL WORLDS

As the term suggests, the *blending* strategy (which parallels creators' strategy of selling their artwork) entails focusing on a single product/category to simultaneously tap into the orders of worth of both the cultural and commercial worlds (see Table 8.1). Firms that use the blending strategy fulfill both institutional logics via the production and distribution of a single product or product line. Such firms earn revenues from selling avant-garde, exclusive, and innovative goods to connoisseurs, who are willing to pay for the privilege of experiencing the artistry. Haute cuisine restaurants, auction houses and galleries, high-end design firms (for example, product and fashion design,

TABLE 8.1.   Producers' strategies for balancing cultural and financial imperatives.

Strategy	Distance between logics	Product/ product lines	Economic capital	Cultural capital	Convertibility of capital (both types)
Blending	Small or none	**A (only one product line)**	Primary	Primary	High
Loose coupling	Moderate	A	Primary	Secondary	Medium
		B	Secondary	Primary	
Portfolio	Moderate	A	Primary	Secondary	Low or none
		B	Secondary	Primary	
Decoupling	Large	A	Primary	N/A	N/A
		B	N/A	Primary	

architecture), and other producers that sell unique and inventive cultural goods to niche markets employ this strategy. With the exception of galleries and auction houses, most firms that use the blending strategy are creator firms.

The ability to adopt the blending strategy is, in many ways, a sweet spot for producers (as making a living by selling artwork is for creators); however, the strategy requires extensive market-creation to ensure sufficient sales of artistic, sometimes esoteric, products. Further, very few products fall into the category of goods that can have both a large financial impact and a significant cultural impact, and the markets for such products tend to be small, consisting of niche groups of consumers. An example of a firm that uses the blending strategy is Noma, the Copenhagen restaurant that serves "New Nordic" haute cuisine. Creative almost to a fault, Chef Redzepi's menu at Noma comprises dishes that are innovative interpretations of the locavore and sustainability movements; these dishes incorporate Nordic ingredients and are presented in unexpected ways. Although Noma now consistently sits at the top of global quality rankings for restaurants, consumers were initially slow to overcome their negative preconceptions of Nordic cuisine and their instinctive resistance to the radical inventiveness of certain dishes (for example. live shrimp, miso made from ground grasshoppers, and dishes containing ants).[12] Although creating a market for these high-concept artistic dishes was not easy, once the market had been developed, the restaurant offered Redzepi, as well as the many interns and trainee chefs who come to Noma to work and learn, a creatively fulfilling and self-actualizing experience. At the same time, the restaurant is profitable (albeit marginally) and thus is able to provide a livelihood for Redzepi and his fellow chefs.

The chief disadvantage of blending is that blended firms, although they may be profitable, can rarely scale beyond a certain point or grow profits rapidly. For example, Noma's elaborate meals cannot be prepared for more than seventy-five people a day, and establishing other locations is difficult, if not impossible, given that Redzepi's culinary creativity is integral to every dish. So although these firms can meet the imperatives of both the cultural world and the commercial world, they may sacrifice their ability to scale. Many firms that adopt blending, therefore, (must) measure success primarily in the metrics of cultural value and place somewhat less emphasis on continually growing or rapidly increasing economic returns. This requirement is much easier for privately owned and privately funded firms to meet.[13] Private businesses do not have to answer to market-oriented growth-driven shareholders and/or analysts and thus can avoid short-term pressure to produce earnings. As a result, they have the luxury of pursuing markets for products that are currently underappreciated and undervalued but may become valuable to consumers once a market has been created. As a corollary, many family-owned Italian design firms that follow the blending strategy, for example, attribute their cultural influence and iconic status to the fact that they are privately owned businesses that are run with patience and passion and seek to serve as a legacy for future generations of the family.[14]

The blending strategy is therefore suitable to firms with managers that are patient, have either artistic ability or credibility with artists, and are willing to measure worth in intangible terms, in addition to financial success. For instance, galleries and restaurants are notoriously slow to become profitable— they often run at a loss for several years, and yet their owners persist even at great financial cost because they derive satisfaction from engaging with artists and artworks and/or from sharing their work with a broader audience. For this same reason (a passion for working in the art world), the blending strategy is particularly applicable to and common among creator-firms such as design houses or restaurants,[15] where creators have strong nonpecuniary motivations and are often willing to collect a relatively low salary if they can create works without compromising their vision.

A MIDDLE GROUND: LOOSE COUPLING
AND BUILDING A PORTFOLIO

Just as blending is the organizational equivalent of creators making a living by selling their art, the next strategy parallels creators' strategy of working in an adjacent creative realm, thus neutralizing the risk inherent in depending on a single source of income from a product with a low likelihood of market success. The *portfolio* and *loose coupling* approaches are two similar but distinct versions of a strategy that falls between blending and segregation (described in the following section)—like artists working in an adjacent rather than entirely unrelated field, both approaches entail some degree of, but not total, separation between the artistic and business worlds (see Table 8.1).

Firms that adopt either the loose coupling or portfolio approaches produce a range of products; some, which have higher sales (though possibly at lower prices) are meant to meet the demands of the market logic, whereas others, which are usually responsible for lower total sales (though likely at higher prices) and less predictable revenue streams, are more artistic and in-novative and therefore more relevant to the cultural standing of the firm. This assortment balances the artistic and financial risks undertaken by the firm, while also helping it build and maintain worth in both worlds. Although both approaches maintain some distance (but not a complete separation) between the market-oriented and culture-oriented sides of the business, the two ap-proaches entail different relationships between these sides. In loose coupling, the (mass) market-oriented product(s) are rendered more desirable to con-sumers because of their association with the avant-garde products produced by the same firm; in the portfolio approach, there is no such effect of one side on the other.

Loose Coupling

Loose coupling is exemplified by the (weak) connections between design-ers' high-fashion collections, which are shown during fashion week, and the corresponding styles available to consumers in stores. The runway collec-tions contain the avant-garde products; intermediaries generate a valuation discourse about these products and evaluate them based on the designer's innovativeness and vision. For producers that adopt loose coupling (in this example, fashion firms), the avant-garde products and the related discourse maintain the firm's artistic standing and prestige while also conveying the value of the firm and its products to consumers.[16] However, the avant-garde products appeal to and are accessible to only a small niche consumer segment—individuals who are both wealthy and fashion forward. The firm's other products—the ready-to-wear lines available in department stores, which are usually toned-down adaptations of the flamboyant runway collections—are targeted toward a much larger consumer base.

The discourse about the runway collections (which appears primarily in fashion magazines) grants the firm visibility and prestige and thus benefits the firm's market-oriented products, which acquire prestige from their associa-tion with the high-concept runway styles that have significant artistic value. This association converts some of the symbolic value from one side of the firm into financial value, because the connection between the two sides of the busi-ness induces consumers to pay more for the mass-market products and thus increases the firm's revenues. Because these styles are consumed by a larger portion of the population, they sustain the financial viability of the firm. In this strategy, the art-oriented products and the market-oriented products are presented under the same label and created by (or at least portrayed as being created by) the same designer.[17] The sales of the ready-to-wear garments fund the production of the avant-garde runway products, and the visibility of the avant-garde products increases the symbolic and commercial value of the ready-to-wear line.

Other than blending, loose coupling is the only strategy that is executable for creator firms. One of the chief problems associated with this approach, however, is the need for the firm to continue activities that may not be producing profits (such as presenting exorbitantly expensive fashion shows, which are considered the cost of entry into the high-culture world for high-end fashion firms). These activities are usually rationalized as "marketing" expenses, and, although they do serve that purpose in a sense, there is not necessarily a clear causal link between financial viability and these expenditures.

Building a Portfolio

The portfolio approach differs from loose coupling in two ways: first, there is less spillover between the firm's product lines; second, the portfolio strategy is suitable only for producer firms, whereas loose coupling is equally suitable for both.[18] In this approach—one of the most widely used strategies among firms in many of the creative industries—firms produce a portfolio of products comprising a judicious combination of works to balance financial and cultural imperatives. Producers using this strategy offer multiple lines of products from many creators, ranging from goods with a high level of market risk as well as a high level of cultural capital to goods that have a predictable and steady market demand but are unlikely to garner much, if any, cultural prestige. Producer firms often employ the portfolio strategy because they can engage with and acquire multiple creators who forge works with varying artistic and symbolic content; in contrast, creator firms are precluded from this strategy because, by definition, they sell works by a single creator.

The portfolio strategy typically entails the existence of several brands/labels/imprints, all of which are business units within a single umbrella firm. Each label or imprint is associated with the production of a certain type of creative work that falls somewhere on a continuum from high artistry to high popularity/market demand. Publishers are excellent examples of this strategic approach, as evidenced by the numerous imprints within any large publishing firm; the erstwhile Penguin Group, for instance, comprised fifty-two separate imprints ranging from the venerable Penguin Classics and Viking Press to the lucrative New American Library (which published historical romances and other genre fiction).[19] Both the so-called highbrow goods (for example, literary fiction) and the so-called lowbrow goods (such as genre fiction) bring a certain degree of either cultural or commercial capital to the firm (and, in exceedingly rare cases, both) without disrupting the firm's status in the other world. Similarly, music companies typically comprise a range of labels, ensuring that the balance between the cultural and business imperatives is maintained.

The portfolio strategy has both tangible and intangible costs. In tangible terms, it is expensive to maintain two or more segments of business because neither segment benefits from economies of scale or scope. Further, adopting this strategy entails the creation of loss-making business units/labels/imprints. Another major challenge of the portfolio strategy is achieving an ideal balance between risky/artistic and populist products: given that each iteration of a creative work is novel and has uncertain demand, it is difficult to derive a "formula" for determining how much of each type of work the firm should produce. However, firms can find one indicator of the optimal mix of products in a comparison of the number of awards/extent of critical acclaim received and the sales revenues (assuming that the two are somewhat orthogonal, which is not always true); moving too far in either direction may create an imbalance, at which point the firm and its management must decide to revise the strategy.

The Conversion of Cultural Capital to Economic Capital

Although the strategy of maintaining some separation between the cultural and commercial arenas within a firm may appear to be one form of the strategy of a firm offering "loss leaders" in their product portfolio (having the production of some products be subsidized by the sales of other products), this is not the case.[20] The main difference lies in the imperfect convertibility between the currencies of the worlds of culture and commerce. For instance, in the classic loss-leader pricing strategy, where some items are underpriced to stimulate sales of other higher- or full-price items, the resource that is the subject of the trade-off is financial capital; in other words, the economic resources that could have been obtained from the sales of one category of goods are obtained from the sales of another category of goods.[21] Because money is fungible, there is no loss due to the transmission of economic resources when these "subsidies" are applied. In contrast, the conversion of economic capital to cultural capital is neither frictionless nor perfectly equivalent. When a firm acquires cultural prestige, that cultural capital does not always convert into economic capital; even when it does produce economic capital, it does not do so in a perfect one-to-one correspondence. For example, although awards for literary novels or alternative films do indeed translate into greater sales and therefore revenues (as discussed in Chapter 4), the increase is relative *to the sales for goods in the same category that did not win awards*, not relative to populist goods that achieve best-seller or blockbuster status. In other words, although an award-winning literary novel would certainly make more money than it would have without the awards, it is rare for such a book, no matter how many awards it wins, to make the same amount of money as the Alex Cross series (or even one novel from the series) written by James Patterson.

In addition, although revenues from sales of best sellers and blockbusters allow the firm to take a chance on goods that are less commercially viable, the difficulty of predicting what products will garner the respect of intermediaries means that firms cannot be always sure that they are betting on the right product. Therefore, the loose coupling and portfolio strategies are less predictable in economic terms than most firms would like. Yet the final strategy— segregation or decoupling, which is described in the following section—is even more unpredictable and difficult to execute.

SEGREGATING THE CULTURAL AND COMMERCIAL WORLDS: DECOUPLING STRATEGIES

The decoupling strategy involves establishing and maintaining a strong (cognitive and/or structural) segregation between the culturally inventive and commercially predictable sides of a firm. There are two primary approaches to the decoupling strategy, offering completely independent product lines and becoming a nonprofit firm.

Offering Independent Product Lines

In this approach, there is a clear divide between the products that enhance the cultural standing of the producer and the products that benefit the firm's financial bottom line, and therefore consumers and other stakeholders do not perceive the dissonance between the two sides. Stakeholders never or rarely become aware of the connection between the two product lines, allowing the firm to reap benefits in both worlds without experiencing the adverse effects of being associated with products from opposite ends of the institutional spectrum. In turn, there is little or no need for the translation of capital be-tween the two arenas. Just as creators who work in an entirely unrelated field are not associated with the creative industries while at work—for example, people do not usually assume their cab driver is the next great novelist—consumers and intermediaries perceive each product line of a firm using the decoupling strategy separately and individually (see Table 8.1).

One firm that utilizes the decoupling approach is Atavist, a digital pub-lisher. Atavist produces both digitally enhanced literary singles (a cultural product) and the software used to create these singles (a technical product). The production of the cultural good is made possible by the funds from sales of the technical product; however, readers of Atavist singles may never know that the two lines are produced by the same firm. The firm's technical prod-uct is culturally irrelevant but commercially competitive, and thus this side of the business focuses solely on fulfilling the directives of the market. The firm's cultural products, in contrast, are literary and innovative and therefore commercially risky; thus, this side of the business focuses almost entirely on fulfilling the directives of the cultural world. Each product succeeds in its re-spective world, garnering value without disrupting or being disrupted by the firm's worth in the other realm. This arrangement allows the firm to maintain its status in both worlds and, by extension, its position as a successful cultural producer.

The decoupling strategy differs from the loose coupling and portfolio approaches with respect to the products' relationships with market and cul-tural institutions. In the loose coupling and portfolio approaches, the artistic and market-oriented works are produced separately and do not affect each other's symbolic status or commercial viability; however, both types of works are subject to both the cultural and commercial imperatives. For example, in a firm using the loose coupling or portfolio strategy, even a commercial product (a ready-to-wear line or a romance novel, for example) created for mass-market consumption has some symbolic/cultural capital. In contrast, the technical product produced by a firm using the decoupling strategy has no cultural capital. In this segregation, one side of a firm is exclusively in the market world, and the other side is exclusively in the artistic world.

Becoming a Nonprofit Firm

Offering two completely independent product lines, as Atavist does, is not possible for all firms. Atavist has the rare fortune of its two product lines being synergistic—Atavist's software both allows for the creation of and funds the publishing of digitally enhanced singles. However, it is rare for a firm to produce two similarly symbiotic products. In the absence of such synergy, a firm risks being spread too thin across the gulf between the market world and the cultural world, which can have the undesired effect of lowering a firm's financial viability. In this case, the segregation of the art and market worlds may be manifest by the firm adopting a nonprofit status and thus limiting commitment to the financial imperative to staying financially viable and covering costs. This limited commitment to the financial imperative allows the firm to produce riskier works that appeal to niche markets as well as philanthropic supporters. Firms that choose to attain nonprofit status produce culturally significant goods but do not support this production by producing a different, tangible, unrelated product; rather, these firms use fund-raising efforts to fill the shortfall between sales revenues and operating costs and in this way segregate their standing in the cultural world from their involvement in the financial world.

The strategies producers use to overcome the challenges inherent in operating in the creative industries are varied, although they are related. Although a producer could, in theory, pursue more than one strategy simultaneously, this is quite uncommon, largely because of the cost—both tangible and intangible (such as coordination and attention)—of doing so, given that each strategy alone comes with costs. The implications for entrepreneurship of the particular costs and challenges of these strategies are described in the next section.

The Management of Distinct Logics in Entrepreneurial Ventures

The role of producers in creative industries is, without question, challenging. However, their work is also exciting and energizing, as evidenced by the large numbers of small independent publishers, studios, design firms, and other firms that, against all odds, pursue entrepreneurial opportunities, both pioneering and not. The motivation behind these entrepreneurial ventures is easy to understand—being involved in the production of creative works offers the chance to interact with artists and ideas; when undertaken in a pioneering position, such involvement also offers the opportunity to influence cultural norms. Exciting as these prospects are, the difficulty of balancing the cultural and financial aspects of being a producer are especially acute in entrepreneurial ventures.

BALANCING STRATEGIES IN NEW VENTURES

When a new creative venture is founded, the opposition between the cultural and financial imperatives is manifest primarily in the difficulty the founder faces in raising money for the new firm, even though most start-ups in creative industries do not require a very large initial capital investment.[22] Producers in creative industries are not typically attractive targets for equity investment because revenues in these industries are uncertain and volatile, and economic returns are slow to emerge (if they emerge at all). Specifically, investors are reluctant in large part because they are aware that the vagaries of the world of art, artists, and intermediaries make it exceedingly difficult to predict strong financial performance and returns. This difficulty is further exacerbated by the limited ability to predict consumer demand for the work as well as a new venture's lack of a track record and reputation.[23] These factors, as well as an opposition between the need for creative independence and the requirements associated with outside funding (which may pull the firm in a direction that the creator/founder does not want to pursue), are the reasons that creative ventures are typically bootstrapped in their early days, and many continue to be self-funded as they grow.

New producer firms in creative industries must decide the relative importance they will assign to the cultural and financial imperatives because their relative significance will influence the type of creators with whom the firm should engage, which is already a fraught decision. In comparison, in creator firms, which are at the mercy of their founding creators' motivations and goals, the balance between the two imperatives is, to some extent, a foregone conclusion, and there may be little room to maneuver regardless of the market reaction (unless the founding creator decides to adapt to the market).

As made clear in the preceding descriptions of the strategies producers use to balance the cultural and financial imperatives in creative industries, these strategies are challenging to execute and require significant resources. Therefore, these strategies are onerous for well-established stable firms, let alone new, small, and inherently fragile start-ups.

Blending the Cultural and Commercial Worlds

Relative to the decoupling, loose coupling, and portfolio strategies, blending does not pose as many cognitive or financial challenges for new producers. However, the blending strategy is limited because it is more feasible for creator firms than for producer firms. The main obstacle for new firms that employ blending is convincing consumers to value the creative work enough to pay a significant price to acquire it. Because new ventures lack a track record, critical recognition, and critical acclaim, consumers are unlikely to discover and/or appreciate the highly artistic (and therefore symbolically complex) and expensive cultural goods produced by these firms. Producer firms do sometimes employ a blending strategy—as explained earlier, galleries and auction houses implement this strategy. However, for most producer firms, blending is a suboptimal use of their particular position because their business model entails access to multiple creators, and thus the portfolio strategy is a much more efficient and effective way of maximizing their artistic and commercial worth.

Loose Coupling and Building a Portfolio

Although less cumbersome than decoupling, the loose coupling and portfolio strategies are still not easy for new producers to implement. Offering a portfolio of cultural products may allow for some economies of scope and may also provide some benefits because the prestige garnered by the culturally complex product line may translate into higher prices for the market-oriented product line. However, these strategies still require the firm to invest significant tangible and intangible resources into building and sustaining multiple operations that are only loosely related. As with decoupling, this task is neither cognitively nor financially simple, especially for a new firm with limited reserves of both energy and funds. Further, adopting a portfolio approach very early in the lifecycle of a venture could have the deleterious effect of confusing the firm's stakeholders and muddying its position in the field, especially if the firm does not maintain a good balance between cultural prestige and commercial viability.

Although a large firm such as Penguin can afford to manage multiple imprints to balance both worlds, this dual (or multiple) focus is less feasible for newer, smaller ventures. Notably, Penguin built a strong reputation on the basis of its line of classics and its curated collections of paperbacks. This reputation allowed the firm to acquire and nurture various imprints in different niches; as a result, the corporation is able to maintain its reputation and continue to garner cultural capital while also owning imprints that accrue financial capital. A new venture attempting to follow a similar portfolio strategy at its inception does not have the advantage of a strong and clear reputation for either artistic discernment or commercial savvy, and its attempts to develop both reputations simultaneously may end in outcomes closer to those of the decoupling strategy (such as cognitive overload, high coordination costs) because the resources are not replicable in both sides of the firm at the same time. Thus, the portfolio strategy, in particular, entails a temporal aspect and will prove most successful for new ventures when they are cognizant of the strategy's possibilities and plan in advance to execute the strategy when the optimal time and conditions arise.

Loose coupling differs from the portfolio strategy in its implications for new ventures in that it is not only feasible but in many ways also advisable for new ventures, especially creator firms such as fashion firms. For example, although it is very expensive to do, showing an innovative runway collection in one of the four prestigious fashion weeks (London, Milan, Paris, or New York) is the surest way for a new designer to gain visibility and prestige (if intermediaries approve of the products) and therefore traction in the marketplace. In the early days of a new producer, therefore, loose coupling provides an optimal way to fulfill the imperatives of both art and market worlds without taking the toll that decoupling or portfolio strategies do.

Decoupling

The decoupling strategy requires firms to effectively run two entirely separate organizations and thus entails a complex and resource-intensive task in the best of circumstances; a firm that employs the decoupling strategy gains almost no economy of scope from its two disparate operations and therefore nearly doubles its costs. A new venture that adopts this strategy will, therefore, add significant coordination costs to its preexisting liabilities of newness.[24] Nevertheless, the strategy is viable for ventures that incorporate an element of technological innovation in the production process, such as Atavist (discussed earlier) because the technological platform provides a path to financial viability for the firm, which the cultural production side alone cannot necessarily provide. The decision to adopt this strategy requires careful thought, and the firm must take measures to avoid complications that could emanate from the principal's attention being divided between the two sides of the firm.

Most new producers that adopt the decoupling strategy seek to have a modicum of synergy between the two sides of the firm. Typically, the cultural product serves to establish the distinctive voice or raison d'être of the new venture and differentiate it from the richer, larger, and more powerful incumbents in the field; once the venture has carved out its own niche, it is able to present a strong case to its stakeholders, riding on the name recognition it has garnered. The hypothetical example of an independent film studio that also holds a patent for searching videos and images on the Internet illustrates this process. Although it might be difficult to attract attention from lay consumers for the latter activity, an interesting, intelligent, and innovative film is much more likely to build a reputation for the firm, which can then be parlayed into greater recognition among funders. A new producer that can take advantage of a scalable business model (like a way to conduct image search), despite (or because of) being decoupled from cultural production (like film production), is more likely to find willing funders who see in the former operations the potential for returns on their investment.

Although synergy across the two sets of products is the most important prerequisite for implementing the decoupling strategy, there are other organizational factors to consider. Running two entirely different businesses is not a straightforward operation and can be debilitating for a newly founded firm. Further, founders of firms in creative industries are unlikely to be interested in running the technical side of the business, and finding a cofounder to take on the task can lead to other problems. Finally, it is critical for firms using this strategy to manage the threat of cannibalization or bolstering competitors (for example, in the case of Atavist, which was described earlier, its software business arguably creates competitors for its publishing business). Given these potential pitfalls, firms must adopt the decoupling strategy with care.

Balancing Strategies: Implications for Growth of New Ventures

With respect to growing and scaling operations, producers seemingly benefit from having relatively straightforward business models in which revenues are derived directly from the sale of the work being produced: selling more will lead to growth. However, the paradox faced by new producer ventures is that although they may adopt a particular structural strategy to balance the cultural and financial imperatives, each of these strategies entails inbuilt constraints on growth (the most important imperative in the market world). Moreover, none of these strategies can fully overcome the limitation on growth imposed by the nature of the creative process, which poses the chief challenge to growth for a new producer in the creative industries—the difficulty of producing works on an industrial scale without an accompanying loss in (real or perceived) quality. Scaling is difficult in the creative industries for two reasons. First, individual creators cannot ramp up the quantity and velocity of creation. Second (and relevant to the issue of the cultural and market logics), it is difficult to pinpoint what makes an idea original, innovative, and high quality, even though this originality is essential to the artistic success of the work. Creating more works (for example, producing a book per year or a song per day), therefore, does not guarantee that intermediaries and consumers will affirm the quality of these works. Creators simply cannot be induced to create in accordance to specifications or volume goals. This is why a producer firm, with access to the works of multiple creators and the resultant availability of several structural strategies to balance the financial and cultural imperatives, has an advantage over a creator firm when it comes to growing both its cultural and commercial impact.

BALANCING STRATEGIES IN PIONEER ENTREPRENEURSHIP

Pioneer-producers (that create markets for radically innovative cultural goods) can be either creator firms or producer firms and either incumbents or new ventures. Although the propensity to produce works that require the revision of prevailing norms does not *necessarily* differ across creator firms and producer firms, it may be reasonable to expect the former to be more likely to produce such works because they provide creators with greater financial and creative independence and control. In addition, whereas being a pioneer producer is a difficult and risky proposition for both established firms and new ventures, incumbents may possess more resources (both tangible and intangible) that can be used to support a novel product category until a new market is established.

Because pioneer entrepreneurs, by definition, introduce a new category of cultural goods to the market, the question of how to balance the logics of the art and business worlds may seem moot in the case of a pioneer producer. Specifically, it may seem that a pioneer has already made the decision to prioritize the cultural imperative, given that establishing a market for a new category is difficult, slow, and often unrewarding. However, this is not necessarily the case, for two reasons. First, not all new categories of creative works meet the value criteria, standards, and specific conventions of the art world. Consider, for instance, the romance and erotica genre in publishing; although the first publisher to introduce this type of book was most certainly a pioneer producer for that category, there was never the possibility that either the publisher or the works would be considered part of the literary canon, even if societal prudishness were not a factor. Thus, the pioneer publisher for this genre was likely either using this category to bolster the financially oriented lines in the firm's portfolio or was never aiming to be considered culturally significant at all. Second, being a pioneer entrepreneur—(one of) the first to introduce a category—can, if the role is strategized and executed well, lead to financial gains from the so-called first mover advantage. However, because the process of building a market for a new category is slow, any financial benefits are part of a long and uncertain game. Given these two conditions, despite pioneer entrepreneurs' notable impact on culture, they too must balance the directives of both the cultural and the market worlds.

In terms of the structural strategies available to pioneer producers, incumbent producer firms are at an advantage relative to both new firms and established creator firms. Existing large producer firms, which have already adopted a portfolio or decoupling strategy, are better able (than new firms) to absorb the cultural or financial (and sometimes both) losses that result from introducing a new category with uncertain prospects to the market.[25] Neither, as already described, can incumbent creator firms take advantage of such separation and its accompanying benefits, because it is difficult for creator firms to produce more than one category of goods. Loose coupling between a radically innovative avant-garde product and its commercial derivative is also difficult for new pioneer producers because, in loose coupling, avant-garde works serve as the foundation for market-oriented works—a position that is difficult to attain when no market exists for the avant-garde goods due to their radical novelty.

Although new ventures have much more difficulty acting as pioneer producers than incumbent firms, paradoxically, new ventures are far more likely than existing firms to be pioneers, betting everything on a single new product or category without regard to the market creation challenges they will face. Because these new pioneer entrepreneurs—producing a novel category of cultural goods—are extremely unlikely to possess the resources to produce more than one product line or to work with several creators, the only truly viable strategy for them is blending, which, in this situation, can be employed by both producer firms and creator firms. Certainly pioneer producers that initially adopt the blending strategy may later adopt the portfolio strategy as they grow and succeed. The record label Def Jam, for instance, followed this path. Although the label was not the first to produce a rap album/single (that honor belonged to Sugar Hill Records), Def Jam is credited with playing an instrumental role in popularizing the genre via their optimal framing of the rap single. The company originally employed the blending strategy but today has grown into a multibillion-dollar conglomerate that deploys both the de-coupling (music and footwear) and portfolio strategies (within the music in-dustry) to great effect, maintaining its status as a cultural innovator while also achieving vast financial success. In contrast, pioneer creator firms almost always employ a blending strategy in the beginning and maintain it, even as they grow, due to the nature of production in a creator firm.

Summing Up and Looking Ahead

Those who operate in the creative and artistic realms often deride the mar-ketplace and its rules for being too calculating and rational and for valuing only things that can be objectively measured. Advocates of market rationality reciprocate by depicting artists as too unwilling to acknowledge the existence of the "real" world in which they reside, where income from sales is essen-tial to everyday life. Producers in creative industries must be willing to enter this zone of mutual antipathy and tension, and they face a series of related obstacles as they seek to achieve financial and/or artistic returns. Although producers have a set of strategies to balance the opposing logics of culture and commerce at their disposal, the balancing act is difficult, especially for new ventures. Yet, individuals are driven to become entrepreneurs in the creative industries, and many succeed in meeting both financial and cultural impera-tives. Indeed, producers have played a key role in nearly all major cultural and artistic breakthroughs in U.S. society in the past century.

Creators, producers, and intermediaries have long coexisted in a some-times uneasy balance in the creative industries, influencing culture and social values via innovations championed by entrepreneurs in the market. However, the world has changed substantially in the last century, particularly in the past two decades—the dual forces of globalization and digitalization have become extremely prominent in the cultural world during this time. The next chapter examines whether and how these two forces have changed the creative industries. The chapter reveals the opportunities this new world offers and the challenges it presents to creators, producers, and intermediaries, with a particular focus on which aspects of these roles have changed in the new context and how the market and entrepreneurs—pioneering and not—in either producer or intermediary positions must adapt to these changes while also highlighting what aspects must remain the same, regardless of the new context.

Part IV

THE CREATIVE INDUSTRIES

Past, Present, and Future

NEW WORLD, OLD RULES

Creative Industries in the Age of Digitalization and Globalization

When a platform is self-service, even the improbable ideas can get tried, because there's no expert gatekeeper ready to say, "That will never work!"
—Jeffrey Bezos, CEO of Amazon.com[1]

The star-making system of the future, it turns out, needs the star-making system of the past . . . The middle men and women have arrived, eroding YouTube's status as the quintessential do-it-yourself enterprise.
—Brooks Barnes and Hunter Atkins[2]

Today, individuals who want to purchase artwork can find an artist or designer to create it on "Unique Board"; they can learn more about art by browsing the vast collections of the venerable Metropolitan Museum of Art (in New York City) from anywhere in the world, either on the museum's own website or on the website for Google's Art Project; and they can buy twentieth-century Indian art from Saffronart.com. Unquestionably, the world is becoming more connected and accessible by the day; economic and technological developments, particularly globalization and digitalization, jointly bridge physical and psychological distances. *Digitalization* refers to the rapid uptake of the Internet and other digital media for creation, commerce, and communication. *Globalization* is the opening of previously closed economies, which has led to widespread economic development and increased interest in these countries from Western firms. Together, these upheavals have significantly changed the way business is conducted and have had a particularly significant (and mostly positive) impact on entrepreneurs. This shift is evidenced by the numerous IPOs (initial public offerings) of digital-native firms, including the Chinese firm Alibaba.com, which had the largest IPO in history.[3] Firms in creative industries have viewed these developments with substantially more caution than firms in other industries. Digitalization and globalization have led to disorder in the creative industries and have challenging consequences for the functioning of established entities. As in other industries, however, in the creative industries the rise of the digital medium and the increasing economic parity among the world's economies have, relative to their impact on incumbents, had positive consequences for entrepreneurs, pioneering and otherwise.

The challenges that digitalization and globalization present for incumbents in the creative industries raise questions about both the viability and relevance of traditional forms of creative works and the validity of old paradigms and practices. In the midst of such large-scale changes, are the established rules and structures still relevant? Or will the disruptions render obsolete old ways of doing things in the creative industries? If so, what new approaches will emerge? This final chapter revisits and critically examines the topics addressed in the previous chapters to understand their relevance, validity, and entrepreneurial implications in the current digitalized and globalized context.

The Implications of Digitalization and Globalization for Creators, Producers, Intermediaries

Digitalization has had both problematic and beneficial consequences for creators. The digital medium is a tremendous hurdle to creators getting paid for their work, as conflicts over online music distribution and sharing have demonstrated.[4] This trouble extends to writers and filmmakers as well.[5] Creators of goods that can be disseminated over the Internet are right to be worried, because electronic versions of books, songs, films, and other works can be easily duplicated, shared, and streamed, although the creators of these works are not necessarily paid for each duplicate that is shared or distributed. This particular concern is less acute among creators of physical goods (for example, fashion designers, visual artists, chefs) that cannot be digitalized. Although a firm may use the Internet to *sell* high-fashion clothing, the actual garment must still be shipped to the consumer in physical form, and thus designers face a lower risk of unauthorized distribution or duplication reducing their incomes than do musicians and writers and the like.[6]

Although uncompensated duplication can be problematic, the rise of the digital medium has also presented creators with a major benefit: the unprecedented opportunity to reach consumers directly, a development that many creators have embraced and celebrated.[7] This shift has increased the number of self-actualized individuals with nonpecuniary motivations who can recapture the artistic ideal of creating for the sake of creation and expression rather than for the market (see, for instance, the many inventive and interesting works on Instagram). Globalization has also had mixed consequences for creators because markets for creators' works are no longer hyperlocalized. Thus, creators can now reach a myriad of consumers across the globe but conversely must contend with both a multitude of other creators who can do the same and enter their own markets and the local creators in those distant markets.

Digitalization has put producers in a situation similar to that of creators. The development of electronic formats of creative works and the digital medium for disseminating content have posed significant challenges, especially in fields such as music, film, and publishing. Producers must worry about everything from copyright protection to the need to produce works in a new format. The main issue for producers, however, is that creators can now reach audiences directly without going through a producer firm (for example, a book publisher or record label), as illustrated by the recent successes of self-published authors such as Amanda Hocking and E. L. James[8] and the popularity of short films made and posted on YouTube by independent creators.[9] As a result, producer firms, especially in the music and publishing sectors, are rightly worried about becoming irrelevant. Yet even as producers worry about impending irrelevance, they also benefit from the opportunities generated by digitalization, which has enabled delivery innovations (such as e-books) and provided a new channel through which producers can bring cultural products to consumers. The reduced cost of doing business, especially in the case of retail operations, has allowed producers to produce, distribute, and scale quickly. In some cases, producer firms have even been able to disrupt traditional industry structure; for example, a large number of online fashion stores and multiple online start-ups in the art space have emerged, casting doubt on the belief that art and high fashion had to be bought and sold in a particular ambience and with a personal touch provided by the seller to the buyer. The impact of globalization on producers also has parallels with the experience of creators. Although the growing economic parity among nations has opened new markets, the ease of cross-border trade and business has increased the level of competition that producers face.

Finally, the growth of the Internet as a medium has had a mixed impact on the nature and work of intermediaries. The chief implication of digitalization has been that consumers have come to expect discursive content on the Internet to be available gratis,[10] which has weakened the financial viability of magazines, newspapers, and other similar intermediaries. It's not all bad news for intermediaries, however; digitalization has also had positive consequences. For example, the Internet offers a new medium for conveying their discourse and has significantly lowered the cost of starting a new intermediary, because publishing text or posting video online is easy and virtually free. As a consequence, new online intermediary ventures have proliferated, and the very existence of their older, costlier physical counterparts is now threatened. These various new digital organizations/sites that provide consumer and/or expert reviews of cultural goods (for example Yelp.com, Goodreads.com,[11] Rottentomatoes.com) are examples of the entrepreneurial vitality in this part of the value chain (see Chapter 1 for a discussion of the value chain). Globalization, too, has created opportunities for intermediaries because the introduction of categories that are new to a particular geography/market/culture requires intermediaries that can provide evaluative and explicatory commentary to encourage the consumption of goods in this category (recall the case of modern Indian art, which is a good example of a new market category made feasible in large part by globalizing forces).

In sum, digitalization has presented significant challenges to incumbents that have presumably not been agile enough to deal with the new digitally mediated context that has disrupted their well-worn ways of doing business. Similarly, globalization has not been a universally positive experience for incumbents—it has enabled firms from previously less developed countries to enter large, developed Western markets while dangling potentially lucrative, but simultaneously extremely challenging, new markets in front of Western firms. However, even as these dual forces have generated challenges for incumbent creators, producers, and intermediaries, they have generated extensive opportunities for pioneer and other entrepreneurs, as previously described. The remainder of this chapter examines the implications of these developments, both opportunities and obstacles, for entrepreneurs.

Entrepreneurial Opportunities Related
to Digitalization and Globalization

These two great upheavals—digitalization and globalization—have generated somewhat different types of opportunities in the creative industries. Digitalization has had a wide-ranging impact across entities (creators, producers, and intermediaries) and has generated market opportunities that can be but are not always pioneering roles, whereas globalization has resulted primarily in opportunities for pioneer entrepreneurs (both pioneer producers and pioneer intermediaries). Specifically, globalization has engendered two types of pioneer entrepreneurship. First, it has allowed cultural products specific to a certain country to be consumed in other countries—goods can be shipped and ideas (and their manifestations) can travel across boundaries to find new markets. Second, globalization has led to the emergence of new markets for certain products within their home country—conventions of value from outside can be adopted in countries to render local cultural products newly valuable. For example, the increased popularity of K-pop from South Korea in both the United States and other Asian countries is a case of the former type of pioneer entrepreneurship (that is, ideas and goods crossing boundaries to reach a new market).[12] Similarly, the entry of Hollywood films into China required pioneer entrepreneurs to create a new market.[13] In an example of the latter type of pioneer entrepreneurship, designers and fashion magazines have applied the modern concept of high-end fashion systems (which entails a market for individualistic, choice-oriented clothing) in African and Latin American countries and India (all regions where clothing had traditionally reflected socioeconomic class rather than fashion trends or individual tastes).[14] New goods from both of these categories are brought to market by pioneer producers and pioneer intermediaries.

Most striking is that the *interaction* of globalization and digitalization has yielded a particularly fertile ground for entrepreneurial opportunities because the digital medium reaches across geographical barriers and enables both commerce and an increased volume of commentary. The opportunities generated by rapid globalization are strengthened by the concurrent trend of digitalization and vice versa. If the Internet did not make cross-national transactions so easy, it would be far more difficult for cultural goods to be sold in geographically and culturally distant markets; conversely, if consumers were not increasingly interested in countries such as India and China (as a result of their recent rapid economic development), there would be no markets for goods from these countries in the Western world. Only as a result of *both* trends occurring simultaneously could an Indian auction house—Saffronart.com—create a market for modern Indian art by providing consumers in various countries access to art from a previously untapped part of the world through online auctions.[15]

In the case of cultural goods, however, cultural distance is more difficult to bridge than physical distance. Because of the influence of nonmarket intermediaries, tastes in goods such as music, food, literature, and art are circumscribed by consumers' social and cultural contexts, which in turn are often geographically determined and differentiated. As a result, there is no guarantee that mere access (enabled by the Internet) to works from different cultures will create a market for these goods—commerce needs commentary to stimulate consumption of cultural goods, especially those that originate in other cultures. (Recall the description of the four elements of a market in Chapter 1). Pioneer producers, therefore, are hampered in their pursuit of a market if there is not sufficient intermediary-driven discourse, and intermediaries must develop expertise and knowledge in the new category before they can effectively create a market for it. Pioneer entrepreneurship is therefore risky for both producers and intermediaries in a globalizing world. However, the concurrent digitalization has increased consumers' willingness and ability to engage in ecommerce transactions and lowered costs of operating online, which mitigates at least the economic aspect of this risk. Pioneer producers, especially those in the sales/retail field, are not required to invest a large amount of money in stores, whereas pioneer intermediaries can take advantage of the vast space available to them for disseminating discourse in a variety of formats (text, audio, visual, video, and so on), which may make their discourse more resonant and therefore more credible and effective. It is not a coincidence that consumers have become increasingly exposed to cultural goods from other countries at the same time that economic conditions have improved among previously less economically developed countries, and the prevalence of and familiarity with the Internet has grown. As a result of these simultaneous trends, a large number of entrepreneurial ventures have recently emerged in the creative industries.

However, with incumbents in the creative industries apparently beleaguered as they endure disruptions in the efficacy of their traditional approaches, it seems that not only the existing firms but also the existing rules of engagement (described as the baseline case in previous chapters) are being or will be rendered obsolete by entrepreneurs and their novel practices in the new environment. Nevertheless, it may be premature to sound the death knell for all things traditional. Although only continued experimentation will fully reveal the best practices for creators, producers, and intermediaries in the new context, many of the challenges and trade-offs described in this book will nonetheless remain relevant and significant, despite these new developments and their repercussions. Therefore, it behooves entrepreneurs to pay heed to the underlying reasons for the structure and functioning of the creative industries; the following descriptions of what has changed and what has not changed for creators, producers, and intermediaries and the entrepreneurial implications of these changes illustrate why such attention is warranted among entrepreneurs.

New Opportunities, New Challenges, Old Rules?

CREATORS

Given that the joint trend of digitalization/globalization is largely a confluence of transformations in the economic, technological, and organizational spheres—which are only remotely germane to the typically solitary pursuit of creating art—it may seem that these forces would have a minimal effect on the creative works produced by individual creators. Indeed, with the exception a few fundamentally digital-only types of works—the "cell-phone novel,"[16] enhanced electronic books,[17] digital art, and possibly electronic dance music— digitalization has not changed the process of creation or the nature of the works created per se. Artworks must still be conceived, developed, and refined, regardless of the medium in which creation occurs. However, the combined influence of digitalization and globalization has had some impact on the works created. In the world of traditional crafts and artisans, for instance, some product designers have attempted to provide a certain degree of guidance to artisans to increase the appeal of their products in the global market.[18] At the same time, given that the interest in these works is the result of their uniqueness, prudent designers will not alter ideas or works of art too significantly in response to market demand. Overall, then, digitalization and globalization have had some (but limited) influence on the nature of the artistic works that are created and brought to market.

In contrast, technological advances, as well as rapid developments in the Internet's ability to enable transactions and interactions of various kinds, have significantly changed *who* can be an artist and aspire to make a living from being a creator of artistic works. Today's aspiring filmmakers can use digital cameras to make films relatively easily; designers, musicians, and singers can use a variety of online platforms to post their work and build an audience; and writers can self-publish online to reach readers.[19] In addition, the creators of works that require a significant sum of money to create and/or distribute—for example, a film, a line of fashion apparel, or a large-scale sculpture—can connect with willing customers/funders/patrons via several Internet platforms. These so-called crowd-funding platforms such as Kickstarter and IndieGogo have made it possible for creators to simultaneously raise money and gauge consumer interest in a product. Finally, once they have created their works, creators can harness the services of online marketplaces such as Etsy.com, which allow them to create a virtual shop and reach customers, regardless of where they are located; by some accounts, Etsy hosts 900,000 creators, who are able to reach 60 million registered buyers from around the world.[20] Thus, the twin forces of digitalization and globalization have jointly changed the everyday lives of artists.

The Possibility of Reverse-Engineering Creative Goods

Although globalization has brought to the fore categories of artworks that were previously unheralded and unseen by consumers in other countries, digitalization's impact on the creation of new market categories has been limited to the few digital-native ones mentioned previously. Further, digitalization has not led to a large shift in the types of works created within existing categories, despite earlier predictions of dramatic changes in the creative process itself due to the availability of "big data" (large amounts of knowledge gleaned from monitoring consumers' habits and actions online). Primary among the promises of big data was the notion that all available information could be analyzed to reveal consumers' preferences and tastes. For example, companies such as Pandora have tried to parse the "music genome" (that is, objective attributes of songs), which could be used to suggest certain music to listeners.[21] More important, such data could be used to make funding decisions and push the creation of works that consumers [would] desire and like, developments that might change the types of works created within existing genres. However, there is no concrete evidence that this has occurred in a meaningful way, even in areas where digitalization has taken hold completely, such as the music industry. Nevertheless, the availability of consumer data has wrought some changes in how creators and their works are assessed and/or commissioned by producer-firms (see the example of Amazon, described in the following pages).[22]

Notably, although the amount of data and the level of detail about customer behavior is a new development, the use of consumer research or buying patterns to reverse engineer products is not new. Moreover, this strategy does not necessarily bring about products that are successful in the artistic or the commercial sense. There is not yet any credible evidence of stable commercial success due to such reverse engineering of creative works. Although some observers have claimed that Netflix and the success of its original series *House of Cards* provides such evidence, it is rumored that Netflix granted the director full creative freedom. Thus, the approach Netflix took was not so different from the "traditional" approach of making programming decisions based on track records and past successes, which the ensemble of creators certainly possessed.[23] Similarly, although Amazon relied on consumer preferences in its initial foray into original programming in 2013—the firm produced only the five series for which its customers voted—the shows debuted to little critical or consumer attention, and a little over a year later only one of the five series had been renewed.[24] Further, in a 2014 article, *The New York Times* reported that Amazon was "conscientiously adding more artistic nuance to its science of programming" and luring creators who "were going with their creative gut . . . despite their employer's algorithm-driven image."[25] Indeed, in the same article, the creators of the firm's new shows emphasized (on record) that they did not engage with comments posted online or use data gleaned by the company and rather focused on being true to their "job" of "being a good storyteller."

The Possibility of Democratizing Artistic Creation

Another prediction that gained considerable traction is related to technology's facilitation of creation and distribution. Some commentators believed that in the new world of creative work, anybody who wanted to would be able to become a writer/artist/singer/musician/filmmaker and reach an audience, and therefore "old world" producers would no longer be needed to take creative works to market. This democratization, which Jeffrey Bezos alluded to in a letter to Amazon's shareholders, was hailed as a way of breaking through the old guard. Bezos opened his letter with eight enthusiastic endorsements, five of which were from individuals who had used Kindle Direct Publishing (KDP), Amazon's self-publishing platform, to become "best-selling" authors. Bezos touted the platform's "radical and transformational innovations that create value for thousands of authors, entrepreneurs, and developers."[26]

That assertion, although marginally true, has not changed the situation of artists in any truly significant way. It has never been easy to make a living as an artist, but, with more artists entering the market and gaining access to customers directly through the Internet, that endeavor is now more difficult than ever because there is a bottleneck of creative goods in the market. In this context, it is extremely difficult for creators' self-distributed works to be discovered among the cacophony of stimuli available to consumers.[27] Authors have lamented the difficulty of being self-published and the struggle to be noticed among the many self-published authors.[28] YouTube has acknowledged that, of the million or so user-produced channels that earn revenues from advertising, only some thousands bring in an annual income topping six figures. The "stars" of these channels have expressed a worry that overcrowding on the platform will mean fewer viewers for each star/channel, which, in turn, will mean diminishing advertising rates and therefore lower revenues.[29]

Although it may seem like the ideal situation, self-publishing, or more generally self-generated connection with a target audience, is not always optimal for artists. Eliminating publishers (or producers more generally) would likely result in the market being flooded by self-published books of variable quality; in this scenario, consumers would have difficulty keeping up and figuring out what to read, whereas individual authors would almost certainly struggle to market their books. Further, contrary to popular belief, such a situation would have the most negative effects on new authors because, although well-known authors such as James Patterson or Stephen King have keen fans who will find the author's next book even if it is not promoted by a large publisher, newcomers do not have such followings, and their works are likely to get lost among the many others.

Although the digital medium has empowered artists, especially writers, those creators who do not enjoy the process of marketing and selling their works (a considerable majority) do not garner stable, long-term gains and/or satisfaction from being self-published. As a result, new authors who did eventually find and build an online fan base would likely sign a formal contract with a publishing firm, which would take over the work of production and promotion, leaving the author free to write. For example, after signing a contract with one of the "Big Five" publishers, the enormously popular, self-published fanfiction writer Amanda Hocking said, "I always knew that if I could get the right deal, I would take it."[30] At this point, many self-published artists seem to have a goal of being discovered and acquired by "old world" producers, thus defying predictions that a totally different and democratic artistic movement is afoot. Thus, the old order lives on, and the role of the producer as risk taker is still necessary. Producers, however, have not been immune to the dramatic changes caused by digitalization and globalization. The following section examines what has changed and what remains unchanged in the role and functions of a producer in creative industries, with particular focus on entrepreneurs.

PRODUCERS

Although Amanda Hocking and E. L. James opted to sign contracts with established publishers, the next self-publishing sensation may forge ahead alone, thus realizing Jeff Bezos's vision of a world without gatekeepers, where the relevance of producers has declined. Yet even in the music industry, where digitalization has had the longest tenure, there are still A&R (artists and repertoire) executives and major labels. Justin Bieber was discovered via the Internet but nevertheless has an agent.[31] Similarly, old-world style producers are emerging in the world of YouTube—multichannel networks and agents have begun to engage with individuals who already have viewers and revenues and therefore would seem not to need help reaching consumers.[32] Even as artists have many more avenues for realizing their work and reaching consumers as a result of the Internet, producers have realized that these digital platforms are venues where they can scout for talented creators who already have an audience.[33] Thus, in the current technology-enabled context, producers remain necessary and relevant in the creative industries, although certain aspects of their duties have changed.

Adjusting to a Digitalized, Globalized Market

The chief impact of digitalization in the context of producers has been the provision of a new distribution method, a platform for both the production of cultural goods and the management of economic transactions. First, the digital medium has allowed the development of innovative cultural goods such as enhanced e-books or short YouTube videos as a format of entertainment; more broadly, advanced technologies have facilitated the emergence of new categories of creative products such as electronic dance music. With regard to these types of goods (film, music, television, and books), which can themselves be digitized, the fear among producers at the start of the digital age focused on two main issues—digital rights management and the difficulty of collecting revenues from online customers. However, the first problem (a technical difficulty) has been addressed, and over time consumers have become more willing to either pay subscription fees to providers such as Netflix or sit through commercials in exchange for free access to the work (as they do for TV). Although incumbent producer firms may still be feeling threatened by the success of Netflix and Hulu, the fundamental order of things has not changed, although the actors are new—recent patterns mirror earlier developments. Like HBO (also originally a subscription service for movies), Netflix has begun to produce original programming to induce customers to return to the platform; other firms, such as Hulu and Amazon, have followed suit. In sum, this process has played out before, and, although it may be occurring on a much larger scale now and thus be more disruptive and frightening for entities vested in the status quo, understanding the fundamental structure of these industries and knowing the underlying reasons for these structures will help entrepreneurs and incumbents survive and thrive.

Examples from the Fashion Industry and the Art Market

One of the best demonstrations of the importance of possessing knowledge of the structure of creative industries is the case of online retail, a sector in which opportunities have flourished due to the new digital medium, which provides a platform for transactions/sales of physical goods. Whereas online retail was accepted (albeit with some reluctance) in the case of books (Amazon.com), there was significant resistance to the idea of online retail among producers in the art and fashion sectors. Industry veterans declared that the online experience would not be able to replicate the real-life experience of shopping for these goods and that the Internet would never deliver the ambience that prized customers desired. Fashion entrepreneurs were the first to challenge the verity of this industry maxim. For example, the website Net-a-Porter.com, which provides an online retail platform for luxury fashion goods and accessories, became very successful despite initial skepticism regarding its viability. The potential of the Internet was again confirmed when so-called born-digital companies such as Warby Parker[34] (eyeglasses), Bonobos[35] (custom trousers for men), Rent the Runway[36] (garment rentals), and Gilt Group[37] (flash sales) received significant press coverage as a result of their seemingly iconoclastic business models and achieved financial success. In addition, online retail has facilitated globalization in fashion—sites such as Farfetch.com and Shoptiques.com (platforms that offer virtual storefronts for boutiques located in cities across the world) and Jaypore.com (a website for fashion clothing and accessories from India) can be accessed by customers all over the world. In sum, the digital medium affords efficiency and convenience to both producers and consumers by serving as a trading platform for all types of goods from any location.

And yet, Warby Parker, Bonobos, and Rent the Runway have each recently constructed brick-and-mortar stores,[38] and Net-a-Porter has begun to publish *Porter*, a print magazine.[39] These developments raise some doubts about the proclaimed victory of virtual sales channels over traditional ones and emphasize the importance of creating a tangible shopping experience with tactile interactions with real products, which, it seems, customers still desire. Producers imbue products with tangible and intangible markers of value (as described in Chapter 8); in the case of high-fashion apparel, the shopping experience and store ambience are very important markers of value. These markers, which are missing in the online shopping experience, play a significant role in creating a market for goods with symbolic value, making the physical stores worth the considerable expense and effort they require. Therefore, online stores must re-create, to at least a certain extent, the same pleasurable shopping experience that consumers have in physical stores. Net-a-Porter, for example, achieves this via the ostentatiously luxurious beautiful packaging that arrives at customers' doorsteps. These accoutrements are expensive for firms to implement and therefore erode some of the cost benefits of not having a physical store. Finally, especially for a new firm/brand (less so for Ralphlauren.com or Bloomingdales.com), it is extremely difficult to be noticed among the crowd of online competitors, and revenues lost from being overlooked (or the marketing expenses required to be noticed) may well counterbalance the savings accrued from being online. As a result, even in the world of online retail, there is a need for flagship physical stores and showrooms. Knowledge of the way consumers perceive value in high-fashion apparel is, therefore, critical to the success of producers, especially entrepreneurs, in the world of online fashion retail.[40]

The notoriously social art market, where seeing and being seen are crucial elements of the experience, has been more resistant to change than the fashion industry. The combined influence of globalization and digitalization resulted in the generation of numerous entrepreneurial opportunities in the art market and a high level of optimism among entrepreneurs, who viewed the success of entrepreneurs in fashion as an indicator of changing consumer behavior and industry dynamics. The Internet's potential to bridge physical distances motivated entrepreneurs to found online galleries that promised to bring art to potential collectors who lived far from the main centers of the art world such as New York, London, Paris, and Berlin.[41] Industry insiders also believed that websites that facilitated retail sales had the potential to bring new artists and their work to the forefront of the market, regardless of where they were located, so that American and European (including those in the United Kingdom) collectors could gain access to art markets in faraway newly modernizing cultures such as China and India and various countries in Africa and Latin America. However, entrepreneurs underestimated both the difficulty of overcoming consumers' need for artworks to be explicated (which is especially acute in the case of new collectors) and the need for trust between the transacting parties. The need for trust and education was a substantial hurdle, especially in the primary market, which testifies to the importance of understanding the structure and functioning of art markets. In the secondary market (sales of artworks that have already undergone the value construction process), the online selling of artworks is easier.

The example of Paddle8.com, a New York–based art venture, provides an illustration.[42] Originally founded as a virtual storefront and platform for art galleries located anywhere in the world to reach distal collectors, the venture underwent two pivots during its first year before finally settling on an online auction model, operating in the secondary market; this model produced financial success for the firm. The case of Paddle8 shows that although the online sales model is not well suited to the primary market due to the complex nature of the art market and the process of value construction in art, it is not a fundamentally untenable proposition in the art market. In fact, for new ventures, and particularly for pioneers of new global art genres, possessing online sales capabilities is especially beneficial because the local universe of collectors may not be sufficiently large to support the venture, and a digital platform provides access to customers based in a wider range of geographical locations.

These examples make it clear that producers in creative industries, especially entrepreneurial ventures, should be wary of excessive optimism about the online business model. The ecosystem remains important because intermediaries and norms have power over producers' fortunes, thus making online retail more difficult in creative industries than in other industries. However, if the *entire* value chain (comprising distinct producers, intermediaries, and consumers) is transplanted to the online world, with clear boundaries between the discourse of producers and that of intermediaries, then the idea of selling art or high fashion (purely) online is, quite possibly, feasible and sustainable.[43,44]

Producers' Interactions with Intermediaries

This importance of trust and education revives earlier discussions (see Chapters 3 and 4) of the interplay between producers and intermediaries—the entities that are responsible for maintaining trust and providing education in the creative industries' value chain. Digitalization and globalization have influenced the interactions between these two entities. One of the main hopes observers had for the Internet was that it would allow producers to connect directly with consumers, ending the need for traditional middlepersons such as wholesalers, brokers, and agents and thereby providing significant savings to consumers. Although this has occurred in other industries, extending this approach to intermediaries in creative industries entails certain problems. Many entrepreneurial producers have made the mistake of assuming that intermediaries in the creative industries, which are crucial to constructing the value of many cultural goods, can be eliminated in the same way that traditional middlepersons in the supply chains of other industries can and have been eliminated. With Kindle Direct Publishing (KDP), Amazon and Jeff Bezos hoped to obviate the need for one of the producer firms that had traditionally vetted the quality of manuscripts and taken on market risks. Although the disruption of the gatekeepers in producer firms in fact warrants an even greater need (see the next subsection) for the other so-called gatekeepers of culture—independent intermediaries—observers have repeatedly predicted their disappearance, too. The seeming inevitability of this outcome, however, must be questioned and critically examined.

INTERMEDIARIES

Proponents of both digitalization and globalization (particularly digitalization) have heralded these dual developments as disruptions that will permanently change how consumers understand, value, and consume cultural goods. Much of this discussion casts these developments in a rosy hue. Notably, these proponents believe that the digital medium's direct conduit to consumers will help eliminate market "inefficiencies," such as the need for expert reviews,[45] and will democratize access to cultural goods. It is, therefore, worthwhile to address the questions: Are intermediaries still relevant, especially in the forms and functional roles they have traditionally occupied, and if so, why?

The Need for Intermediaries in the Age of Digitalization and Globalization

An examination of the traditional entities that have long served as the predominant intermediaries for valuation discourse—namely magazines and newspapers—would expose struggles and difficulties, suggesting that intermediaries' relevance and raison d'être are steadily diminishing. Nonetheless, that conclusion would be premature and arises from conflating medium and message; magazines and newspapers were indeed the chief loci for intermediary discourse (especially discourse fulfilling the introduction and instruction functions; see Chapter 4 for a detailed discussion of the functions of intermediaries), and the print versions of these entities are indeed suffering. However, the demise of these printed publications does not preclude the possibility that the magazine or newspaper format cannot enjoy a second incarnation online. The specific magazines and newspapers may be different, and new digital-only start-ups may become the norm, but these developments would signal only the demise of the print medium, not the death of the entire form. In fact, the emergence of a digital medium has made it easier and less expensive to start a new venture that performs intermediary functions.[46]

Intermediaries are just as necessary, if not more necessary, than before the advent of digitalization and globalization for three reasons—the properties of cultural goods, the increasing number of creators and producers in the market, and the need for explication of new global cultural goods. As seen in Chapter 3, the need for intermediaries in the creative industries is driven by the properties of cultural goods—the vast numbers and variety of goods produced, their experiential nature, and their inherent symbolism—and none of these properties has been fundamentally or even marginally transformed in a way that would mitigate the challenge of consuming creative works. If anything, because digital platforms such as YouTube, Pinterest, and Vimeo, as well as online publishing sites, have increased the number of individuals creating a large number of works that can be presented to consumers with relative ease, digitalization has exacerbated the need for intermediaries. Moreover, not *all* of these goods are less complex or require less explication and/or evaluation merely because they are virtual or because they are created by a larger portion of the population.[47] Far from being obsolete, therefore, intermediaries are now even more necessary; consumers need intermediaries to sift through the goods available in the market and interpret and evaluate these goods so they can make informed choices. Globalization has further intensified this need. As creators from all countries and corresponding cultural contexts gain the ability to access digital platforms and reach far-flung consumers who live in different cultural contexts, and thus are unfamiliar with the codes and symbolism in these works, entities on both sides of the transaction need the interpretive and evaluative commentary of intermediaries more acutely than ever before.

In 2011, the Sundance Institute became the first "curatorial partner" of the crowd-funding website Kickstarter; this partnership and other similar arrangements indicate that the Internet has created a greater need for an objective intermediary's endorsement.[48] In addition to its joint work with Sundance, Kickstarter has several other "curated pages" that allow interested funders to view only projects that have received some sort of endorsement from a traditional intermediary and thus feel more comfortable when they decide to fund the creative projects of unknown individuals. Somewhat similarly, Rottentomatoes.com, an aggregator of user reviews of films, also presents professional reviews, further tagging some of those as the reviews of so-called top critics. The more artists consumers can access, the more they need the guidance of an entity that can help them navigate the selection of creative goods, apply relevant metrics for evaluation (for example, should a YouTube artist be evaluated differently than a TV or movie actor?), learn about these goods, and identify the best products. In short, consumers still need traditional intermediaries.

Not only has the pool of creators expanded, producers have proliferated, too; for instance, there is an abundance of online retailers in the fashion sector. These retail firms still face the problem of reaching consumers, and the emergence of the digital medium has not changed the fact that consumers discount producers' discourse because producers have a profit motive. Thus, the work of intermediaries cannot be eliminated by producers placing their own commentary and discourse on their websites, and online producers continue to need the *independent* value-constructing discourse of intermediaries to spur consumption. The Internet has therefore not yet lived up to its proclaimed potential to render intermediaries obsolete.

Neither have any of the specific functions of intermediaries—introduction, instruction, or inclusion—been eliminated. Indeed, as discussed earlier, the need for introduction to enable discovery of goods has increased, as has the need for the interpretation and the explication of the meaning of esoteric works that now traverse cultural and geographical borders. In the world of art, for instance, collectors who want to discover promising new artists in locales such as Africa or Latin America (because, in the art market, as in the financial market or real estate, it pays to spot a diamond in the rough) must first understand the entire context, including the history and trajectory of artistic movements in these areas and the meanings and subtexts embedded in the locale's artistic works. The inclusion function, which identifies works and creators with significant promise and value, is also important in the globalized market because it allows consumers to identify the best and most valuable items in a category. Although particularly applicable to works with a high level of symbolic complexity, intermediary functions remain important (to varying degrees) in all creative industries.

In the case of pioneer intermediaries, the changes wrought by globalization have increased the need for such intermediaries, whereas digitalization has provided nearly endless space for the discourse of these intermediaries. Further, just as they were before the advent of digitalization and globalization, independence and expertise are absolutely crucial in the case of pioneer intermediaries, regardless of the category.

Who Can Act as an Intermediary in the New World?

The issue of prerequisites is particularly significant for online intermediaries, whose number is high and growing. Many of these entities take advantage of the fact that the Internet makes it very easy for any and all individuals to contribute to the valuation discourse, mainly via user-generated discourse and reviews from lay consumers. This development, in turn, has been portrayed as a benefit for consumers, who can now, finally, take matters into their own hands rather than being subjected to the dictates of elite critics. Especially in the case of user reviews, there is growing support for giving power back to consumers and not permitting elite experts, who are far removed from the lay consumer, to determine the quality and therefore the fortunes of creators and their works.[49] At its core, this is a postmodern worldview that asserts that everyone is an expert, and therefore everyone's opinion and evaluation matters and thus brings the ideas of democracy and self-governance into the professional arena.

Although this move toward democratization may sound appealing, it is not clear that it is the best path for civil society. Because customers lack the training and/or experience of professional critics/reviewers, their reviews are not always informed and objective. Just as the expansion of opportunities to create artwork does not make every individual an artist, the consumption of creative works does not make an individual a critic. This is clear, for example, in reviews of books on Amazon.com; readers often limit their reviews to their final judgment ("Awesome!!!" "Amazing read. Must-buy!!"), without explaining why they believe the book is good. Such reviews do not help consumers cultivate their taste in or knowledge about writing, or, for that matter, help them reach a decision, because it is not clear why the book is being praised. Similarly, consumers who post negative reviews of books often do not provide in-depth reasons and analysis to explain why the book does not meet quality standards. These shallow reviews undermine the efforts of the writers by not giving their work due consideration, thought, and analysis.

The erroneous notion that the Internet takes power away from hegemonic elite intermediaries and places it in the hands of consumers arises from the conflation of high standards and expertise with elitism. Although consumers may or may not agree with critics' criteria and their picks and most certainly are not required to abide by these judgments, they cannot and should not ignore intermediaries simply because they have high standards. Replacing the reviews of professional critics (formal intermediaries) with user reviews or algorithmic filters and suggestions will create a world in which, potentially, the lowest common denominator will carry the day. A civil society needs professional, independent (that is, having no vested interest in the sale of the work), and knowledgeable critics who can push the boundaries of thinking and thus make members of society see beyond their limited worldview and understand and accept great works of art that challenge prevailing norms.

"Content Should Be Free":
A Problematic Expectation for Intermediaries

A major stumbling block to maintaining the independence of online intermediaries is the general perception among consumers that "content should
be free" on the Internet. Because of this perception, intermediaries are often
forced to generate revenues in ways (for example, collecting affiliate [sales]
commissions via hyperlinks) that result in the seamless interpenetration of
reviews and sales. Such practices undermine the independence and objectivity of the review and thus the credibility and influence of intermediaries.
For example, observers allege that these revenue collection methods are at
the root of Buzzfeed's questionable decision to not publish negative reviews.[50]
Compounding this problem is the fact that new intermediaries that operate
solely online have yet to formally establish industry-wide professional ethics
and standards (such as the separation of copy and advertisements in magazines and newspapers). Thus, although formal intermediaries remain central
to the existence of markets for cultural goods, entrepreneurs in the field must
remember that long-run success as an intermediary still depends on performing the fundamental functions with independence and expertise.

However much it may appear that consumers are not particularly concerned about apparent conflicts of interest and that they welcome the opinions of other consumers, some recent incidents suggest that consumers are
not so blinded by the easy and free access to reviews and critiques that they
become oblivious to the prerequisites of intermediaries. For instance, an up-
roar ensued when consumers noticed that revenues from advertising (from
restaurants) had influenced the reviews and information available on Yelp
.com.[51] In another case, consumers became upset when they found out that a
sharply negative review of (the rather unflattering book) *The Everything Store:
Jeff Bezos and the Age of Amazon* was written by MacKenzie Bezos, Jeff's wife.

Consumers are right to be suspicious of user reviews. The possibility of
gaming the system is so insidious and so high—especially since the advent
of "mechanical turks,"[52,53] which can write multiple (positive or negative) reviews on demand in exchange for a fee—that ventures founded purely on the
basis of social engagement and reviews contributed by lay users are in dan-
ger of becoming obsolete as consumers become disillusioned by their lack of
objectivity. A *New York Times* report on Penske Media's purchase of *Variety*
emphasized the pertinence and significance of credibility and reputation in its
assertion that the magazine's old-fashioned principles continue to be of value

to new world intermediaries and its conclusion that "despite its ailing state, *Variety* lends credibility to Penske Media."[54]

Restoring Faith in Formal Intermediaries

Because the twin properties of independence and expertise are so essential, intermediaries will survive, albeit in a modified format. However, entrepreneurs must restore consumers' faith in formal intermediaries, regardless of where (that is, through which medium) the discourse is presented. To that end, the FCC has made attempts to regulate conflict-of-interest issues in blogs and other individual-driven websites that evaluate and endorse goods. In addition, entrepreneurs have begun to self-impose disclosure and disclaimer requirements. Many bloggers and other online entities are aware of such problems and are taking steps to develop the same safeguards and abide by the same principles and norms that exist in the world of physical media, although the issue of credibility will persist until those norms are widely accepted and adopted. One example of an online intermediary who has emphasized independence is brainpickings.org, founded and run by writer/commentator Maria Popova, who reviews thematically grouped books (in the style of *The New York Review of Books*). The site contains no advertisements and is run as a nonprofit, with revenues solicited from readers in the form of donations/ subscriptions. Rather than drawing an income from affiliate revenues (from publishers), Popova links to the public library page of the book and thus maintains separation between her discourse and sales.[55,56]

THE ROLE OF CONSUMERS

Finally, any discussion of the changes in the ecosystem of the creative industries would be incomplete without a close examination of the role of consumers in the process of creating a market for cultural goods. As mentioned at several points earlier, some of the problems faced by the entities in creative industries emerged because consumers lost sight of the economic realities that constrain all members of society: artists need to earn a living, and sharing and duplicating works without proper payment defies both the law and ethical norms. Similarly, the expectation that discourse should be free forces entrepreneurial intermediaries to compromise their integrity to generate revenues sufficient to provide an income. This situation is neither economically sustainable nor beneficial for the future of civic society. As consumers, individuals must understand and accept that, although the Internet has made it possible for anyone to create and contribute, not everything posted on the Internet is of equivalent quality. Society must recognize high-quality contributions and foster economic and social conditions that enable the continued creation of both high-quality artistic works and expert independent discourse that identifies such works and establishes their economic and cultural value. Heeding this clarion call is the only way to ensure the promulgation of new ideas and innovative creative goods that can rejuvenate and transform society.

Conclusion

Although the advent of digitalization and globalization has engendered significant changes in the markets for cultural goods, the traditional structure and functioning of the value chain in creative industries remains relevant and important. Thus, old rules prevail in the new world, albeit with some modifications. The goal of the moment, then, is to judiciously blend the advantages of the new world with the foundational elements of the old world to generate broader and deeper access to new cultural goods in a sustained manner.

Contemporary society stands at a juncture where the possibilities for cultural change are numerous and significant—indeed, these possibilities are a business imperative for pioneer entrepreneurs seeking to avail themselves of the market-creation opportunities generated by globalization and/or digitalization. This is an exciting but delicate moment, as established practices in the creative industries are reexamined, challenged, and sometimes adjusted as a result of the upheavals caused by the intensively interconnected nature of today's digitalized and globalized world. Willfully ignoring rules and practices that serve primarily to protect and elevate consumers, in pursuit of a gold rush of entrepreneurial opportunities, will result in a race to the bottom from a civil society perspective. One of the objectives of this book is to illuminate the hazards of such behavior while also offering a way to prevent this potential downfall. Despite the misgivings expressed in certain parts of the book, it is intended to serve as an optimistic portrait of the creative industries that highlights both the pitfalls and plaudits awaiting those pioneer entrepreneurs who successfully create markets for radically innovative cultural goods, changing culture in the process. These are interesting times, and the onus is on all members of society to understand and establish the foundations of a world in which artists and artworks, and above all the novel ideas and unique visions embedded in these works, enjoy unfettered access to minds ready for change.

NOTES

PREFACE

1. Wilson, E. 2012. "Moving Past Fierce." *The New York Times*. February 9, 2012; retrieved on June 30, 2016, from www.nytimes.com/2012/02/09/fashion/christian-siriano-seeks-fashion-industrys-approval.html)

2. D. H. Bowen, J. P. Greene, and B. Kisida. 2014. "Learning to Think Critically: A Visual Art Experiment." *Educational Researcher* 34(1).

CHAPTER 1

1. Yoko Ono, 1971. "What Is the Relationship between the World and the Artist?" Retrieved on December 29, 2016, from http://imaginepeace.com/archives/2622.

2. H. E. Aldrich and C. M. Fiol. 1994. "Fools Rush In? The Institutional Context of Industry Creation." *Academy of Management Review* 19: 645–670; H. S. Becker. 1982. *Art Worlds*. Berkeley: University of California Press; A. Danto. 1964. "The Artworld." *The Journal of Philosophy*, 61(19): 571–584; and Mukti Khaire and R. Daniel Wadhwani. 2010. "Changing Landscapes: The Construction of Meaning and Value in a New Category—Modern Indian Art." *Academy of Management Journal* (Special Issue on Organizations and Their Institutional Environments: Bringing Meaning, Culture, and Values Back In); 53(6): 1281-1304

3. Paul M. Hirsch. 1972. "Processing Fads and Fashions by Culture Industry Systems: An Organization-Set Analysis." *American Journal of Sociology* 77(4): 639–659.

4. It is possible to overstate this distinction between cultural goods and other utilitarian items, especially because in the current context producers layer symbolism and status signals on top of commodified goods to command premium pricing. That said, the underlying utility of these objects is greater than that of most cultural goods, which possess primarily intangible value.

5. Lewis Hyde. 2009. *The Gift: Creativity and the Artist in the Modern World*. New York: Random House; Patricia Thornton, W. Ocasio, and M. Lounsbury. 2012. *The Institutional Logics Perspective: A New Approach to Culture, Structure, and Process*. Oxford, UK: Oxford University Press; and M. Glynn and M. Lounsbury. 2005. "From the Critics' Corner: Logic Blending, Discursive Change and Authenticity in a Cultural Production System." *Journal of Management Studies* 42: 1031–1055.

6. Pierre Bourdieu. 1993. *The Field of Cultural Production: Essays on Art and Literature*. New York: Columbia University Press.

7. Harrison C. White. 1981. "Where Do Markets Come From?" *American Journal of Sociology*, 87(3): 517–547; and V. A. Zelizer. 1988. "Beyond the Polemics on the Market: Establishing a Theoretical and Empirical Agenda." *Sociological Forum* 3: 614–634.

8. Mukti Khaire, 2010. "Fashioning an Industry: Socio-cognitive Processes in the Construction of Worth of a New Industry." *Organization Studies* 35(1): 41–74.

9. Ibid.

10. John Dewey. 1939. *Theory of Valuation*. Chicago: The University of Chicago Press.

11. D. Stark. 2011. *The Sense of Dissonance: Accounts of Worth in Economic Life*. Princeton, NJ: Princeton University Press.

12. R. Daniel Wadhwani and Mukti Khaire. 2014. "Valuation as a Social Process: How Market Contexts, Actors, and Texts Interact to Construct the Value of Goods." Working Paper.

13. John Dewey. 1939. *Theory of Valuation*. Chicago: University of Chicago Press; V. A. Zelizer. 1989. "The Social Meaning of Money: 'Special Monies.'" *The American Journal of Sociology* 95(2): 342–377; V. A. Zelizer. 1988. "Beyond the Polemics on the Market: Establishing a Theoretical and Empirical Agenda." *Sociological Forum* 3: 614–634; and Lester Thurow. 1983. *Dangerous Currents*. New York: Random House.

14. N. Phillips and C. Oswick. 2012. "Organizational Discourse: Domains, Debates, and Directions." *Academy of Management Annals* 6: 435–481; also R. Daniel Wadhwani and Mukti Khaire. 2014. "Valuation as a Social Process: How Market Contexts, Actors, and Texts Interact to Construct the Value of Goods." Working Paper.

15. N. Phillips and C. Oswick. 2012. "Organizational Discourse: Domains, Debates, and Directions." *Academy of Management Annals* 6: 435–481; and R. Daniel Wadhwani and Mukti Khaire. 2015. "Valuation as a Social Process: Organizational and Managerial Implications of the Social Construction of Value." Working Paper.

16. D. Dranove and G. Z. Jin. 2010. "Quality Disclosure and Certification: Theory and Practice." *Journal of Economic Literature* 48(4): 935–963. For a more detailed conceptual exposition on the process of value construction in markets and the role of such disinterested intermediaries, please see Daniel R. Wadhwani and Mukti Khaire. 2014. "Valuation as a Social Process: How Market Contexts, Actors, and Texts Interact to Construct the Value of Goods." Working Paper; also see M. Khaire. 2014. "Fashioning an Industry: Socio-cognitive Processes in the Construction of Worth of a New Industry." *Organization Studies* 35(1): 41–74.

17. However, as writer and design critic Virginia Postrel noted, it has become difficult of late to identify a strictly utilitarian good, one that has no design elements that infuse the object with symbolic cachet and increase its market price; an illustrative example is toasters with a "retro" look, conceived by well-known designers and sold in the market at a higher price than other equally functional "regular" toasters that are undifferentiated and commoditized. The premium such designed objects command is presumably the result of not only superior aesthetics but also the emotional connec-

tion to a bygone era they evoke among consumers. For more information, see Virginia Postrel. 2004. *The Substance of Style: How the Rise of Aesthetic Value Is Remaking Commerce, Culture, and Consciousness.* New York: HarperCollins.

18. Pierre Bourdieu. 1993. *The Field of Cultural Production: Essays on Art and Literature.* New York: Columbia University Press.

19. M. Eisenman 2013. "Understanding Aesthetic Design in the Context of Technological Evolution." *Academy of Management Review* 38(3): 332–351; V. Postrel. 2009. *The Substance of Style.* New York: HarperCollins; and M. Khaire. 2014. "Entrepreneurship by Design: The Construction of Meaning and Markets for Craft Goods." Working Paper.

20. Details about this definition are discussed later in the chapter. Suffice it here to say that this broad definition allows existing firms to be considered entrepreneurial, not limiting entrepreneurship as the purview of new ventures. Moreover, the specific conceptualization of markets used in this book allows individuals also to be characterized as entrepreneurs, if their commentary (see the following discussion) is responsible for creating a market for a new good.

21. The importance of a shared understanding of a good and broad acceptance of its meaning to enabling market exchange of the good has been the cornerstone of the literature on the centrality of cognition to the study of markets and organizations. See, in particular, J. F. Porac, H. Thomas, and C. Baden-Fuller. 1989. "Competitive Groups as Cognitive Communities: The Case of Scottish Knitwear Manufacturers." *Journal of Management Studies* 26: 397–416; and J. F. Porac, H. Thomas, F. Wilson, D. Paton, and A. Kanfer. 1995. "Rivalry and the Industry Model of Scottish Knitwear Producers." *Administrative Science Quarterly* 40: 203–227.

22. Margaret C. Campbell. 1995. "When Attention-Getting Advertising Tactics Elicit Consumer Inferences of Manipulative Intent: The Importance of Balancing Benefits and Investments." *Journal of Consumer Psychology* 4(3): 225–254.

23. R. Barthes. 1983. *The Fashion System.* New York: Hill & Wang.

24. Paul M. Hirsch. 1972. "Processing Fads and Fashions by Culture Industry Systems: An Organization-Set Analysis." *American Journal of Sociology* 77(4): 639–659.

25. R. Barthes. 1983. *The Fashion System.* New York: Hill & Wang.

26. Although not the same as wearing two *blouses* per se, consider the practice of wearing a suit jacket or blazer over a shirt. Although it is perfectly legitimate and appropriate to do so and although the custom needs no explanation or justification any more, it is not inconceivable that the added significance of a jacket (in some ways, a blouse by a different name) had to be constructed through commentary.

27. R. E. Caves. 2000. *Creative Industries: Contracts between Art and Commerce.* Cambridge, MA: Harvard University Press; Pierre Bourdieu. 1993. *The Field of Cultural Production: Essays on Art and Literature.* New York: Columbia University Press; and Herbert J. Gans. 1999. *Popular Culture and High Culture: An Analysis and Evaluation of Taste.* New York: Basic Books.

28. In the context of fashion, for instance, this individual desire to "fit in" is an almost axiomatic belief. The television network equivalent of this is the so-called

water-cooler show, which pervades social interactions and conversation so much that individuals feel compelled to watch it, largely to be part of the conversation.

29. See Georg Simmel. 1957. "Fashion." *American Journal of Sociology* 62(6): 541–558.

30. Georg Simmel. 1998. *Simmel on Culture: Selected Writings.* Edited by David Frisby and Mike Featherstone. London: Sage Publications.

31. Howard Becker. 1982. *Art Worlds.* Berkeley: University of California Press.

32. This example is based on research jointly conducted with R. Daniel Wadhwani and published as a case study (see following note), and a scholarly journal article; see Mukti Khaire and R. Daniel Wadhwani. 2010. "Changing Landscapes: The Construction of Meaning and Value in a New Market Category Modern Indian Art." *Academy of Management Journal* 53(6). (Special Issue on Organizations and Their Institutional Environments: Bringing Meaning, Culture, and Values Back In).

33. Mukti Khaire and Daniel Wadhwani. "Saffronart.com: Bidding for Success." HBS No. 9-807-114. Boston: Harvard Business School Publishing.

34. Mukti Khaire and R. Daniel Wadhwani. 2010. "Changing Landscapes: The Construction of Meaning and Value in a New Market Category Modern Indian Art." *Academy of Management Journal* 53(6). (Special Issue on Organizations and Their Institutional Environments: Bringing Meaning, Culture, and Values Back In.)

35. Indeed, de novo goods and the creation of a market for such goods usually receive the most scholarly and popular attention, but, as will become clearer in the latter sections of this book, the creation of markets for existing goods is a unique form of pioneer entrepreneurship that has significant cultural implications.

36. Mukti Khaire and Eleanor Kenyon. 2014. "The Development of the Markets for Natural, Organic, and Health Foods in the U.S." Harvard Business School Module Note 815-054. Boston: Harvard Business School Publishing.

37. See the teaching case on Noma: Mukti Khaire and Elena Corsi. 2014. "Noma: A Lot on the Plate." Harvard Business School Case 814-097. Boston: Harvard Business School Publishing.

38. René Redzepi. 2009. *Noma Time and Place.* London: Phaidon; and Helen Greenwood. 2012. "Going Wild in the Kitchen." *The Sidney Morning Herald.* September 4. Also see H. Byrkjeflot, J. S. Pedersen, and S. Svejenova. 2013. "From Label to Practice: The Process of Creating New Nordic Cuisine." *Journal of Culinary Science & Technology* 11(1): 36–55.

39. Peter Gay. 2008. "Modernism: The Lure of Heresy from Baudelaire to Beckett and Beyond." New York: W. W. Norton & Company.

40. Lewis Hyde. 2009. *The Gift: Creativity and the Artist in the Modern World.* New York: Random House; and Pierre-Michel Menger. 2014. *The Economics of Creativity.* Cambridge, MA: Harvard University Press.

41. Lewis Hyde. 2009. *The Gift: Creativity and the Artist in the Modern World.* New York: Random House.

42. R. E. Caves. 2000. *Creative Industries: Contracts between Art and Commerce.* Cambridge, MA: Harvard University Press; Pierre Bourdieu, 1993. *The Field of Cul-*

tural Production: Essays on Art and Literature. New York: Columbia University Press; Herbert J. Gans. 1999. *Popular Culture and High Culture: An Analysis and Evaluation of Taste*. New York: Basic Books; and Wesley Shrum. 1991. "Critics and Publics: Cultural Mediation in Highbrow and Popular Performing Arts." *American Journal of Sociology* 97(2): 347–375.

43. Billboard Charts Archive. The Hot 100 1979 Archive. Retrieved on December 29, 2016, from www.billboard.com/archive/charts/1979/hot-100.

44. Given the importance of intersubjective agreement on norms and value within a market, more than one entity will inevitably be involved in market creation. That said, a single entity is often closely and inextricably linked with particular categories of goods and markets for those categories. Failure to create a market is also likely to be a common and frequent outcome for pioneer entrepreneurs, due to the difficulties inherent to the process, but, like all failures, this is difficult to detect and analyze systematically.

45. Dan Charnas. 2010. *The Big Payback: The History of the Business of Hip-Hop*. New York: New American Library; see also Mukti Khaire and Kerry Herman. "Hip Hop (B): Can't Stop Won't Stop." HBS No. 9-812-116. Boston: Harvard Business School Publishing.

46. S. Craig Watkins. 2005. *Hip Hop Matters: Politics, Pop Culture and the Struggle for the Soul of a Movement*. Boston: Beacon Press.

47. Tricia Rose. 1994. *Black Noise: Rap Music and Black Culture in Contemporary America*. Hanover and London: Wesleyan University Press.

48. Peter Gay. 2008. *Modernism: The Lure of Heresy from Baudelaire to Beckett and Beyond*. New York: W. W. Norton & Company.

49. Ibid.

50. Kevin Birmingham. 2014. *The Most Dangerous Book: The Battle for James Joyce's Ulysses*. New York: The Penguin Press.

51. It is also, more generally, imprudent and dangerous to make anachronistic judgments about the moral superiority of certain beliefs and the cultural works that may influence those beliefs; as an illustration, note that James Joyce's *Ulysses* was considered blasphemous, and therefore morally heinous, when it was first published but today is part of the literary canon and believed to have been a harbinger of modernism.

CHAPTER 2

1. From Lincoln's first debate with Stephan A. Douglas, 1958.

2. For details and background information about the prize, see website of the Man Booker Foundation, retrieved in November 2013 from www.themanbookerprize.com.

3. Adam LeBor. 2011. "I Spy, with My Literary Eye." *Financial Times*. October 14.

4. Julie Bosman. 2013. "Under New Guidelines, Man Booker Prize to Be Open to Americans." *The New York Times*. September 18; and Philip Hensher. 2013. "Well That's the End of the Booker Prize, Then." *The Guardian*. September 18.

5. Julie Bosman. 2013. "Under New Guidelines, Man Booker Prize to Be Open to Americans." *The New York Times*. September 18; and Philip Hensher. 2013. "Well That's the End of the Booker Prize, Then." *The Guardian*. September 18.

6. The term *pioneer* is used here in the traditional, dictionary meaning:

[a] person who goes before others to prepare or open up the way; one who begins, or takes part in beginning, of some enterprise, course of action, etc.; an original worker in a particular field or department of knowledge; a founder (*of* some activity, industry, movement, etc.); a person who is amongst the first to explore or settle a new country, territory, or region. (From the Oxford English Dictionary; retrieved in December 2016 from www.oed.com/view/Entry/144355?rskey=2co1qX&result=1&isAdvanced=false #eid)

Thus, a pioneer entrepreneur does not have to be the first of its kind (that is, the first fashion magazine or first record label or first auction house) but rather *the first in a territory, the first to take on the task of creating a new market for a new category of goods*. Neither are pioneer entrepreneurs limited to the creative industries; Microsoft was a pioneer in the personal computing market.

7. Of course, the perceived appropriateness and value of a category of goods or an idea can also be decreased, but the process typically will not result in the creation of a market for that category. Lowering the appropriateness of a good is often the result of social movements; the antismoking campaign that reduced the perceived value of cigarettes is an exemplar. Additionally, recategorizing as valuable one particular item may simultaneously involve lowering the value of another item; this occurred in the process of creating a market for organic foods, which lowered the perceived value of produce and grains grown using chemical pesticides and fertilizers.

8. Box Office Mojo,."Jaws Summary." Retrieved in August 2011 from http://boxofficemojo.com/movies/?id=jaws.htm; and Gary R. Edgerton. 1983. *American Film Exhibition and an Analysis of the Motion Picture Industry's Market Structure, 1963–1980*. New York: Garland Publishing.

9. Pierre Bourdieu. 1993. *The Field of Cultural Production: Essays on Art and Literature*. New York: Columbia University Press.

10. R. Daniel Wadhwani and Mukti Khaire. 2014. "Valuation as a Social Process: How Market Contexts, Actors, and Texts Interact to Construct the Value of Goods." Working Paper.

11. Aldrich, Howard E. 1999. *Organizations Evolving*, London: Sage; and H. E. Aldrich and C. M. Fiol. (1994). "Fools Rush In? The Institutional Context of Industry Creation." *Academy of Management Review* 19: 645–670.

12. P. M. Hirsch. 1972. "Processing Fads and Fashions: An Organization-Set Analysis of Cultural Industry Systems." *American Journal of Sociology*: 639–659.

13. R. E. Caves. 2000. *Creative Industries: Contracts between Art and Commerce*. Cambridge, MA: Harvard University Press; and Herbert J. Gans. 1999. *Popular Culture and High Culture: An Analysis and Evaluation of Taste*. New York: Basic Books.

14. C. L. Brown and A. Krishna. 2004. "The Skeptical Shopper: A Metacognitive Account for the Effects of Default Options on Choice." *Journal of Consumer Research*

31(3): 529–539; and P. Wright. 2002. "Marketplace Metacognition and Social Intelligence." *Journal of Consumer Research* 28(4): 677–682.

15. R. Daniel Wadhwani and Mukti Khaire. 2014. "Valuation as a Social Process: How Market Contexts, Actors, and Texts Interact to Construct the Value of Goods." Working Paper; and Mukti Khaire and R. Daniel Wadhwani, 2010. "Changing Landscapes: The Construction of Meaning and Value in a New Market Category—Modern Indian Art." *Academy of Management Journal* 53(6).

16. R. E. Caves. 2000. *Creative Industries: Contracts between Art and Commerce.* Cambridge, MA: Harvard University Press; Pierre Bourdieu. 1993. *The Field of Cultural Production: Essays on Art and Literature.* New York: Columbia University Press; and Herbert J. Gans. 1999. *Popular Culture and High Culture: An Analysis and Evaluation of Taste.* New York: Basic Books.

17. R. Daniel Wadhwani and Mukti Khaire. 2014. "Valuation as a Social Process: How Market Contexts, Actors, and Texts Interact to Construct the Value of Goods." Working Paper; and Mukti Khaire and R. Daniel Wadhwani. 2010. "Changing Landscapes: The Construction of Meaning and Value in a New Category—Modern Indian Art." *Academy of Management Journal* (Special Issue on Organizations and Their Institutional Environments: Bringing Meaning, Culture, and Values Back In) 53(6): 1281–1304.

18. Ibid.

19. Robert Clark. 1993. *James Beard: A Biography.* New York: HarperCollins Publishers.

20. Guy Henle. 1978. "Critic's Choice for Fine Fare." *The New York Times.* January 1; and Craig Clairborne. 1959. "$4.5 Million Restaurant to Open Here." *The New York Times.* July 16.

21. Fiona M. Scott Morton and Joel M. Podolny. 2002. "Love or Money? The Effects of Owner Motivation in the California Wine Industry." *The Journal of Industrial Economics* 50(4): 431–456; and Javier Gimeno, Timothy B. Folta, Arnold C. Cooper, and Carolyn Y. Woo. 1997. "Survival of the Fittest? Entrepreneurial Human Capital and the Persistence of Underperforming Firms." *Administrative Science Quarterly* 42(4): 750–783.

22. Kevin Birmingham. 2014. *The Most Dangerous Book: The Battle for James Joyce's Ulysses.* New York: The Penguin Press.

23. H. E. Aldrich and C. M. Fiol. 1994. "Fools Rush In? The Institutional Context of Industry Creation." *Academy of Management Review* 19: 645–670; Robert D. Benford and David A. Snow. 2000. "Framing Processes and Social Movements: An Overview and Assessment." *Annual Review of Sociology* 26: 611–639; and A. B. Hargadon and Y. Douglas. 2001. "When Innovations Meet Institutions: Edison and the Design of the Electric Light." *Administrative Science Quarterly* 46(3), 476–501.

24. Mukti Khaire and R. Daniel Wadhwani. 2010. "Changing Landscapes: The Construction of Meaning and Value in a New Market Category—Modern Indian Art." *Academy of Management Journal* 53(6): 1281–1304.

25. James Greenberg. 1984. "Sundance Institute Shot in Arm for Indie Prod'n," *Variety*, June 11: 22; Ray Loynd 1983, "How a Sundance Step Spawned a 'Ballad,'" *Variety*, June 13: 72; and Geoff King. 2009. *Indiewood, USA: Where Hollywood Meets Independent Cinema*. New York: I. B. Tauris & Co. For a comprehensive history of independent cinema in the United States, also see Yannis Tzioumakis. 2006. *American Independent Cinema: An Introduction*. Edinburgh, UK: Edinburgh University Press; Emanuel Levy. 1999. *Cinema of Outsiders: The Rise of American Independent Film*. New York: New York University Press; and Lory Smith. 1999. *Party in a Box: The Story of the Sundance Film Festival*. Salt Lake City, UT: Gibbs Smith.

26. M. F. Callan. 2011. *Robert Redford: The Biography*. New York: Alfred A. Knopf.

27. Edmonde Charles-Roux. 1975. *Chanel: Her Life, Her World—and the Woman behind the Legend She Herself Created*. New York: Knopf; and Justine Picardie. 2010. *Coco Chanel: The Legend and the Life*. London: Harper Collins.

28. Edmonde Charles-Roux. 1975. Chanel: Her Life, Her World—and the Woman behind the Legend She Herself Created. New York: Knopf; and Justine Picardie. 2010. *Coco Chanel: The Legend and the Life*. London: Harper Collins.

29. Geoffrey A. Moore. 1999. *Crossing the Chasm: Marketing and Selling High-Tech Products to Mainstream Customers*. New York: HarperCollins.

30. H. E. Aldrich and C. M. Fiol. 1994. "Fools Rush In? The Institutional Context of Industry Creation." *Academy of Management Review* 19: 645–670; Robert D. Benford and David A. Snow. 2000. "Framing Processes and Social Movements: An Overview and Assessment." *Annual Review of Sociology* 26: 611–639; and A. B. Hargadon and Y. Douglas. 2001. "When Innovations Meet Institutions: Edison and the Design of the Electric Light." *Administrative Science Quarterly* 46(3): 476–501.

31. This description of the framing strategy of designers in India is based on a multiyear qualitative research project on the Indian fashion industry that I conducted and that yielded two journal papers and a chapter in an edited volume. The paper that most closely describes this framing and the advantages designers derived from it was published as Mukti Khaire. 2014. "Fashioning an Industry: Socio-cognitive Processes in the Construction of Worth of a New Industry." *Organization Studies* 35(1): 41–74.

32. Five yards of fabric draped in a specific style. Saris are traditionally hand-woven but not embroidered.

33. A clothing ensemble or "suit" consisting of a loosely fitted tunic (the *kameez*) worn over loose drawstring trousers (the *salwar*) and a scarf (*dupatta*).

34. Mukti Khaire. 2014. "Fashioning an Industry: Socio-cognitive Processes in the Construction of Worth of a New Industry." *Organization Studies* 35(1): 41–74.

35. An ensemble that resembles a long, full skirt worn with a blouse of varying length and a large scarf, usually draped across the torso.

36. Author interview with Sabyasachi Mukherjee. New York, September 1, 2006.

37. Mukti Khaire and Eleanor Kenyon. 2014. "The Development of the Markets for Natural, Organic, and Health Foods in the U.S." Harvard Business School Module Note 815-054, September. Boston: Harvard Business School Publishing; and Nick Paumgarten. 2010. "Food Fighter." *The New Yorker*. January 4.

38. W. C. Rhoades. 1963. "The History and Use of Agricultural Chemicals." *The Florida Entomologist* 46(4): 275–277.

39. Robert D. Benford and David A. Snow. 2000. "Framing Processes and Social Movements: An Overview and Assessment." *Annual Review of Sociology*, 26: 611–639.

40. Lewis Hyde. 2009. *The Gift: Creativity and the Artist in the Modern World*. New York: Random House.

41. This is the primary distinction between market making or market creation and marketing, which primarily comprises producers' attempts to communicate the value of their products.

42. Lucien Karpik. 2010. *Valuing the Unique: The Economics of Singularities*. Princeton, NJ: Princeton University Press.

CHAPTER 3

1. Jonathan Landman, quoted in Arthur S. Brisbane, 2016. "The View from the Critic's Seat." *The New York Times*. July 14.

2. R. Serge Denisoff. 1991. *Inside MTV*. New Brunswick, NJ: Transaction Publishers: 34.

3. Gabriel Weimann. 2000. *Communicating Unreality: Modern Media and the Reconstruction of Reality*. Thousand Oaks, CA: Sage Publications: 193.

4. Jack Banks. 1996. *Monopoly Television: MTV's Quest to Control the Music*. Boulder, CO: Westview Press: 37.

5. In most creative industries, creators can and do work and create outside the bounds of producers, but the structure of some industries, such as fashion and food, allows for creators themselves to found firms to take their creations to market. This distinction and its implications are explored in greater detail in the section of the book on producers.

6. H. C. White. 1981. "Where Do Markets Come From?" *American Journal of Sociology* 87(3): 517–547; and V. A. Zelizer. 1988. "Beyond the Polemics on the Market: Establishing a Theoretical and Empirical Agenda." *Sociological Forum* 3: 614–634.

7. Ibid.

8. D. Dranove and G. Z. Jin. 2010. "Quality Disclosure and Certification: Theory and Practice" *Journal of Economic Literature* 48(4): 935–963. For a more detailed conceptual exposition on the process of value construction in markets and the role of such disinterested intermediaries, please see Daniel R. Wadhwani and Mukti Khaire. 2014. "Valuation as a Social Process: How Market Contexts, Actors, and Texts Interact to Construct the Value of Goods." Working paper; also see M. Khaire. 2014. "Fashioning an Industry: Socio-cognitive Processes in the Construction of Worth of a New Industry." *Organization Studies* 35(1): 41–74.

9. C. Shapiro. 1983. "Premiums for High Quality Products as Returns to Reputations." *The Quarterly Journal of Economics*: 659–679; and S. Salop and J. E. Stiglitz. 1977. "Bargains and Ripoffs: A Model of Monopolistically Competitive Price Dispersion." *Review of Economic Studies* 44(October): 493–510.

10. C. Shapiro. 1983. "Premiums for High Quality Products as Returns to Reputations." *The Quarterly Journal of Economics*: 659–679.

11. P. Wright. 1986. "Schemer Schema-Consumers Intuitive Theories about Marketers Influence Tactics." *Advances in Consumer Research* 13: 1–3; S. K. Balasubramanian. 1994. "Beyond Advertising and Publicity: Hybrid Messages and Public Policy Issues." *Journal of Advertising* 23(4): 29–46; M. A. Jolson and F. A. Bushman. 1978. "3rd Party Consumer Information Systems: Case of the Food Critic." *Journal of Retailing* 54(4): 63–79; C. L. Brown and A. Krishna. 2004. "The Skeptical Shopper: A Metacognitive Account for the Effects of Default Options on Choice." *Journal of Consumer Research* 31(3): 529–539; P. Wright. 2002. "Marketplace Metacognition and Social Intelligence." *Journal of Consumer Research* 28(4): 677–682; and M. Friestad and P. Wright. 1994. "The Persuasion Knowledge Model: How People Cope with Persuasion Attempts." *Journal of Consumer Research*: 1–31; for an overall review of consumers' beliefs about the market, see C. P. Duncan. 1990. "Consumer Market Beliefs: A Review of the Literature and an Agenda for Future Research." *Advances in Consumer Research* 17(1): 729–736.

12. P. R. Darke, L. Ashworth and R. J. Ritchie. 2008. "Damage from Corrective Advertising: Causes and Cures." *Journal of Marketing* 72(6), 81–97; R. D. Petty and J. C. Andrews. 2008. "Covert Marketing Unmasked: A Legal and Regulatory Guide for Practices That Mask Marketing Messages. *Journal of Public Policy & Marketing* 27(1): 7–18; P. R. Darke and R. J. Ritchie. (2007). "The Defensive Consumer: Advertising Deception, Defensive Processing, and Distrust." *Journal of Marketing Research* 44(1): 114–127; C. Obermiller and E. R. Spangenberg. 2000. "On the Origin and Distinctness of Skepticism toward Advertising." *Marketing Letters* 11(4): 311–322; R. M. Kramer. (1998). "Paranoid Cognition in Social Systems: Thinking and Acting in the Shadow of Doubt." *Personality and Social Psychology Review* 2(4): 251–275; J. E. Calfee and D. J. Ringold. 1994. "The 70% Majority: Enduring Consumer Beliefs about Advertising." *Journal of Public Policy & Marketing*: 228–238; and M. Friestad and P. Wright. 1994. "The Persuasion Knowledge Model: How People Cope with Persuasion Attempts." *Journal of Consumer Research*: 1–31.

13. D. Dranove and G. Z. Jin. 2010. "Quality Disclosure and Certification: Theory and Practice." *Journal of Economic Literature* 48(4): 935–963. For a more detailed conceptual exposition on the process of value construction in markets and the role of such disinterested intermediaries, please see Daniel R. Wadhwani and Mukti Khaire. 2014. "Valuation as a Social Proess: How Market Contexts, Actors, and Texts Interact to Construct the Value of Goods." Working paper; also see Mukti Khaire. 2014. "Fashioning an Industry: Socio-cognitive Processes in the Construction of Worth of a New Industry." *Organization Studies* 35(1): 41–74.

14. Notably, producers, too, influence the perceived value of creative works (and not just through advertisements, brochures, and promotional materials). This is especially evident in the art market, where, despite their direct stake in the value of art works, gallery owners have a significant amount of influence on buyers' perceptions of the meaning and value of the art. As discussed later in the book, specific features

of the underlying structure of the art market render this possible. Similarly, nonprofit producers have, for obvious reasons, a greater impact on value construction and market creation than for-profit producers. In particular, large public institutions such as Lincoln Center in New York have played significant roles in influencing tastes and constructing the value of the category of goods they produce. In part, the reasons for this are historical, especially because public institutions were typically set up with a mission to promote civic society by instilling "high" culture among citizens. Further, the absence of a profit motive renders the value-constructing discourse of these producers more "pure" in intent and untainted by the desire to profit at any cost, in the eyes of consumers. As a result, nonprofit producers often occupy the same exalted position as intermediaries in the value chain, with a similar amount of influence on the market value of a good. These issues are explored in greater detail later in the book.

15. Stefanie Cohen. 2013. "'Spider-Man: Turn off the Dark' to Close in January, Sources Say." *The Wall Street Journal.* November 18; and Internet Broadway Database. "Spider-Man: Turn off the Dark." Retrieved in April 2015 from www.ibdb.com /production.php?id=488485.

16. There is precedent for using the term in this way. Scholars have previously used the term to denote third-party (that is, neither producers nor consumers) market entities, whose discourse provides crucial objective and independent assessments (such as reviews, rankings, awards, and so on) of goods in a market. See, for example, P. Aspers and Jens Beckert. 2011. "Introduction." In Jens Beckert and Patrick Aspers. *The Worth of Goods: Valuation and Pricing in the Economy.* Oxford, UK: Oxford University Press; Wendy N. Espeland and Michael Sauder. 2007. "Rankings and Reactivity: How Public Measures Recreate Social Worlds." *The American Journal of Sociology* 113(1): 1–40; Michael Sauder. "Interlopers and Field Change: The Entry of U.S. News into the Field of Legal Education." *Administrative Science Quarterly* 53: 209–234; and M. Sauder and Gary Alan Fine. 2008. "Arbiters, Entrepreneurs, and the Shaping of Business School Reputations." *Sociological Forum* 23(4): 699–723.

17. Mark Granovetter. 1985. "Economic Action and Social Structure: The Problem of Embeddedness." *The American Journal of Sociology* 91(3): 481–510; H. C. White. 1981. "Where Do Markets Come From?" *American Journal of Sociology* 87(3): 517–547; and V. A. Zelizer. 1988. "Beyond the Polemics on the Market: Establishing a Theoretical and Empirical Agenda." *Sociological Forum* 3: 614–634. Indeed, one of the contributions of this section in the book is the systematic definition and description of the various functions and properties of intermediaries to enable a rigorous analytical understanding of markets and entrepreneurship in the creative industries.

18. P. M. Hirsch. 1972. "Processing Fads and Fashions: An Organization-Set Analysis of Cultural Industry Systems." *American Journal of Sociology:* 639–659.

19. Pierre Bourdieu. 1993. *The Field of Cultural Production: Essays on Art and Literature.* New York: Columbia University Press.

20. Ibid.

21. Ibid.

22. Ibid.

23. Adam Gopnik. 2012. "Postscript: Robert Hughes." *The New Yorker*, August 2.

24. Thorstein Veblen. 1899. *The Theory of the Leisure Class: An Economic Study of Institutions*. New York: Macmillan.

25. R. E. Caves. 2000. *Creative Industries: Contracts between Art and Commerce*. Cambridge, MA: Harvard University Press.

26. R. Daniel Wadhwani and Mukti Khaire. 2015. "Valuation as a Social Process: Organizational and Managerial Implications of the Social Construction of Value." Working paper.

27. Stanley Lieberson. 2000. *A Matter of Taste: How Names, Fashions, and Culture Change*. New Haven, CT: Yale University Press.

28. Ibid.

29. Herbert J. Gans. 1999. *Popular Culture and High Culture: An Analysis and Evaluation of Taste*. New York: Basic Books.

30. R. E. Caves. 2000. *Creative Industries: Contracts between Art and Commerce*. Cambridge, MA: Harvard University Press.

31. Ceramic artist Grayson Perry referred to this phenomenon in his 2013 Reith lecture: "It's like when we go on holiday, all we really want to do is take the photograph that we've seen in the brochure."

32. Pierre Bourdieu. 1993. *The Field of Cultural Production: Essays on Art and Literature*. New York: Columbia University Press.

33. R. E. Caves. 2000. *Creative Industries: Contracts between Art and Commerce*. Cambridge, MA: Harvard University Press.

34. Importantly, the number of book titles is much larger than the number of other creative goods produced in a given year (and was selected as an example for this reason) because of the number of creators and producers writing and publishing books. In "high arts" such as opera or avant-garde theater, the number of pieces written (not to mention published and performed) is much lower, due to the nature of these art forms.

35. This is based on print ISBN counts of books with a U.S. publication date from 2002 to 2013. See Bower, "ISBN Output"; retrieved in January 2014 from www.bowker.com/assets/downloads/products/isbn_output_2002_2013.pdf.

36. Don Thompson. 2008. *The $12 Million Stuffed Shark: The Curious Economics of Contemporary Art*. New York: Palgrave Macmillan.

37. In fact, there is a vast literature on this topic, probably sufficient for an entire book by itself. However, I am not expending much space on the issue because the focus of this book is the *business* of culture.

38. This truth forms the basis of a movement on the part of firms to insert themselves (and their products) into these webs and personal social networks through "word of mouth" marketing efforts and the use of social networking sites and tools such as Facebook and Twitter. See S. Sengupta and B. Sisario. 2011. "Facebook as Tastemaker." *The New York Times*. September 22. Such efforts are effectively attempts to formalize previously informal avenues of influence that have existed beyond the control of firms, more so than even formal intermediaries.

39. Julia Robson. 2011. "Not Just for Weddings." *Financial Times*. July 1.

40. Thomas R. Eisenmann. 2008. "Managing Proprietary and Shared Platforms." *California Management Review* 50(4, summer): 31–53.

41. N. Phillips and C. Oswick. 2012. "Organizational Discourse: Domains, Debates, and Directions." *Academy of Management Annals* 6: 435–481.

42. These are all forms of discourse; in the literature on organizations and institutions, discourse comprises not just texts (written and spoken) but also actions and events that are intended to convey meaning and serve as a means of engagement and dialogue among several entities.

43. Hannah Seligson. 2015. "The Brands in Art Basel's Orbit." *The New York Times*. March 8.

44. Personal communication with Karen Jolna, faculty associate at *Ms. Magazine* and lecturer at UCLA, May 17, 2011.

45. Paul Goldberger, phone interview by author, Cambridge, MA, July 19, 2012; Diane Grey, phone interview by author, Cambridge, MA, June 11, 2012; Martha Thorne, phone interview by author, Cambridge, MA, May 18, 2012; Peter Palumbo, phone interview by author, Cambridge, MA, June 21, 2012; Karen Stein, phone interview by author, Cambridge, MA, June 20, 2012; Bill Lacy, phone interview by author, Cambridge, MA, June 2012; Ada Louise Huxtable, phone interview by author, Cambridge, MA, September 14, 2012; Renzo Piano, phone interview by author, Cambridge, MA, September 10, 2012; Frank Gehry, phone interview by author, Cambridge, MA, July 24, 2012; Glenn Murcutt, phone interview by author, Cambridge, MA, June 27, 2012; Thom Mayne, phone interview by author, Cambridge, MA, September 2012; and Peter Zumthor, interview by author, Risch, Switzerland, July 9, 2012.

46. Theodore Libbey. 2006. "Bach, Johann Sebastian." *The NPR Listener's Encyclopedia of Classical Music*. New York: Workman Publishing.

47. Thomas Kelly. "Igor Stravinsky's 'The Rite of Spring.'" *NPR's Peformance Today: Milestones of the Millenium*. Retrieved in April 2015 from www.npr.org/programs/specials/milestones/991110.motm.riteofspring.html.

48. Danny Heitman. 2014. "The Big Easy Slacker's Manual." *The Wall Street Journal*. May 16.

49. All analyses of the Sundance Institute and its impact on creating a market for independent cinema in the United States (here and elsewhere in the book) are based on integrated field research and information from secondary sources. All details of primary and secondary data sources are available in the teaching case study (and corresponding teaching note): Mukti Khaire and Eleanor Kenyon. "The Kid Grows Up: Decisions at Sundance Institute." HBSP 812-051. Some of these ideas are also explored in a forthcoming (in 2017) chapter "The Importance of Being Independent: The Role of Intermediaries in Creating Market Categories," in *Research in Sociology of Organizations*. Bingley, UK: Emerald Insight.

50. Box Office Mojo, "Jaws Summary." Retrieved in August 2011 from http://boxofficemojo.com/movies/?id=jaws.htm.

51. Alex Ross. 2014. "The Opera Lab." *The New Yorker*, February 3.

52. Craig Claiborne. 1959. "$4.5 Million Restaurant to Open Here." *The New York Times.* July 16; and Guy Henle. 1978. "Critic's Choice for Fine Fare." *The New York Times.* January 1.

53. M. Khaire and R. D. Wadhwani. 2010. "Changing Landscapes: The Construction of Meaning and Value in a New Market Category—Modern Indian Art." *Academy of Management Journal* 53(6): 1281–1304.

54. Such a reorientation of value has occurred for art from a variety of countries/regions that were overlooked in the past. Examples include Latin American art, Chinese art, Native American art, and African art.

55. At the same time, it is worth noting that an intermediary firm that determines that the risk of trying to create a new market is too high to contemplate is making a self-fulfilling prophecy because a strong commitment to explicating the category and constructing its value can lead to market creation.

56. In a recent example of this phenomenon, the editor-in-chief of *Vice Magazine* left to create a new literature quarterly *Apology*, where he has adopted a very different sensibility.

57. Dan Charnas. 2010. *The Big Payback: The History of the Business of Hip-Hop.* New York: New American Library.

CHAPTER 4

1. Arthur Danto. 1964. The Artworld. *The Journal of Philosophy* 61(19): 571–584.

2. Julie Bosman. 2012. "Pulitzer Fiction Snub Has Book Publishers Fuming." *The New York Times.* April 16.

3. Mark Granovetter. 1985. "Economic Action and Social Structure: The Problem of Embeddedness." *The American Journal of Sociology* 91(3): 481–510; B. Uzzi. 1997. "Social Structure and Competition in Interfirm Networks: The Paradox of Embeddedness." *Administrative Science Quarterly* 42(1): 35–67; H. C. White. 1981. "Production Markets as Induced Role Structures." *Sociological Methodology* 12(1): 1–57; H. C. White. 1981. "Where Do Markets Come From?" *American Journal of Sociology* 87(3): 517–547; and V. A. Zelizer. 1988. "Beyond the Polemics on the Market: Establishing a Theoretical and Empirical Agenda." *Sociological Forum* 3: 614–634.

4. John Dewey. 1939. *Theory of Valuation.* Chicago: The University of Chicago Press; and D. Stark. 2011. *The Sense of Dissonance: Accounts of Worth in Economic Life.* Princeton, NJ: Princeton University Press.

5. J. Courtney Sullivan. 2013. "How Diamonds Became Forever." *The New York Times.* May 3.

6. Mark Granovetter. 1985. "Economic Action and Social Structure: The Problem of Embeddedness." *The American Journal of Sociology* 91(3): 481–510; H. C. White. 1981. "Production Markets as Induced Role Structures." *Sociological Methodology* 12: 1–57; H. C. White. 1981. "Where Do Markets Come From?" *American Journal of Sociology* 87(3): 517–547; V. A. Zelizer. 1988. "Beyond the Polemics on the Market: Establishing a Theoretical and Empirical Agenda." *Sociological Forum* 3: 614–34; and

B. Uzzi. 1997. "Social Structure and Competition in Interfirm Networks: The Paradox of Embeddedness." *Administrative Science Quarterly*, 35–67.

7. Specific individual preferences, however, may not always align perfectly with broader culture, for a variety of reasons. Thus, for instance, an individual may accept that heavy metal music is a valid market category with established value (at least in a certain section of society) but may not desire to listen to this music, perhaps because he or she grew up in a home where classical music was considered the pinnacle of musical achievement and heavy metal, with its entirely different attributes, was not similarly appreciated and valued.

8. Much of this section on value construction is based on work on valuation more generally in markets beyond creative industries, developed jointly with R. Daniel Wadhwani. Details are articulated in R. Daniel Wadhwani and Mukti Khaire. 2015. "Valuation as a Social Process: Organizational and Managerial Implications of the Social Construction of Value." Working paper. Some parts of it have been expanded in other papers (joint work, as well as single-author studies, such as Mukti Khaire and R. Daniel Wadhwani. 2010. "Changing Landscapes: The Construction of Meaning and Value in a New Category—Modern Indian Art." *Academy of Management Journal* 53(6): 1281–1304; Mukti Khaire. "Fashioning an Industry: Socio-Cognitive Processes in the Construction of Worth of a New Industry." *Organization Studies* 35(1): 41–74; Mukti Khaire. 2015. "Art without Borders? Online Firms and the Global Art Market." In *Cosmopolitan Canvases: The Globalization of Markets for Conemporary Art*. Edited by Olav Velthuis and Stefano Baia-Curioni. Oxford, UK: Oxford University Press: 102–118; and Mukti V. Khaire. 2017. "The Importance of Being Independent: The Role of Intermediaries in Creating Market Categories." Special Issue: Categories to Categorization: Studies in Sociology, Organizations and Strategy at the Crossroads. Research in the Sociology of Organizations 48.

9. R. Daniel Wadhwani and Mukti Khaire. 2015. "Valuation as a Social Process: Organizational and Managerial Implications of the Social Construction of Value." Working paper.

10. M. Callon, C. Méadel, and V. Rabeharisoa, V. 2002. "The Economy of Qualities." *Economy and Society* 31(2): 194–217.

11. M. Callon, Y. Millo, and F. Muniesa, eds. 2007. *Market Devices*. Malden, MA: Blackwell Publishing; M. Callon and F. Muniesa. 2005. "Peripheral Vision: Economic Markets as Calculative Collective Devices." *Organization Studies* 26(8): 1229–1250; J. F. English. 2005. *The Economy of Prestige: Prizes, Awards, and the Circulation of Cultural Value*. Cambridge, MA: Harvard University Press; and Y. Millo, 2007. "Making Things Deliverable: The Origins of Index-Based derivatives." *Sociological Review* 55(s2): 196–214.

12. Producers' commentary also establishes valuation elements and value, but, due to producers' economic incentives, their commentary is entirely valorizing, whereas intermediaries evaluate as well as valorize. For instance, an artwork placed in a well-known gallery such as the Gagosian is implicitly categorized as "fine art," and

a gallery owner may stress to potential buyers the attributes of the work that meet the criteria of evaluation applicable to fine art. Intermediaries' discourse, however, should ideally also inform consumers about the quality criteria that are not met by the work and thus help explain where the work falls on the quality gradient. These distinctions will become clearer in this chapter and the next.

13. The distinctions and definitions here are, for purposes of analytical parsimony and clarity, somewhat reductive or schematic, although I have attempted to highlight nuances whenever possible.

14. U.S. Census Bureau, *Statistical Abstract of the United States 2010. Profile America: Facts for Features*; retrieved in January 2012 from www.census.gov/newsroom /releases/archives/facts_for_features_special_editions/cb10-ff15.html; and U.S. Census Bureau, *Statistical Abstract of the United States. Labor Force, Employment, and Earnings 2012*; retrieved in January 2012 from www.census.gov/prod/2011pubs/12statab /labor.pdf.

15. Joshua P. Friedlander. 2013. *News and Notes on 2013 RIAA Music Industry Shipment and Revenue Statistics*. The Recording Industry Association of America. Available at http://riaa.com/media/2463566A-FF96-E0CA-2766-72779A364D01.pdf.

16. Association of American Publishers. *BookStats 2013*. Accessed in 2015 from http://bookstats.org/pdf/BOOKSTATS_2013_GENERAL_PUBLIC_WEBSITE _HIGHLIGHTS.pdf.

17. Emily Holt. 2011. "And at Long Last, It's Showtime: J.Crew's Runway Debut at NYFW." *Vogue*. September 13; and "J. Crew." Mercedes-Benz Fashion Week. Retrieved in April 2015 from http://mbfashionweek.com/designers/jcrew.

18. Mukti Khaire. 2012. "*Variety*: Taking the Biz Overseas." Harvard Business School Case.

19. Mark Granovetter. 1985. "Economic Action and Social Structure: The Problem of Embeddedness." *The American Journal of Sociology* 91(3): 481–510; H. C. White. 1981. "Production Markets as Induced Role Structures." *Sociological Methodology* 12: 1–57; H. C. White. 1981. "Where Do Markets Come From?" *American Journal of Sociology* 87(3): 517–547; V. A. Zelizer. 1988. "Beyond the Polemics on the Market: Establishing a Theoretical and Empirical Agenda." *Sociological Forum* 3: 614–634; and B. Uzzi. 1997. "Social Structure and Competition in Interfirm Networks: The Paradox of Embeddedness." *Administrative Science Quarterly*: 35–67.

20. Although the terms *critic* and *reviewer* tend to be used interchangeably, there is a difference between a review, "a brief composition, reacting to a specific work," and a piece of criticism, which is "longer and more reflective, on a variety of themes, even departing from [the] artworks themselves." (See Wesley Shrum. 1991. "Critics and Publics: Cultural Mediation in Highbrow and Popular Performing Arts." *American Journal of Sociology* 97(2): 347–375.) Accordingly, *The New York Review of Books* typically publishes criticisms, whereas *The New York Times* publishes reviews (of books or films). Further, per these definitions, criticisms would be more instructive than reviews, owing to the greater contextualization and elaboration in the former. That said, it seems unlikely that this distinction would be meaningful to the majority of

consumers, even though the two formats may have different impacts at the subconscious level.

21. The Razzies (as the ceremony and awards presented annually by the Golden Raspberry Foundation are unofficially known) are an exception (see the Razzie website; retrieved on December 30, 2013, from www.razzies.com). Founded by John Wilson in 1980 to "Dishonor Worst Achievements in Film," the foundation parodies award shows and derides and sometimes humiliates the self-important denizens of Hollywood. At the same time, by unequivocally identifying and publicizing low-quality performances, these awards too can be seen as upholding standards of quality in the art of filmmaking. However, "winning" a Golden Raspberry Award is unlikely to bring the same benefits to an individual or firm that winning another legitimate generally accepted award would bring.

22. M. Adler. 1985. "Stardom and Talent." *American Economic Review*, 75(1): 208–212; and Peter Hedström. 1998. "Rational Imitation." In *Social Mechanisms: An Analytical Approach to Social Theory*, edited by P. Hedstrom and R. Swedberg. Cambridge, UK: Cambridge University Press. For more on social influences on tastes and consumption, see Matthew J. Salganik and Duncan J. Waats. 2009. "Social Influence: The Puzzling Nature of Success in Cultural Markets." In Peter Hedström and Peter Bearman, eds., *The Oxford Handbook of Analytical Sociology*: 315–341, Oxford, UK: Oxford University Press; and Duncan J. Waats. 2007. "The Collective Dynamics of Belief." In Victor Nee and Richard Swedberg, eds. *On Capitalism*: 241–272. Stanford, CA: Stanford University Press.

23. With all these individuals, it is important to distinguish between their work as independent intermediaries and their paid work as spokespersons or models for brands. DeGeneres, for instance, is the face of Cover Girl cosmetics and in that capacity is not acting as an intermediary. That said, brands that employ such influential individuals as spokespersons are clearly trying to piggyback on the individuals' credibility among consumers. Naturally, such individuals must be careful to not overexploit their stature for monetary gain, lest they lose their credibility entirely.

24. Wesley Shrum. 1991. "Critics and Publics: Cultural Mediation in Highbrow and Popular Performing Arts." *American Journal of Sociology* 97(2): 347–375.

25. James English. 2008. *The Economy of Prestige: Prizes, Awards, and the Circulation of Cultural Value*. Cambriddge, MA: Harvard University Press: 7.

26. Box Office Mojo. "2013 Domestic Grosses: Total Grosses of All Movies Released in 2013." Retrieved on December 30, 2016, from http://boxofficemojo.com/yearly/chart/?yr=2013.

27. Box Office Mojo. "Oscar Past Winners and Nominees." Retrieved in April 2015 from www.boxofficemojo.com/oscar.

28. In the twenty years from 1994 to 2014, only three films were both top box office and Best Picture winners (at the Academy Awards): *Forrest Gump* (1994), *Titanic* (1997), and *Lord of the Rings: Return of the King* (2003).

29. In the ten years between 2001 and 2011, books that were awarded the Man Booker Prize experienced, on average, a sixtyfold increase in cumulative sales after

they were named winners (see Katy Stoddard. "Booker Prize Datablog." *The Guardian*. Retrieved in April 2013 from www.theguardian.com/news/datablog/2012/oct/10/booker-prize-2012-winners-sales-data#data. Original data source: Nielsen Bookscan).

30. Robert K. Merton. 1968. "The Matthew Effect in Science." *Science* 159 (3810): 56–63.

31. Coined by sociologist Robert Merton, the term refers to the self-reinforcing cycle of status gains observed in evaluative situations and is derived from a verse in the Book of Matthew: "For unto every one that hath shall be given, and he shall have abundance: but from him that hath not shall be taken even that which he hath."

32. Roger Friedland and Robert R. Alford. 1991. *Bringing Society Back In: Symbols, Practices, and Institutional Contradictions. The New Institutionalism in Organizational Analysis*. Chicago: University of Chicago Press.

33. It is, however, possible to overstate the distinction between individual intermediaries and firms. For all practical purposes, an intermediary is an entity—whether an individual or a firm—that performs the functions previously described in order to construct the value of cultural goods. Both the functions of the intermediary and consumers' expectations regarding these functions remain the same whether the intermediary is an individual or a firm.

34. James English. 2008. *The Economy of Prestige: Prizes, Awards, and the Circulation of Cultural Value*. Cambridge, MA: Harvard University Press.

35. "Film Festivals in the United States." Retrieved in April 2014 from www.festivalfocus.org/breakdown.php.

36. Jackie Wullschlager. 2009. "Painted Love: The Threadneedle Prize Aims to Free Figurative Art from a Generation of Conceptual Taste." *The Financial Times*. September 5.

37. See *The Village Voice* and the American Theater Wing at www.villagevoice.com/obies/about/; accessed on various dates during April 2015.

38. This is so much so that the National Book Award (U.S.) is reportedly trying to make its award ceremony more exciting to stimulate more interest among lay consumers and thus increase the visibility, and consequently the sales, of the award-winning book. For more information, see Leslie Kaufman. 2012. "Book Awards Seek a Bigger Splash, Red Carpet and All." *The New York Times*. November 11.

39. Kaufman, Leslie. Book Awards Seek a Bigger Splash, Red Carpet and All. *The New York Times*. November 11, 2012.

40. See two deep case studies of the Booker Prize and the Grammy Awards on the role of awards and award ceremonies in "configuring" new fields, constructing value, and creating markets. N. Anand and Mary R. Watson. 2004. "Tournament Rituals in the Evolution of Fields: The Case of the Grammy Awards." *The Academy of Management Journal* 47(1): 59–80; and N. Anand and B. Jones. (2008). "Tournament Rituals, Category Dynamics, and Field Configuration: The Case of the Booker Prize." *Journal of Management Studies* 45(6): 1036–1060.

41. See Performa Arts, founded by Roselee Goldberg, at http://performa-arts.org/; Accessed on various dates during April 2015.

CHAPTER 5

1. Ezra Pound. 2010 (1934). *The ABC of Reading*. Reprint with introduction by Michael Dirda. New York: New Directions Paperbacks.

2. In 1905, the first issue of *Variety* declared:

We want you to read it. It will be interesting if for no other reason than that it will be conducted on original lines for a theatrical newspaper. The first, foremost and extraordinary feature of it will be FAIRNESS. Whatever there is to be printed of interest to the professional world WILL BE PRINTED WITHOUT REGARD TO WHOSE NAME IS MENTIONED OR THE ADVERTISING COLUMNS. . . . The reviews will be written conscientiously, and the truth only told. If it hurts it is at least said in fairness and impartiality. . . . a paper to which anyone connected with or interested in the theatrical world may read with the thorough knowledge and belief that what is printed is not dictated by any motive other than the policy above outlined. (Capital letters in original)

3. M. Friestad and P. Wright. 1994. "The Persuasion Knowledge Model: How People Cope with Persuasion Attempts." *Journal of Consumer Research*: 1–31; C. L. Brown and A. Krishna. 2004. "The Skeptical Shopper: A Metacognitive Account for the Effects of Default Options on Choice." *Journal of Consumer Research* 31(3): 529–539; A. Kirmani and M. C. Campbell. (2004). "Goal Seeker and Persuasion Sentry: How Consumer Targets Respond to Interpersonal Marketing Persuasion." *Journal of Consumer Research* 31(3): 573–582; and A. C. Morales. (2005). "Giving Firms an 'E' for Effort: Consumer Responses to High_Effort Firms." *Journal of Consumer Research* 31(4): 806–812.

4. For all market-related intents and purposes, the *perception* of independence is necessary *and* sufficient. Indeed, producers use many "workarounds" to buy intermediaries' attention and favor while allowing intermediaries to maintain a veneer of independence (for more details, see work by Gabriel Rossman, including G. Rossman. 2014. "Obfuscatory Relational Work and Disreputable Exchange." *Sociological Theory* 32(1): 43–63). However, as shown later in this chapter and in Chapter 9, a mere façade of independence is ultimately deleterious to markets and is always bad for society.

5. Although FCC (the Federal Communications Commission, which, in the United States regulates communications by radio, television, wire, satellite, and cable) directives strictly stipulate that advertisements or commercial promotions be clearly identified as such, this separation between copy and ads is not subject to specific regulations and is enforced only via voluntary adherence to a collective norm.

6. Margaret Sullivan. 2014. "Beyond Blank Slates: Writers under Fire." *The New York Times*. February 8.

7. P. Wright. 1986. "Schemer Schema-Consumers Intuitive Theories about Marketers Influence Tactics." *Advances in Consumer Research* 13: 1–3; S. K. Balasubramanian. 1994. "Beyond Advertising and Publicity: Hybrid Messages and Public Policy Issues." *Journal of Advertising* 23(4): 29–46; M. A. Jolson and F. A. Bushman. 1978. "3rd Party Consumer Information Systems: Case of the Food Critic." *Journal of Retailing* 54(4): 63–79; C. L. Brown and A. Krishna. 2004. "The Skeptical Shopper: A Metacognitive Account for the Effects of Default Options on Choice." *Journal of Consumer Research* 31(3): 529–539; P. Wright. 2002. "Marketplace Metacognition and

Social Intelligence." *Journal of Consumer Research* 28(4): 677–682; and M. Friestad and P. Wright. 1994. "The Persuasion Knowledge Model: How People Cope with Persuasion Attempts." *Journal of Consumer Research*: 1–31; for an overall review of consumers' beliefs about the market, see C. P. Duncan. (1990). "Consumer Market Beliefs: A Review of the Literature and an Agenda for Future Research." *Advances in Consumer Research* 17(1): 729–736.

8. Lois Wicken. 2009. "'Pay for Play': The Redistribution of Payola for Music Diversity in New York State and Its Implications for Sustainability in Music." *The World of Music* 51(1): 55–74.

9. Don Thompson. 2008. *The $12 Million Stuffed Shark: The Curious Economics of Contemporary Art.* New York: Palgrave Macmillan.

10. Rebecca Mead. 2011. "Alice's Wonderland: A Walmart Heiress Builds a Museum in the Ozarks." *The New Yorker.* June 27.

11. The jury comprises invited esteemed individuals. The prize is organized and run by the Pritzker Foundation, a nonprofit organization. The prize has not been free of controversy, the most recent being the awarding of the 2016 prize to Chile's Alejandro Aravena, who stepped down from the jury in 2015, after serving six years. This and other controversies further attest to the importance of maintaining a clear perception of independence because such actions do not go unnoticed; consumers and producers must view the intermediary as unimpeachable to be able to trust it.

12. Peter Besas. 2000. *Inside* Variety: *The Story of the Bible of Show Business, 1905–1987, Unauthorized.* New York. Ars Millenii: 35–37.

13. *Variety* Editorial Policy. Company archives.

14. Personal communication with Neil Stiles, president, *Variety* Inc., in March 2013.

15. "Trade Papers for 25 Years." *Variety*, December 31, 1990: 15.

16. M. A. Jolson and F. A. Bushman. (1978). "3rd Party Consumer Information-Systems: Case of the Food Critic." *Journal of Retailing* 54(4): 63–79; R. B. Fireworker and H. H. Friedman. 1977. "The Effects of Endorsements on Product Evaluation." *Decision Sciences* 8(3): 576–583; and D. H. Dean. 1999. "Brand Endorsement, Popularity, and Event Sponsorship as Advertising Cues Affecting Consumer Pre-Purchase Attitudes." *Journal of Advertising* 28(3): 1–12.

17. Consider the unrelated example of expert testimony at trials; because they are paid by the side that summoned them, the expertise of these witnesses is typically received with skepticism.

18. M. A. Jolson and F. A. Bushman. 1978. "3rd Party Consumer Information Systems: Case of the Food Critic." *Journal of Retailing* 54(4): 63–79; R. B. Fireworker and H. H. Friedman. 1977. "The Effects of Endorsements on Product Evaluation." *Decision Sciences* 8(3): 576–583; and D. H. Dean. 1999. "Brand Endorsement, Popularity, and Event Sponsorship as Advertising Cues Affecting Consumer Pre-Purchase Attitudes." *Journal of Advertising* 28(3): 1–12.

19. Alexandra Alter. 2015. "When Mark Zuckerberg Likes a Book, Sales Soar." *The New York Times.* January 5.

20. Lizzie Widdicome. 2015. "The Zuckerberg Bump." *The New Yorker*. January 19.

21. It can also be argued, however, that, in yet another instance of the intimate and mutually reinforcing linkages between independence and expertise, a truly independent intermediary, not beholden to powerful incumbents, would possess the flexibility and objectivity necessary to acknowledge and endorse an innovation, even if it upsets the prevailing equilibrium.

22. Max Weber. 1968. *Economy and Society: An Outline of Interpretive Sociology*. New York: Bedminster Press.

23. Vanessa Friedman. 2012. "Be Grateful for Grace." *Financial Times*. November 16.

24. Ibid. Also see Troy Patterson. 2011. "Critical Mass." *W*. September.

25. Judith H. Dobrzynski. 2011. "Honoring Art, Honoring Artists." *The New York Times*. February 3.

26. Although much of the information about the *Michelin Guide* in this book comes from my interviews with company officials (for the purpose of writing a teaching case), the *Guide* and its stars have been the subject of scholarly studies too. See Christel Lane. 2014. *The Cultivation of Taste: Chefs and the Organization of Fine Dining*. Oxford, UK: Oxford University Press; and Bo T. Christensen and Jesper Strandgaard Pedersen. 2013. *Restaurant Rankings in the Culinary Field*. In *Exploring Creativity: Evaluative Practices in Innovation, Design and the Arts*, edited by B. Christensen and B. Moeran. Cambridge, UK: Cambridge University Press.

27. Mukti V. Khaire. 2017. "The Importance of Being Independent: The Role of Intermediaries in Creating Market Categories." *Special Issue: Categories to Categorization: Studies in Sociology, Organizations and Strategy at the Crossroads. Research in the Sociology of Organizations* 48.

28. Erik Piepenburg. 2014. "Smut, Refreshed for a New Generation." *The New York Times*. January 26.

29. It may seem that in a new category, where nobody knows anything, a pioneer new venture has the potential to gain from being a first mover, regardless of expertise. However, when a new category arouses hostility or resistance, the discourse of a new venture is less likely to inspire confidence than that of an established one.

30. Wanda Orlikowsky and Susan Scott. 2013. "What Happens when Evaluation Goes Online? Exploring Apparatuses of Valuation in the Travel Sector." *Organization Science, Articles in Advance*: 1–24.

31. Although not the same because the company is a producer, the recent actions of Amazon.com provide a useful example of the power of algorithms. In response to a contractual disagreement with the publishing house Hachette, Amazon's collaborative filters were tweaked to display "similar books at a lower price" next to books from Hachette, leading to outrage and protests from readers. However, the dispute only escalated to the point where Amazon stopped selling Hachette books altogether. Similarly, the question of how variables are weighted in algorithms for consumer-generated content on website ratings of hospitality services has had significant implications for

hotels with regards to pricing, especially when websites offer vastly different rankings of the same service.

32. Eric Wilson. 2011. "Magazines Begin to Sell the Fashion They Review." *The New York Times*. September 25.

33. Intermediaries that are not online (magazines, for example) do also face the same Catch-22 but do not face the alluring temptation of earning revenues through hyperlinks.

34. Wayne Robins. 1983. "A Thriller: Pop Battles Race Barrier." *Los Angeles Times*. August 7: R56.

CHAPTER 6

1. Peter Gay. 2008. *Modernism: The Lure of Heresy from Baudelaire to Beckett and Beyond*. New York: W. W. Norton and Company.

2. Jeremy Lewis. 2005. *Penguin Special: The Story of Allen Lane, the Founder of Penguin Books and the Man Who Changed Publishing Forever*. New York: Penguin Books: 84.

3. Ibid.

4. Deirdre David. 2001. *The Cambridge Companion to the Victorian Novel*. Cambridge, UK: Cambridge University Press: 22; and Jeremy Lewis. 2005. *Penguin Special: The Story of Allen Lane, the Founder of Penguin Books and the Man Who Changed Publishing Forever*. New York: Penguin Books: 73.

5. To be clear, this is true of Western civilizations, although the situation may well have been similar in other parts of the world.

6. Although the democratization trope is commonly used today in the context of the wide penetration of the Internet and its ability to serve as a medium of distribution and sales for cultural goods, the rise of creative industries and producers had a similarly democratizing effect.

7. Viviana Zelizer. 2010. *Economic Lives: How Culture Shapes the Economy*. Princeton, NJ: Princeton University Press; and Jens Beckert and Patrick Aspers. 2010. *The Worth of Goods: Valuation and Pricing in the Economy*. Oxford, UK: Oxford University Press.

8. Lewis Hyde. 2009. *The Gift: Creativity and the Artist in the Modern World*. New York: Random House.

9. Patricia Thornton, W. Ocasio, and M. Lounsbury. 2012. *The Institutional Logics Perspective: A New Approach to Culture, Structure, and Process*. New York: Oxford University Press; and Roger Friedland and Robert R. Alford. 1991. "Bringing Society Back In: Symbols, Practices, and Institutional Contradictions." In *The New Institutionalism in Organizational Analysis*, edited by Walter W. Powell and Paul J. Dimaggio: 232–263. Chicago: University of Chicago Press.

10. B. Townley. 2002. "The Role of Competing Rationalities in Institutional Change." *Academy of Management Journal* 45(1): 163–179; and Patricia Thornton, W. Ocasio, M. Lounsbury. 2012. *The Institutional Logics Perspective: A New Approach to Culture, Structure, and Process*. New York: Oxford University Press.

11. Pierre Bourdieu. 1983. "The Field of Cultural Production, or: The Economic World Reversed." *Poetics* 12(4–5): 311–356; and Pierre Bourdieu. 1985. "The Market of Symbolic Goods." *Poetics* 14(1–2): 13–44.

12. L. Boltanski and L. Thevenot. 2006/1991. *On Justification: Economies of Worth*. Translated bt C. Porter. Princeton, NJ: Princeton University Press. Original French edition published in 1991.

13. Pierre Bourdieu. 1983. "The Field of Cultural Production, or: The Economic World Reversed." *Poetics* 12(4–5): 311–356; and Pierre Bourdieu. 1985. "The Market of Symbolic Goods." *Poetics* 14(1–2): 13–44.

14. L. Boltanski and E. Chiapello. 2006. *The New Spirit of Capitalism*. London: Verso; and L. Boltanski and L. Thevenot. 2006. *On Justification: Economies of Worth*. Princeton, NJ: Princeton University Press.

15. Lewis Hyde. 2009. *The Gift: Creativity and the Artist in the Modern World*. New York: Random House; and Peter Gay. 2008. *Modernism: The Lure of Heresy from Baudelaire to Beckett and Beyond*. New York: W. W. Norton & Company.

16. Lewis Hyde. 2009. *The Gift: Creativity and the Artist in the Modern World*. New York: Random House.

17. Consider as evidence, for instance, some writers' strong wish to adopt pseudonyms when writing books for Alloy Media, an entertainment company that sells novels, TV shows, and some films as fully formed packages. Ideas for novels, for instance, are pitched at meetings and then forwarded to writers, who are asked to write sample chapters based on the idea. Writers whose sample chapters are approved by Alloy executives receive contracts. Not surprisingly, most aspiring authors seeking to write the next "great American novel" are wary of having their names associated with books that are published in this manner; however, these contracts help pay their bills. For more on Alloy Media, see Rebecca Mead. 2009. "The Gossip Mill." *The New Yorker* 85(33, October 19).

18. In contrast, utilitarian goods with objective and measurable attributes can be reverse engineered because it is feasible for producers to predict the kinds of useful attributes desired by consumers.

19. Paul M. Hirsch. 1972. "Processing Fads and Fashions by Culture Industry Systems: An Organization-Set Analysis." *American Journal of Sociology* 77: 639–659.

20. Pierre-Michel Menger. 2014. *The Economics of Creativity*. Cambridge, MA: Harvard University Press; and Howard Becker. 1982. *Art Worlds*. Berkeley: University of California Press.

21. J. B. Thompson. 2010. *Merchants of Culture*. Cambridge, UK: Polity Press.

22. An article in *The New York Times*, for instance, asserts that self-publishing was seen as "once a small backwater of vanity presses for authors who could not get contracts with mainstream houses." For more, see Leslie Kaufman. 2013. "New Publisher Authors Trust: Themselves." *The New York Times*. April 16.

23. Although self-publishing does occur, it is infrequently carried out by a firm established for the purpose and almost never involves employing other people; in fact, before the advent of the digital medium, self-publishing was exceedingly difficult and

rare. Similarly, a group of artists may, on a rare occasion, team up to organize a show or establish a collective studio that operates as a gallery, but these are generally exceptions rather than the rule, whereas chefs and fashion designers routinely found their own firms.

24. Dreamworks Studios. Retrieved in March 2015 from www.dreamworks studios.com.

25. Thomas J. McLean. 2006. "Section Eight Goes up in Smoke." *Variety*. October 12.

26. Heather Haveman and Mukti Khaire. 2004. "Survival beyond Succession? The Contingent Impact of Founder Succession on Organizational Failure." *Journal of Business Venturing* 19(May): 437–463. For more on collaboration and complementarities in top management teams, please refer to José Luis Alvarez and Silviya Svejenova. 2005. *Sharing Executive Power: Roles and Relationships at the Top*. Cambridge, UK: Cambridge University Press.

27. R. E. Caves. 2000. *Creative Industries: Contracts between Art and Commerce*. Cambridge, MA: Harvard University Press; and J. B. Thompson. 2010. *Merchants of Culture*. Cambridge, UK: Polity Press.

28. P. Wright. 1986. "Schemer Schema-Consumers Intuitive Theories about Marketers Influence Tactics." *Advances in Consumer Research* 13: 1–3; S. K. Balasubramanian. 1994. "Beyond Advertising and Publicity: Hybrid Messages and Public Policy Issues." *Journal of Advertising* 23(4): 29–46; M. Jolson and F. A. Bushman. 1978. "3rd Party Consumer Information Systems: Case of the Food Critic." *Journal of Retailing* 54(4): 63–79; C. L. Brown and A. Krishna. 2004. "The Skeptical Shopper: A Metacognitive Account for the Effects of Default Options on Choice." *Journal of Consumer Research* 31(3): 529–539; P. Wright,. 2002. "Marketplace Metacognition and Social Intelligence." *Journal of Consumer Research* 28(4): 677–682; and M. Friestad and P. Wright. 1994. "The Persuasion Knowledge Model: How People Cope with Persuasion Attempts. *Journal of Consumer Research* 21(1): 1–31; for an overall review of consumers' beliefs about the market, see C. P. Duncan. (1990). "Consumer Market Beliefs: A Review of the Literature and an Agenda for Future Research." *Advances in Consumer Research* 17(1): 729–736.

29. Mukti Khaire. 2012. "Variety: Taking the Biz Overseas." HBS No. 812-111. Boston: Harvard Business School Publishing: 10; and personal communication with Steven Gaydos, executive editor, *Variety*, September 2011.

30. Mukti Khaire. 2012. "Variety: Taking the Biz Overseas." HBS No. 812-111. Boston: Harvard Business School Publishing: 10; and personal communication with Peter Bart, editor, *Variety*, September 2011.

31. This is not to say that marketing is irrelevant or useless in the creative industries. Marketing budgets for films and music albums are notoriously high and certainly do result in higher sales, sometimes even with bad reviews, as described in the previous section on intermediaries (especially in Chapter 4). However, unlike utilitarian goods, sales of cultural goods cannot be ensured on the strength of producers' promotional discourse alone. Not only does market making require complementary

intermediaries' discourse, but even producers' discourse takes on a more experiential and circumspect tone, as with book tours and film premieres followed by conversations with the director.

32. Michiko Kakutani. 2005. "Misery's Company for a Confederacy of Depressives in London." *The New York Times*. June 20.

33. R. E. Caves. 2000. *Creative Industries: Contracts between Art and Commerce*. Cambridge, MA: Harvard University Press.

34. This is evident, for example, in the use of excerpts from reviews or reviewers' reactions quoted in film posters—" 'Extraordinary!' says *The New York Times*"—or trailers.

35. Personal communication with Karl Lagerfeld, creative director, Chanel, September 2012.

36. Personal communication with John Galantic, U.S. chief operating officer, Chanel, September 2012.

37. Sam Roberts. 2015. "Sherry Arden, Publisher with a Passion for Best Sellers, Dies at 91." *The New York Times*. February 3.

38. Creators do sometimes, of their own volition, try their hand at something new; this is different, however, from being asked by producers/managers, in the service of improving sales, to emulate a popular creators' work or to start working in a different category.

39. Not many consumers can or choose to buy very expensive artworks, and, even if there were a larger group of consumers, the dynamics of art markets are such that galleries prefer to work with a small group of collectors they can trust not to engage in dubious practices such as "flipping" artworks.

40. Mukti Khaire. 2005. "Great Oaks from Little Acorns Grow: Strategies for New Venture Growth." *Academy of Management Annual Meeting Proceedings*, August.

41. Heather Haveman and Mukti Khaire. 2004. "Survival beyond Succession? The Contingent Impact of Founder Succession on Organizational Failure." *Journal of Business Venturing* 19(May): 437–463.

42. Jeremy Lewis. 2005. *Penguin Special: The Story of Allen Lane, the Founder of Penguin Books and the Man Who Changed Publishing Forever*. New York: Penguin Books: 71, 90.

43. *The Atavist Magazine*; retrieved in November 2011 from http://magazine.atavist.com/team; and Mukti Khaire and Mary Tripsas. 2012. "The Atavist: Reinventing the Book." HBS No. 812-177. Boston: Harvard Business School Publishing.

44. Matthew Garrahan. 2012. "Return of the Punisher." *The Financial Times*. February 25.

45. H. E. Aldrich and C. M. Fiol. 1994. "Fools Rush In? The Institutional Context of Industry Creation." *Academy of Management Review* 19: 645–670; and Howard Aldrich. 1999. *Organizations Evolving*. Thousand Oaks, CA: Sage Publishing.

46. J. B. Thompson. 2010. *Merchants of Culture*. Cambridge, UK: Polity Press.

47. Chapter 8 contains a further examination of this strategy for managing risk in a creative industry. In brief, a producer may bring crowd-pleasing works to market

to acquire sufficient revenues to fund the production of more artistic and/or esoteric works. For instance, London West End producer Sonia Friedman cherishes both commercial success and artistic experimentation and innovation; Friedman has produced both *Legally Blond* (a musical based on an enormously popular Hollywood film of the same name) and Harold Pinter's play *Old Times*. For more on Friedman, see Sarah Hemming, 2013. "I Don't Want the West End Left Behind," *The Financial Times*. February 9.

48. Peter Gay. 2008. *Modernism: The Lure of Heresy from Baudelaire to Beckett and Beyond*. New York: W. W. Norton & Company.

49. Craig Watkins. 2005. *Hip Hop Matters: Politics, Pop Culture, and the Struggle for the Soul of a Movement*. Boston: Beacon Press; and Mukti Khaire and Kerry Herman. 2013. "Hip Hop (A): Rapper's Delight, Producer's Dilemma." HBS No. 812-106. Boston: Harvard Business School Publishing.

50. Jeremy Lewis. 2005. "Penguin Special: The Story of Allen Lane, the Founder of Penguin Books and the Man Who Changed Publishing Forever." New York: Penguin Books.

51. Mukti Khaire and Daniel Wadhwani. "Saffronart.com: Bidding for Success." HBS No. 9-807-114. Boston: Harvard Business School Publishing.

52. Charles Isherwood. 2014. "Off Off Off Broadway at Your Multiplex." *The New York Times*. January 26.

53. Mukti Khaire and Mary Tripsas. 2012. "The Atavist: Reinventing the Book." HBS No. 9-812-177. Boston: Harvard Business School Publishing.

CHAPTER 7

1. Margaret Sullivan. 2015. "In Big Media Town, Core Beat in Flux." *The New York Times*. February 21.

2. Mary Lynn Stewart. 2005. "Copying and Copyrighting Haute Couture: Democratizing Fashion, 1900–1930." *French Historical Studies* 28(1): 103–130; Valerie Steel. 2006. *Paris Fashion: A Cultural History*. Oxford, UK: Oxford University Press: 248.

3. R. E. Caves. 2000. *Creative Industries: Contracts between Art and Commerce*. Cambridge, MA: Harvard University Press.

4. P. Wright. 1986. "Schemer Schema-Consumers Intuitive Theories about Marketers Influence Tactics." *Advances in Consumer Research* 13: 1–3; S. K. Balasubramanian. 1994. "Beyond Advertising and Publicity: Hybrid Messages and Public Policy Issues." *Journal of Advertising* 23(4): 29–46; M. A. Jolson and F. A. Bushman. 1978. "3rd Party Consumer Information Systems: Case of the Food Critic." *Journal of Retailing* 54(4): 63–79; C. L. Brown and A. Krishna. 2004. "The Skeptical Shopper: A Metacognitive Account for the Effects of Default Options on Choice." *Journal of Consumer Research* 31(3): 529–539; P. Wright. 2002. "Marketplace Metacognition and Social Intelligence." *Journal of Consumer Research* 28(4): 677–682; and M. Friestad and P. Wright. 1994. "The Persuasion Knowledge Model: How People Cope with Persuasion Attempts." *Journal of Consumer Research*: 1–31. For an overall review of consumers' beliefs about the market, see C. P. Duncan. 1990. "Consumer Market Beliefs: A

Review of the Literature and an Agenda for Future Research." *Advances in Consumer Research* 17(1): 729–736.

5. P. M. Hirsch. 1972. "Processing Fads and Fashions: An Organization-Set Analysis of Cultural Industry Systems." *American Journal of Sociology* 77(4): 639–659.

6. Patricia Thornton, W. Ocasio, and M. Lounsbury. 2012. *The Institutional Logics Perspective: A New Approach to Culture, Structure, and Process.* New York: Oxford University Press; and M. Glynn and M. Lounsbury. 2005. "From the Critics' Corner: Logic Blending, Discursive Change and Authenticity in a Cultural Production System." *Journal of Management Studies* 42: 1031–1055.

7. Pierre Bourdieu. 1993. *The Field of Cultural Production: Essays on Art and Literature.* New York: Columbia University Press.

8. The fact that firms in the creative industries are often managed by individuals who have motivations beyond the pecuniary places this scenario within the realm of possibility.

9. Pierre Bourdieu. 1993. *The Field of Cultural Production: Essays on Art and Literature.* New York: Columbia University Press; and L. Boltanski and L. Thevenot. 2006. *On Justification: Economies of Worth.* Princeton, NJ: Princeton University Press.

10. Despite seeming similarities, this choice is different from the question of whether to produce popular or highbrow goods. The putative popular forms of cultural production can still redirect norms (as explained in the following discussion) by choosing to tackle unconventional ideas in a conventional format.

11. An additional challenge posed by such goods is that, in fact, not finding a market is not only a financial problem but also a cultural one; a radical, redirective work that is not widely seen (consumed) will have minimal cultural impact.

12. Sarika Bansal. 2012. "Soap Operas with a Social Message." *The New York Times.* January 26.

13. A. B. Hargadon and Y. Douglas. 2001. "When Innovations Meet Institutions: Edison and the Design of the Electric Light." *Administrative Science Quarterly* 46(3): 476–501; H. E. Aldrich and C. M. Fiol. 1994. "Fools Rush In? The Institutional Context of Industry Creation." *Academy of Management Review* 19(4): 645–670.

14. Brian Stelter. 2011. "Season 5 of 'Mad Men' Is Delayed until 2012." *The New York Times.* March 29.

15. R. Daniel Wadhwani and Mukti Khaire. 2015. "Valuation as a Social Process: Organizational and Managerial Implications of the Social Construction of Value." Working paper.

16. Herbert J. Gans. 1999. *Popular Culture and High Culture: An Analysis and Evaluation of Taste.* New York: Basic Books; and Dwight Macdonald. 1960. "Masscult and Midcult: An Inquiry into American Popular Culture and the Role of the Middlebrows in the Distortion of Cultural Values." *The Partisan Review* 27(2): 203–233 and 27(4): 589–631.

17. Pierre Bourdieu. 1993. *The Field of Cultural Production: Essays on Art and Literature.* New York: Columbia University Press; and Stanley Lieberson. 2000. *A Matter*

of Taste: How Names, Fashions, and Culture Change. New Haven, CT: Yale University Press.

18. Rebecca Mead. 2014. "Written Off: Jennifer Weiner's Quest for Literary Respect." *The New Yorker.* January 13.

19. Ben Brantley. 2014. "Those Brand-Name Musicals." *The New York Times.* February 23.

20. Pierre-Michel Menger. 2014. *The Economics of Creativity.* Cambridge, MA: Harvard University Press.

21. Although this emphasis on quality is not unique to creative industries, the uncertainty of evaluation, the subjective qualities of the works, and the inherent absence of utilitarian features in cultural goods renders intermediaries crucial and simultaneously precludes the use of any meaningful predictive models.

22. R. E. Caves. 2000. *Creative Industries: Contracts between Art and Commerce.* Cambridge, MA: Harvard University Press.

23. Ibid.

24. Founding a creator firm is not always available as an option, especially in some industries, as described in Chapter 6.

25. Mukti Khaire. 2005. "Great Oaks from Little Acorns Grow: Strategies for New Venture Growth." *Academy of Management Annual Meeting Proceedings*, August; and Heather Haveman and Mukti Khaire,. 2004. "Survival beyond Succession? The Contingent Impact of Founder Succession on Organizational Failure." *Journal of Business Venturing* 19(May): 437–463.

26. A similar dynamic occurs in a very different context when a well-liked television talk-show host retires, a scenario that has played out several times, most recently when Jon Stewart stepped down as the host of "The Daily Show with Jon Stewart."

27. Eric Wilson. 2013. "It's Valentino's Name, but Their Vision." *The New York Times.* March 8.

28. Shiv Malik. 2011. "Harry Potter Author JK Rowling Leaves Her Agent." *The Guardian.* July 3.

29. For academic research on this topic, please see Joseph P. Broschak and Emily S. Block. 2014. "With or without You: When Does Managerial Exit Matter for the Dissolution of Dyadic Market Ties?" *Academy of Management Journal* 57(3): 743–765.

30. Ian Parker. 2012. "Mugglemarch." *The New Yorker.* October 1.

31. Harrison C. White. 1970. *Chains of Opportunity.* Cambridge, MA: Harvard University Press; and Aage Sorenson. 1977. "The Structure of Inequality and the Process of Attainment." *American Sociological Review* 42(6): 965–978.

32. Mukti Khaire. "From Paperback to the Future: The Penguin Group and Book Country." HBS No. 812-109. Boston: Harvard Business School Publishing; and The Association of American Publishers. "Book Stats." Available at www.bookstats.org.

33. Although these independent publishers certainly struggle, their very existence is a prime example of the nonpecuniary motivations that drive so many individuals that enter these industries. The existence and diversity of multiple independent entre-

preneurial ventures is, however, not true of other kinds of producers, such as booksellers, in the publishing supply chain, primarily because efficiency, which accompanies scale, rather than novelty, is the key to success in these functions.

34. American Repertory Theater. 2015. Available at www.americanrepertory theater.org.

35. Even in industries such as fashion, where several hundred copies of a given garment can be manufactured once the design has been finalized, the originality of the idea embodied in the design is not a limitless resource.

36. An editor and/or publishing firm that accepts such a radically novel book would also be a pioneer-producer (in addition to the agent). With the value chain being so complex and iterative in creative industries, it takes a village to bring goods to market, a situation that is only exacerbated in the case of new and unfamiliar categories of goods.

CHAPTER 8

1. Lewis Hyde. 2007. *The Gift: Creativity and the Artist in the Modern World.* New York: Vintage.

2. David Kirkpatrick. 2001. "'Oprah' Gaffe by Franzen Draws Ire and Sales." *The New York Times.* October 29.

3. J. F. English. 2005. *The Economy of Prestige.* Cambridge, MA: Harvard University Press.

4. Lewis Hyde. 2009. *The Gift: Creativity and the Artist in the Modern World.* New York: Random House.

5. Pierre Bourdieu. 1993. *The Field of Cultural Production: Essays on Art and Literature.* New York: Columbia University Press.

6. Ibid.

7. Lewis Hyde. 2009. *The Gift: Creativity and the Artist in the Modern World.* New York: Random House.

8. Ibid.

9. Victor Bockris. 1989. *The Life and Death of Andy Warhol.* New York: Bantam Publishing: 366.

10. Adam Gopnik. 2015. "Trollope Trending." *The New Yorker.* May 4.

11. This section on strategies builds on principles discussed in the literature on organizations and institutional logics more generally. Although the strategies are described using the same terminology as the rest of the literature, for the sake of consistency the descriptions and specifics are idiosyncratic to creative industries. For the foundational exposition, see Patricia Thornton, W. Ocasio, and M. Lounsbury. 2012. *The Institutional Logics Perspective: A New Approach to Culture, Structure, and Process.* New York: Oxford University Press.

12. René Redzepi. 2009. *Noma Time and Place.* London: Phaidon; Helen Greenwood, 2012. "Going Wild in the Kitchen." *The Sidney Morning Herald.* September 4. Retrieved via Factiva in January 2014; Mukti Khaire and Elena Corsi. "Noma: A Lot on the Plate." HBS No. 814-097. Boston: Harvard Business School Publishing.

13. Belén Villalonga. 2000. "Privatization and Efficiency: Differentiating Ownership Effects from Political, Organizational, and Dynamic Effects." *Journal of Economic Behavior and Organization* 42: 43–74.

14. "The Family Way: Italy's Dynamic Design Dynasties and the Empires They Rule." *Wallpaper Magazine*. August 8, 2012.

15. John Colapinto. 2012. "Check, Please: Annals of Gastronomy." *The New Yorker* 88(27, September 10).

16. Mukti Khaire. 2010. "Young and No Money? Never Mind: The Material Impact of Social Resources on New Venture Growth." *Organization Science* 21 (January–February): 168–185.

17. When this type of spillover occurs between the avant-garde clothing and market-oriented accessories (such as handbags and jewelry), the firm is similar to a portfolio producer because such accessories are usually designed by other individuals. The distinction between the loose coupling and portfolio strategies, therefore, is blurred, and the two approaches fall along a continuum rather than existing as two clearly separate strategies.

18. An example of loose coupling in a producer firm would be the case of a gallery that sells mugs with prints of artworks or other designed objects that derive from the artworks in the gallery.

19. Penguin. 2011. "Meet Our Authors and Publishers." Available at www .penguin.com/meet/browse/16/publishers; Mukti Khaire. "From Paperback to the Future: The Penguin Group and Book Country." HBS No. 812-109. Boston: Harvard Business School Publishing.

20. M. C. Kemp. 1955. "An Appraisal of Loss Leader Selling." *Canadian Journal of Economics and Political Science* (May): 245–250; J. D. Hess and E. Gerstner. 1987. "Loss Leader Pricing and Rain Check Policy." *Marketing Science* 6(4): 358–374; R. Lal and C. Matutes. 1994. "Retail Pricing and Advertising Strategies," *The Journal of Business* 67(3): 345–370. Thomas T. Nagle. 1987. *The Strategy and Tactics of Pricing*. Englewood Cliffs, NJ: Prentice-Hall; Delbert Duncan, Stanley Hollander, and Ronald Savitt. 1983. *Modern Retailing Management*. Homewood, IL: Irwin; and Rodney G. Walters and Scott B. McKenzie.1988. "A Structural Equation Analysis of the Impact of Price Promotions on Store Performance." *Journal of Marketing Research* 25 (February): 51–63.

21. M. C. Kemp. 1955. "An Appraisal of Loss Leader Selling." *Canadian Journal of Economics and Political Science* (May) 245–250; J. D. Hess and E. Gerstner. 1987. "Loss Leader Pricing and Rain Check Policy." *Marketing Science* 6(4): 358–374; R. Lal and C. Matutes. 1994. "Retail Pricing and Advertising Strategies." *The Journal of Business* 67(3): 345–370; Thomas T. Nagle. 1987. *The Strategy and Tactics of Pricing*. Englewood Cliffs, NJ: Prentice-Hall; Delbert Duncan, Stanley Hollander, and Ronald Savitt. 1983. *Modern Retailing Management*. Homewood, IL: Irwin; and Rochney G. Walters, and Scott B. McKenzie. 1988. "A Structural Equation Analysis of the Impact of Price Promotions on Store Performance." *Journal of Marketing Research* 25 (February): 51–63.

22. Mukti Khaire. 2010. "Young and No Money? Never Mind: The Material Impact of Social Resources on New Venture Growth." *Organization Science* 21 (January–February): 168–185.

23. Although the demand for new products introduced by new ventures is uncertain in all industries, the features of cultural goods, especially the high degree of symbolism and subjectivity of consumers' evaluation, significantly increase the uncertainty in the creative industries. Similarly, the lack of reputation and track record, common to all new ventures (see Arthur L. Stinchcombe. 1965. "Social Structure and Organizations." In *Handbook of Organizations*, edited by J. G. March. Chicago: Rand McNally: 153–193) has particularly severe repercussions for new producers in creative industries because of the obstacles it puts in the way of gaining access to high-quality creators, as seen in Chapter 6. This uncertainty and resulting difficulties in fund raising are the chief reason for the success of crowd-funding platforms (such as Kickstarter) that enable demand testing and fundraising at the same time.

24. Arthur L. Stinchcombe. 1965. "Social Structure and Organizations." In *Handbook of Organizations*, edited by J. G. March. Chicago: Rand McNally: 153–193.

25. J. Freeman, Glenn R. Carroll, and Michael T. Hannan. 1983. "The Liability of Newness: Age Dependence in Organizational Death Rates." *American Sociological Review* 48(5): 692–710; Michael T. Hannan, Glenn R. Carroll, Stanislave Dobrev, and Joon Han. 1998. "Organizational Mortality in the European and American Automobile Industries, Part 1: Revisiting the Effects of Age and Size." *European Sociological Review* 14(3): 279–302; Gael Le Mens, Michael T. Hannan, and Laszlo Polos. 2011. "Founding Conditions, Learning, and Organizational Life Chances: Age-Dependence Revisited." *Administrative Science Quarterly* 56(2011): 95–126; and Michael T. Hannan, Gael Mens, and Laszlo Polos. 2010. "On the Dynamics of Organizational Mortality: Age-Dependence Revisited." Working paper.

CHAPTER 9

1. Jeffrey Bezos. 2011. Letter to shareholders. Available at http://phx.corporate-ir .net/phoenix.zhtml?c=97664&p=irol-reportsannual.

2. Brooks Barnes and Hunter Atkins. 2014. "Hollywood's Old-Time Star Makers Are Swooping in on YouTube's Party." *The New York Times*. September 15.

3. Ryan Mac. 2014. "Alibaba Claims Title for Largest Global IPO Ever with Extra Share Sales." *Forbes*. September 22.

4. These spats reached peak levels of publicity when popular singer-writer Taylor Swift announced in November 2014 that not only would her new album, "1989," be unavailable on streaming service Spotify but that her label would remove her entire back catalogue from Spotify. In an op-ed she wrote at the time, Swift went so far as to equate streaming with piracy at least insofar as revenues to artists were concerned. For more context on online piracy and low royalty rates from streaming services, please see Robert Levine. 2012. *Free Ride: How Digital Parasites Are Destroying the Culture Business, and How the Culture Business Can Fight Back*. Toronto: First Anchor Books; John Seabrook. 2014. "Revenue Streams." *The New Yorker*. November 24; Stephen

Witt. 2015. "The Man Who Broke the Music Business." *The New Yorker*. April 27; Clyde Haberman. 2014. "Grappling with the 'Culture of Free' in Napster's Aftermath." *The New York Times*. December 7; and Ben Sisario. 2015. "Pandora Readies for Another Royalties Battle, This Time with BMI." *The New York Times*. February 7.

5. Robert Levine. 2012. *Free Ride: How Digital Parasites Are Destroying the Culture Business, and How the Culture Business Can Fight Back*. Toronto: First Anchor Books.

6. This is not to say that there is no risk of unauthorized knockoffs of designs. However, such infringement was occurring even before the Internet, although it is certainly harder to enforce property rights in the world of e-commerce.

7. Melena Ryzik. 2012. "Web Sites Illuminate Unknown Artists." *The New York Times*. June 17.

8. Julie Bosman. 2012. "Discreetly Digital, Erotic Novel Sets American Women Abuzz." *The New York Times*. March 9; Julie Bosman. 2011. "Self-Publisher Signs Four-Book Deal with St. Martin's." *The New York Times*. March 24; and Sarah Millar. 2011. "How a Failed Author Made $2 Million from E-Books." *The Toronto Star*, March 3. For a more general description of the recent popularity of self-publishing, see Leslie Laufman. 2013. "New Publisher Authors Trust: Themselves." *The New York Times*. April 16.

9. John Anderson. 2012. "Sundance Offers a Web Afterlife for Its Alumni." *The New York Times*. January 4; and Rob Walker. 2012. "Youtubers." *The New York Times Magazine*. July 1.

10. Robert Levine. 2012. *Free Ride: How Digital Parasites Are Destroying the Culture Business, and How the Culture Business Can Fight Back*. Toronto: First Anchor Books. For a writer's firsthand account of how this widespread expectation is affecting him, see Tim Kreider. 2013. "Slaves of the Internet, Unite." *The New York Times*. October 27.

11. Goodreads is now owned by Amazon.com.

12. John Seabrook. 2012. "Factory Girls." *The New Yorker*. October 8.

13. Michael Cieply and David Barboza. 2012. "In China, Foreign Films Meet a Powerful Gatekeeper." *The New York Times*. April 29.

14. Vincent Bevins. 2011. "London, Paris, New York, Lima? Peru and Iceland Are the Latest Countries to Pursue the 'Fashion Week' Effect." *The Financial Times*. May 14. For a detailed description of the development of the Indian fashion industry, see Mukti Khaire. 2014. "Fashioning an Industry: Socio-cognitive Processes in the Construction of Worth of a New Industry." *Organization Studies* 35(1): 41–74.

15. Mukti Khaire and Daniel Wadhwani. 2010. "Saffronart.com: Bidding for Success." HBS No. 9-807-114. Boston: Harvard Business School Publishing.

16. Dana Goodyear. 2008. "I [Heart] Novels." *The New Yorker*. December 22.

17. Jenna Wortham. 2011. "Shorter E-Books for Smaller Devices." *The New York Times*. February 13.

18. V. Friedman. 2011. "Good Luxe: What Is Luxury Fashion Doing to Help the Developing World?" *The Financial Times* (Weekend Supplement). November 19.

19. Hobbyists, too, have many more opportunities to try their hand at creating works and can even receive feedback from online viewers/readers. This ability likely

increases the amount of experimentation in the artistic fields. However, hobbyists and enthusiasts are very different from the artists and creators that have been considered in this book, which is about creative industries and markets, and therefore will not be explored in any detail here.

20. Sue Hapern. 2014. "The Creepy New Wave of the Internet." *The New York Review of Books*. November 20; Hiroko Tabuchi. 2015. "Etsy's Success Gives Rise to Problems of Credibility and Scale." *The New York Times*. March 15; and Michael J. de la Merced and Peter Eavis. 2015. "Etsy, Online Bazaar for Handmade Goods, Files for Initial Offering." *The New York Times*. March 4.

21. Wilson Rothman. 2007. "A Radio Station Just for You." *The New York Times*. March 29; and Rob Walker. 2009. "The Song Decoders." *The New York Times Magazine*. October 18.

22. David Carr. 2013. "For 'House of Cards,' Using Big Data to Guarantee Its Popularity." *The New York Times*. February 24.

23. Laura Prudom. 2014. "'House of Cards': Beau Willimon on Netflix's Rule-Breaking Creativity." *Variety*. June 20; Donald Sull and Kathleen M. Eisenhardt. 2015. "Netflix's 'House of Cards' Secrets: The Real Story behind Kevin Spacey and Frank Underwood's Meteoric Ascent." *Salon*. April 26; and Dorothy Pomerantz. 2013. "The Producer behind 'House of Cards' on How Netflix Offered Creative Freedom." *Forbes*. July 18.

24. Mike Hale. 2013. "Original Pilots, Judged by the Masses." *The New York Times*. April 22.

25. Emily Steel. 2014. "For Its New Shows, Amazon Adds Art to Its Data." *The New York Times*. August 15.

26. Jeffrey P. Bezos. 2011. "Letter to Shareholders." Available at www.sec.gov /Archives/edgar/data/1018724/000119312512161812/d329990dex991.htm.

27. Indeed, the increased access to information and works is itself a result of digitalization.

28. Tony Horwitz. 2014. "I Was a Digital Best Seller!" *The New York Times*. June 19.

29. Rob Walker. 2012. "Youtubers." *The New York Times Magazine*. July 1.

30. Strawberry Saroyan. 2011. "Storyseller." *The New York Times Magazine*. June 17.

31. Lizzie Widdicombe. 2012. "Teen Titan." *The New Yorker*. September 3.

32. Brooks Barnes. 2014. "Media Companies Join to Extend the Brands of YouTube Stars." *The New York Times*. May 22.

33. Although this ability helps producers improve their revenues, it is worth keeping in mind that producers cannot fulfill only their financial imperative and exclusively produce best sellers unless they are willing to lose their status among intermediaries as cultural producers.

34. Warby Parker. "Online Eyeglasses and Sunglasses." Available at www.warby parker.com.

35. Bonobos. "Better Fitting Men's Clothing." Available at www.bonobos.com.

36. Rent the Runway. Available at www.renttherunway.com.

37. Gilt Groupe. Available at www.gilt.com.

38. Stephanie Clifford. 2012. "Shopping Sites Open Brick-and-Mortar Stores." *The New York Times*. December 18.

39. Alexandra Jacobs. 2013. "The World at Her Fingertips." *The New York Times*. December 22.

40. Note that neither this knowledge nor consumers' perceptions of value in fashion is equivalent to branding issues or marketing tactics but rather is related to the underlying processes of value construction and their role in creating a market.

41. See "A Whole New World." 2009. *The Economist*. November 26; Pernilla Holmes. 2009. "Art of Africa." *The Financial Times*. November 7; Robin Pogrebin. 2011. "China's New Cultural Revolution: A Surge in Art Collecting." *The New York Times*. September 7; and Ellen Gamerman and Kelly Crow. 2011. "Clicking on a Masterpiece: Are Some Serious Collectors Ready to Buy Million-Dollar Art Works Online?" *The Wall Street Journal Asia*. January 19. For a more academic treatment of the increasingly globalized art market and the interaction between globalization and digitalization in the art market, see Mukti Khaire. "Art without Borders? Online Firms and the Global Art Market." In *Contemporary Canvases: The Globalization of Markets for Contemporary Art*, edited by O. Velthuis and S. B. Curioni. Oxford, UK: Oxford University Press.

42. Mukti Khaire. "Paddle8: Painting a New Picture of the Art Market." HBS No. 9-812-047. Boston: Harvard Business School Publishing.

43. I first developed this idea in detail in a chapter on online startups in the art market. See Mukti Khaire, 2015. "Art without Borders? Online Firms and the Global Art Market." In *Canvases and Careers in a Cosmopolitan Culture: On the Globalization of Contemporary Art Markets*, edited by Olav Velthuis and Stefano Baia-Curioni. Oxford, UK: Oxford University Press.

44. The key word here is *distinct*. The problems with blurring the boundaries between producers and intermediaries in the art market is described succinctly by Carol Vogel. 2012. "The Art World, Blurred." *The New York Times*. October 28.

45. To be clear, the position of this book is that the existence of intermediaries is not an "inefficiency" but rather is necessary for the smooth functioning of markets for cultural goods. However, the presence of numerous entities, especially entities other than buyers and sellers, is generally taken to be a sign of inefficient markets, where price is not the only coordinating mechanism.

46. Steven Kurutz. 2011. "The Thriving (Online) Shelter Magazine Industry." *The New York Times*. June 1; and Julie Bosman. 2010. "New Site for Teenagers with Literary Leanings." *The New York Times*. December 6.

47. Of course, it is important to acknowledge the preponderance of home videos of cats, puppies, and kids/babies on YouTube; the bulk of the works created and available in the virtual world are, in fact, not very complex or infused with symbolism.

48. Sundance Institute Artists. Available at www.kickstarter.com/pages/sundance institute.

49. This sentiment is dramatically exemplified by Neal Gabler's op-ed in *The Boston Globe*, which proclaims "The End of Cultural Elitism" because audiences are "no longer interested" in the opinions of elite tastemakers and critics. Neal Gabler. 2001. "The End of Cultural Elitism. *The Boston Globe*, January 6. Available at http://archive.boston.com/bostonglobe/editorial_opinion/oped/articles/2011/01/06/the_end_of_cultural_elitism/. A critical analysis of this assertion was provided in A. O. Scott. 2011. "Defy the Elite! Wait, Which Elite?" *The New York Times*. January 13.

50. Ann Friedman. 2013. "BuzzFeed's All-Positive Books Section." *Columbia Journalism Review*. November 14.

51. Claire Cain Miller. 2009. "The Review Site Yelp Draws Some Outcries of Its Own." *The New York Times*. March 3.

52. Shelley Podolny. 2015. "If an Algorithm Wrote This, How Would You Even Know?" *The New York Times*. March 7.

53. A distinct but related development that should cause concern is the use of algorithmic narrative generators that convincingly mimic the natural language produced by humans. This technology raises the issue of the damage that could result from the potential existence of unknown and hidden biases in the algorithms and the underlying data that are analyzed to produce discourse.

54. Brooks Barnes and Michael Cieply. 2012. "In Fire Sale, Penske Media Buys Variety." *The New York Times*. October 9.

55. Popova has, however, also been accused of hypocrisy because she began linking to Amazon.com and earning affiliate revenues (see Kelly Faircloth. 2013. "Maybe Don't Talk Shit about Ads if You Make Money on Affiliate Links." *The Observer*, February 12. Retrieved in March 2016 from http://observer.com/2013/02/maria-popova-brain-pickings-affiliate-links-amazon-on-advertising-tumblr-ads-ads-ads/. Although she retains the link to the public library, she has recently added images of book covers, which hyperlink to the Amazon sales page. She responded to these allegations by denying receiving sizeable affiliate commissions. Either way, her hyperlinking to Amazon reiterates the difficulty of making a living through traditional business models when the intermediary function is transferred online, whereas her overall trajectory suggests how new online intermediaries can build trust among consumers, which could give them leeway to add revenue streams at a later date. In this sense, Popova's situation is not that different (albeit occurring along a highly compressed timeline) from *Vogue* and *Allure* and other magazines pointing to their track record of independence and objectivity as a safeguard against being corrupted, when they added hyperlinks to their websites (see Chapter 5).

56. Bruce Feiler. 2012. "Maria Popova Has Some Big Ideas." *The New York Times*. November 30.

INDEX

Academy Awards, 73, 85, 89, 98, 225n28
adaptations, 152
advertisements, 49, 59, 94, 110, 227n5; as
    commentary, 8, 9, 13–14, 16, 50, 51, 74,
    150; in magazines, 61–62, 63–64, 100,
    102, 103, 118, 206; in newspapers, 65,
    100, 118, 206; on YouTube, 196
affiliate revenue, 117, 206, 207, 243n55
agents, 132–34, 154–55, 161, 197, 237n36
algorithms, 115–17, 205, 229n31, 243n53
Alibaba.com, 187
Alloy Media, 231n17
Allure, 117, 243n55
Amazon.com, 116, 195, 196, 198, 205, 206,
    229n31, 243n55
American Bandstand, 101
American Repertory Theater (A.R.T.), 158
Apology, 222n56
Aravena, Alejandro, 228n11
architecture, 65, 85, 102, 127
Arden, Sherry, 136
Art Basel, 63
art historians, 33–34
art market, 136, 198, 200–201, 204, 222n54,
    242n44; Impressionism, 3–4, 18; Indian
    art, 17–18, 33–34, 37, 69, 142, 187, 190,
    192; and private museums, 102. *See also*
    auction houses; galleries
Atavist, 140, 143, 174–75, 178, 179
auction houses, 13, 18, 37, 53, 101, 167–68,
    177, 192, 214n6
awards, 84, 111, 219n16, 226n38; Academy
    Awards, 73, 85, 89, 98, 225n28; Cannes
    Palme d'Or, 85; Grammy Awards, 73,

85; by industry/trade associations, 105;
    James Beard Award, 85; Man Booker
    Prize, 27–28, 78, 85, 88, 90, 93, 225n29;
    MTV Movie Awards, 89; National Book
    Award, 85, 88, 226n38; Obie Awards, 93,
    96; People's Choice Awards, 78, 89, 90,
    107; prestige of, 73, 85–86, 89–90, 152,
    173; Pritzker Prize, 65, 78, 85, 89, 102,
    105–6, 228n11; Pulitzer Prize, 73, 88;
    Teen Choice Awards, 89; Tony Awards,
    93, 158

Bach, J. S., 66
Ballets Russes, 6
Barthes, R., 14
Bazin, André, 92
Beach, Sylvia, 5, 35
Beard, James, 34, 69
Beatles, 42
belief changes: vs. behavior changes, 22,
    24, 43; relationship to market creation,
    14–15, 17–18, 19, 21, 29, 32–33, 38, 43,
    54, 60, 148. *See also* cultural norms
Bergdorf Goodman, 138
Bergé, Pierre, 131, 139
Berklee College of Music, 23
best-seller lists, 86, 90, 107
Beyoncé, 67
Bezos, Jeffrey, 196, 197, 201
Bezos, MacKenzie, 206
Bieber, Justin, 197
Billboard magazine, 49
Bloomingdales.com, 199
Bloomsbury (UK), 155

Sundance Institute, 58, 62, 63, 68, 95, 109,
112, 113, 203, 221n49
supply and demand, 16
supply chain: supply-chain firms, 132; vs.
value chain, 8
Swift, Taylor, 239n4

talent scouts, 132–34
Tallmer, Jeffrey, 96
Target, 11
Teen Choice Awards, 89
Telluride, 62
theater, 13, 93, 96, 158, 220n34
Threadneedle Prize, 95–96
Tony Awards, 93, 158
Toole, John Kennedy: *A Confederacy of
Dunces*, 67
"Top 10" lists, 86, 90
trade intermediaries, 80–81, 133, 161
Tribeca Film Festival, 111
Trollope, Anthony, 166
trouser suit, 18
Turner Prize, 85
TV Guide, 79
TV shows, 149
TV studios, 156
12 Years a Slave, 89
Twilight novels, 152

Ulysses, 5, 20, 29, 35, 104–5, 120–21,
213n51
"Unique Board," 187
user-generated content, 78, 115–16,
229n31; user reviews, 20, 94–95, 98,
107–9, 115, 116, 203, 204–5, 206

Valentino, 154
value: intersubjective agreement on, 8,
12, 14, 18, 21, 33, 34, 36, 41–42, 43, 44,
76–77, 82, 83, 211n28, 213n44; material
value, 6, 10, 22, 54, 126–27; symbolic
value, 5–6, 10, 11, 22, 31, 52, 54, 74,
81, 96, 108, 127, 150–51, 199, 202–3,
239n23. *See also* cultural norms; market
values

vampire novels, 137
Variety, 78, 114, 133–34; editorial policy,
99, 102–3, 227n2; purchase by Penske
Media, 206–7; "Ten to Watch" feature,
80
Vibe, 71
Vice Magazine, 222n56
Village Voice, 96
Vimeo, 203
Vogel, Carol, 242n44
Vogue, 58, 62, 63, 81, 112; affiliate revenue
generated by, 117, 243n55; "Must-Watch
Artists" list, 87

Wallace, David Foster: *Infinite Jest*, 104–5
Wall Street Journal, 91
Walton, Alice, 102
Warby Parker, 199
Warner Amex Cable Communications
(WACC), 49
Washington Post, 91
water-cooler show, 211n28
Waters, Alice, 34
ways of thinking, 18–19, 21, 22, 24. *See also*
cultural norms
Weber, Max, on bureaucracy, 108
Weiner, Jennifer, 151
Weinstein, Harvey, 140
Western art, 17, 18, 34
"What's On [Broadway]," 79
Whole Foods, 28, 41
Will & Grace, 149
William, Prince, 59
Wilson, John, 225n21
Wine Advocate, 92
Winfrey, Oprah: book list, 78, 87, 106–7,
163–64, 165; as intermediary, 163, 165
W Magazine, 64, 81, 87
Wood, James, 58

Yelp.com, 94, 98, 107, 116, 190, 206
YouTube, 189, 196, 197, 198, 203,
242n47

Zuckerberg, Mark, 107